S0-AKZ-100

Literature and the American Tradition

LEON HOWARD is Professor of English at the University of California at Los Angeles. He received an M.A. from the University of Chicago and a PH.D. from Johns Hopkins University. A former Guggenheim Fellow and Fullbright lecturer, he has written many articles on American literature. Among his books are *The Connecticut Wits, Herman Melville: A Biography, Victorian Knight-Errant: A Study of the Early Literary Career of James Russell Lowell,* and, with Louis B. Wright and Carl Bode, *American Heritage.*

Literature and the American Tradition

LEON HOWARD

Doubleday & Company, Inc.
Garden City, New York

Copyright © 1960 by Leon Howard
All Rights Reserved
Printed in the United States of America

For
Michiko and Toshio, Guido, Pat, Tauno, Bernard Kao,
Monique and Isabelle, Mustafa, Broder,
and the many others
with whom I have sought the ethos of America
beneath the surface of its literature

Preface

THIS book had its origin in an experiment in the writing of literary history, and it was completed under pressure. The experiment was made in response to a challenge, issued by an eastern university a good many years ago, to discover and define in a public lecture the distinctively American qualities of a seemingly incongruous group of nineteenth-century writers who were strongly affected by the European literary tradition yet maintained an independent existence within it. The pressure developed in later years when I lectured in various universities in Japan, England, France, and the Scandinavian countries and realized how eagerly many foreigners looked to imaginative literature for an understanding of the United States and how confused or misguided they often were by the raw facts with which the imaginative writer deals and the raw ideas he sometimes expresses. Would it be possible, I wondered, to write a short history of American literature which would be comprehensive and at the same time analytic enough to seek out those attitudes of mind which controlled the creative imagination and helped shape the country's literature toward a recognizable national character?

Imaginative literature is one of the richest and most

revealing expressions of the human mind; but an attempt to survey its whole national history, for this particular purpose, created its own problems. The first involved the concept of history itself. Should it be simply a philosophical interpretation of known facts and such new ones as I could discover? The older writers on national characteristics in literature had assumed so, reasoning in terms of analogy and causation or from some arbitrary critical approach. Yet it seemed to me that such a concept placed artificial boundaries on our knowledge of the past, diverting part of its richness into a predesigned channel to serve some useful purpose, perhaps, but without attempting to estimate its natural force. As I continued to experiment with the problem, most directly in a series of lectures at a midwestern university, I began to see the past less as a stream of water which the historian could observe or control and more in terms of a shifting flow of lava, consisting of a hardening surface and of undercurrents of energies and unformed beliefs which were the true basis of what I sought to describe. The history of America was to be found as much in these undercurrents of impulse and belief as in their recorded expression, their solid surface and visible symbols; and the peculiar value of literature, as the material for historical research, lay in its impulsive energy, which kept it alive and distinguished it from the less imaginative records of its time.

Such a concept of history, however, was not easy to handle. Its special difficulty was that the lava stream behaved too naturally: near its source it was all impulse and no solid surface, near its end it was still roiling with lumps whose solidity was not yet determined. In short, the first two centuries of America, when the national character was in the process of formation, produced little pure literature in the conventional sense of the word; whereas the canon of literature for the last half century, at least, is so unsettled that it is impossible to determine which authors reflect the values which posterity will call "permanent." Only in the middle period was there a solid body of writing beneath which one could perceive a dominant and reasonably consistent moving impulse. Accordingly I was forced to divide my investigation into three major sections. The first followed the pattern of what is often called intellectual history. The second consisted of somewhat conventional literary interpretation. The third is an exploration of the mass of recent writing in an effort to see whether my interpretation of the earlier period revealed a force of sufficiently enduring character to continue into the present the recognizable power of the past.

The story I have finally tried to tell was inevitably affected by the pattern of investigation upon which it was based. It differs from the research pattern, though, because of the conflicting currents of impulse and belief which became evident in America after the Civil War, when an earlier attitude of mind had come to the surface and become hardened into a symbol, the visible evidence of an established tradition. Consequently I felt compelled to devote the third part of my narrative to the evidences of conflict between the older tradition and a new one which threatened to emerge and dominate it. I reserved for an Epilogue such evidence as I could find among recent writers which bore firmly upon the question I originally set out to answer: Does the literary history of America reveal the existence of an attitude of mind consistent and durable enough to be called an aspect of the national character?

I would not have spent so much time upon so short

and in some respects so ordinary a book (filled, as it is, with dates and titles) had it not been for my experience in teaching abroad. My dedication of this volume to a representative group of foreign students and personal friends expresses something of the gain one feels in seeing his own country through other eyes. But my indebtedness to the many students in this country whose researches and reactions have improved my knowledge and judgment is great, and I want to acknowledge a special debt to those friends who read the manuscript—Ralph Cohen in part, and Robert Falk, Robert Kirsch, Norman Holmes Pearson, and Walter Rideout *in toto*—whose suggestions and corrections have improved its quality and would have improved it more had I been capable of following all of them.

L. H.

Los Angeles, May 12, 1959

Contents

Contents

Background and Beginning 1608–1828

CHAPTER ONE

The Law and the Land

I

THE story of American literature begins deviously, for to be told it must begin with a developing attitude of mind of which the earliest writings were evidence rather than products—an attitude which developed over a period as long as that of the memorable literature itself. Yet without this attitude the literature would never have acquired the distinctive national character that makes a coherent story possible, and so we must begin with a people whose minds were more involved in religious, economic, and political problems than in matters of esthetics, in order to see what they acquired and left to posterity as an intellectual and cultural heritage upon which a literature could be based.

The first writers were explorers, one of whom (George Sandys of Jamestown) was engaged in what was to become a famous translation of Ovid, although most of them were like Captain John Smith, who reported on his Jamestown experiences in *A True Relation* (1608), encouraged new settlers in *A Description of New England* (1616), and defended and romanticized his activities in *A General History of Virginia* (1624). After them came the Pilgrims from the English colony in Holland under the leadership of William Bradford, whose *History of Plymouth Plantation* was written for posterity rather than for a contemporary public and perhaps for that reason proved to be one of the most moving of early American narratives when the manuscript was eventually published in 1856. Finally came the Puritans of the Massachusetts Bay Colony, a thousand strong in the summer of 1630, bringing with them their own charter and therefore a greater independence than the other colonies possessed as well as a firm determination to establish a new way of life in the exile they chose in preference to oppression at home.

These were people with a peculiar heritage which had given them the name they had just begun to accept as a term of distinction rather than of contempt. They were devoted to the great reformation which would prepare the way for the second coming of Christ on earth, and they represented its second phase. As self-designated "Doctrinal" Puritans, they had inherited the fruits of the first reformation in the form of the Calvinistic doctrines which had recently been systematized by the Synod of Dort: they believed that mankind was totally depraved in its heritage of Adam's original sin but that a limited portion of the race had been mercifully and unconditionally elected to salvation by the vicarious atonement of Christ, and they believed that for these chosen Saints God's merciful grace was a gift which could be neither refused nor abandoned. As English followers of such "Old" Puritans as Thomas Cartwright, William Perkins, and William Ames, they carried their doctrinal reform further by insisting that they were New Testament Christians who lived under a "Covenant of Grace" (made with Abraham and confirmed in Christ) rather than under the "Covenant of Works" (made with Adam and violated by him), which they identified with the Roman Catholics, Lutherans, and Arminian heretics. Yet, useless though they considered good works to be as a means of salvation, as "Moral" Puritans they were obedient to Biblical law as the revealed will of God, convinced that it was binding upon the unsanctified mass of mankind and disposed to make it the only law of the new colony.

But as representatives of the second stage of reformation they were mostly preoccupied with their role as "Ecclesiastical" or "Church" Puritans, whose great calling was to remake the church in the image of the primitive New Testament congregations, which were gatherings of confirmed believers rather than catholic assemblages like the Old Testament Jewish church to which all members of the nation were initiated in infancy. Their acceptance of this aim—into which they were hastened by the mere fact of their voluntary emigration and by the necessity for taking with them the unsanctified servants and artisans needed in the wilderness—was actually somewhat premature, for the English Puritans as a whole had not yet decided whether the Bible dictated a "gathered" church of Saints or a reformed "national" church like that of Scotland. Some, who were called "Political" or "State" Puritans by their contemporaries, believed that the state itself would have to be purified before the character of the church could be established, and the only firm area of agreement at the time of the migration was opposition to such relics of Romanism in the church as the episcopal hierarchy and clerical vestments, although there was widespread opposition to a set liturgy and kneeling for communion.

The earliest literature of the emigrants reflected their dominant interests. Quite properly, their responsibilities as Moral Puritans were set forth before their departure by the Reverend John Cotton, who was to join them later and become the most prolific writer in the early settlement. In a sermon on "The Christian Calling," later printed in *The Way of Life* (1641), he summarized the Puritan ethical system inherited from the previous generation. Its primary virtue was industry. A good man would not rest until he had found some warrantable calling—a particular employment which would enable him to serve the public good as well as his own, which would be agreeable to his talents, and into which he could enter readily without deceit and without undermining others. Their second virtue was dependence upon their Divine Creator: "Faith saith not," explained Cotton, "give me such a calling and turn me loose to it; but faith looks up to heaven for skill and ability." Having found his calling and sincerely committed himself to God, the Puritan had other formal virtues to practice—the virtue, which Shakespeare had allowed Sir John Falstaff to mock, of laboring faithfully in his profession; the virtue of humility, which he practiced by embracing "any homely service" he was called to give, "although a carnal heart would blush to be seen in" it; the virtues of cheerfulness, modesty, and, when he came to lay down his work, resignation.

These seven Puritan virtues were the guiding principles which the colonists were expected to accept in the same way that John Milton was to accept them in his sonnet "On His Blindness." They constituted a stabilizing system of ethics, designed for a conservative

society in which God's immutable law was supreme.
For those who lived under the dispensation of God's
mercy as well as his law, the Reverend Thomas Shepard set forth a higher ideal in *The Sincere Convert*
(1641), which was to prove the most popular of all
collections of early colonial sermons. In one of the most
memorable of these discourses he preached against
sloth, carelessness, and formality in religion and taught
that "the way of self-love"—in which a man, out of fear,
"useth diligently all means whereby he shall be saved"
—was an "easy" way to hell. There were easier ways,
of course, for the irreligious strangers who had joined
the colony for material reasons and were more interested in economic than in religious freedom. But the
leaders believed that all men should be kept acutely
aware of their insignificance before God.

Such sermons as these (and there were many of
them on ethical and spiritual subjects) were printed
for the edification of all readers, English and American
alike. But there was one subject, often labored in extensive manuscripts circulated for years before being
printed, which became of primary importance because
of English curiosity concerning the New England way
of doing things. This was the new reformation in
church government. Richard Mather's *Church Government and Church Covenant Discussed* (1643),
John Cotton's *The Keyes of the Kingdom of Heaven*
(1644) and *The Way of the Churches of Christ in New-
England* (1645), John Norton's Latin *Responsio ad
Guliel. Apollonii* (1648), Thomas Hooker's *A Survey
of the Summe of Church Discipline* (1648)—these
were the books from the new world which caused excitement in England, for the Americans expounded
and defended a new way of church government, which
freed each congregation from all external state or ec-

clesiastical control and guaranteed that freedom by allowing each to call and ordain its own ministers and officers and by giving each the absolute power to admit, release, admonish, or excommunicate its own members. Such freedom was unimaginable to most Englishmen, who were accustomed to a church regulated by the state and who found it difficult to distinguish between the "New England Way" and the Independency of the Brownists, or Separatists (represented in America by the Plymouth Colony), who refused communion with the Church of England because of its "impurity," and the independence of the various sects who refused communion with each other because of differences in doctrine.

The New Englanders, however, maintained that theirs was a middle way between Independency and a national establishment, and they were convinced that they were following the Lord's way of maintaining a uniform discipline without institutionalized control. Their confidence was based upon an absolute acceptance of the will of God as revealed in the Scriptures as the supreme law and upon a belief in the law-abiding sincerity of those Saints who formed the churches and whose exclusive right to the franchise made them the only full-fledged citizens of the new commonwealth. Their problem, as it quickly developed, was the purely human fact that a sincere Saint might also be a zealot who placed his own interpretation of the law above that of his fellows. Their first unfortunate experience was with the Reverend Roger Williams who became "teacher" (or minister of doctrine) of the church at Salem in 1631 but soon removed to Plymouth, only to return and engage in so many attacks upon the legality of the colonial charter, the rights and responsibilities of the magistrates, and the propriety of communing or even praying with unregenerate persons that he was banished from Massachusetts Bay in 1635 and became the founder of the Rhode Island Colony. Their second was with Mrs. Anne Hutchinson, a cousin of the English poet John Dryden and a woman of ready wit and great energy. She followed John Cotton to New England in 1634 and became the private interpreter of his sermons to a large group of followers whom she convinced that Cotton was the only minister preaching the true Covenant of Grace in a colony of legalistic heretics. She, in turn, was accused of antinomianism (or of denying the binding force of Biblical moral law) and after much turmoil—which included the public disarming of her followers—was exiled to Connecticut.

Both affairs stirred the colony deeply, for each involved numerous meetings of ministers in an effort to convince the troublemakers of their errors and each provided a test of the Puritan confidence in the efficacy of revealed law. In one affair, Williams at first admitted error and then returned more stubbornly than ever to his own interpretation of the law. In the other, neither Mrs. Anne Hutchinson nor the Reverend John Wheelwright was convinced; but John Cotton was, and he participated in Mrs. Hutchinson's excommunication and became the official spokesman for orthodox New England in the later controversy which followed the publication in 1644 of Williams' *The Bloody Tenent of Persecution, for Cause of Conscience*. The crux of this basic Puritan problem, originally so involved in personalities and now so surrounded by historical implications that it can hardly be seen clearly, was the meaning of "conscience." Williams and Mrs. Hutchinson evidently thought of conscience as a somewhat intuitive quality, which in Mrs. Hutchinson's mind

came very close to private revelation. Cotton accepted
the more widespread Puritan view that it was a rational
faculty, subject to information from without, and that
a "rightly informed conscience" was informed primarily by the Word of God. Furthermore, he tacitly
accepted, as Williams emphatically did not, the principle of a judicious review of his own individual interpretation of the Word.

The civil action of banishment which concluded each
affair also had its effect in helping convince the leaders
of the Bay Colony that the power of the churches, even
over their own members, was not sufficient to keep the
peace. For eight years they tried to get along without
a body of civil laws, handling all problems by means
of a General Court of citizens who met to elect a governor and other magistrates and deal with such civil
problems as were important enough to come before it.
But the growing extent and population of the colony
and the increasing amount of business made a democratic assembly inconvenient and unwieldy and compelled a decision that the General Court was "like
a parliament" to which representatives should be
elected. By the end of a decade, in short, State Puritanism had been forced upon the refugees from English politics, and it was becoming easier to have recourse to a secular arm in any effort to put down
troublemakers.

II

It was against this background that the Americans
responded to the Puritan Revolution, which began in
England in 1640 when the ill success of King Charles I
in his Scottish war forced him to assemble a Parliament

for the first time in eleven years. The New Englanders had worked hard to establish themselves as a Christian commonwealth. They had founded Harvard College in 1636 for the education of future ministers, brought over a printing press, and published their first book—a new metrical translation of the Psalms from the original Hebrew, called *The Bay Psalm Book*—in 1640. They had been obliged to fight the Indians in the Pequot War of 1637 and had suffered internal troubles, but, in general, they had managed to keep peace and were prepared to look with sympathy upon their English brethren when active civil war broke out between Parliament and King in 1642.

But their sympathy was not wanted, they discovered, as they found themselves in a completely unexpected psychological relationship to their mother country. Instead of being pioneers in the second stage of the reformation, the Puritans in exile discovered that they were considered escapists by the Puritans of the resistance. State Puritanism became the dominant movement in the England of the Long Parliament, and, when the Westminster Assembly of Divines was called in 1643 to make recommendations for a reformed church, the Scots moved in with their Presbyterian discipline, and the idea of a national church came to dominate both the assembly and Parliament. Only five "dissenting brethren" at Westminster were willing to advocate the New England way of Congregationalism, and they never brought in a formal report, because, as they protested, the assembly violated its instructions by seeking guidance from human experience rather than exclusively from the Word of God. But political expediency was the order of the English day, and when the battle of Marston Moor, in July 1644, effectively demonstrated the superiority of Oliver Cromwell's sectarian Ironsides not only to other English troops but to the Presbyterian Scots, the military leader of the Revolution was under practical compulsion to tolerate a variety of sects which made Anne Hutchinson and Roger Williams seem comparatively orthodox. The New England middle way of church government thus found itself in the middle of a violent political controversy, damned by the Presbyterians for its independence and by the Independents for its intolerance; and it is not surprising that the New Englanders should have gone on the defensive in their writings and actions.

Their defensiveness was both particular and general. Cotton replied to Williams' attack in *The Bloody Tenent* with *The Controversie Concerning Liberty of Conscience in Matters of Religion Truly Stated and Distinctly and Plainly Handled* (1646) and *The Bloody Tenent Washed and Made White in the Blood of the Lambe* (1647), and he and others supplemented and defended the expositions of the New England way of church government which had been circulating in manuscript and were beginning to appear in print at this time. The latter also sometimes contained a more general defense of New England, most explicitly in a little pamphlet called *A Defense of the Answer* prepared by Thomas Shepard and John Allin and published in London in 1648. The Preface protested against the settlers being "judged as deserters of our Brethren, and the Cause of Christ in Hand: with whom (excuse us if we now speak plainly) it had been far more easy unto many of us to have suffered, than to have adventured hither upon the wilderness sorrows we expected to have met withal." The American settlers "surely all were not rash, weak-spirited, inconsiderate of what they left behind, or of what it was to go into a Wilderness," they assured the critical stay-at-homes. What was needed was a proper history of the settlement: "If we were able to express and recount the singular workings of divine Providence for bringing on this work to what it has come unto, it would stop the mouths of all that have not an heart to accuse and blaspheme the goodness of God in his glorious works."

Certainly no writer at that time had produced or was in the process of producing the sort of history Shepard required. Francis Higginson, for example, who had come over in 1629 and written his *New-Englands Plantation* (1630) in order to encourage others to follow him, bore no witness to the hardships and sorrows of wilderness adventure when he boasted of his improved health and digestion in America—even though he died before his book was published. Nor did William Bradford or John Winthrop in their histories do more than barely list the undeniable sufferings they had witnessed. Shepard's call was answered two years later, however, when Edward Johnson began his *Wonder-Working Providence of Sions Saviour in New England*, which was completed and published in 1654. His account of the building of Concord made the soldiers of Christ in America appear as heroic as those in England who had captured the town of Bristol. Lying in the open air or in smoky dugouts, wet and cold in day and night, the men and their wives and children—"every one that can lift a hoe to strike it into the Earth"—struggled with the land while they "cut their bread very thin for a long season." Johnson's settlers had not escaped to the land of peace of which Shepard had boasted only ten years before. The English had no grounds for criticizing the sort of people he portrayed.

A certain amount of self-righteousness was implicit

in this defensive portrayal of the settlements, but it was more apparent in the official New England attitude toward the religious toleration which was spreading in the mother country. During the middle forties, when John Cotton and others were regularly advertising the New England way or middle way of church government as a way of compromise between the English Presbyterians and Independents, the colonists made no secret of their feeling of superiority to their contentious brethren at home. In a letter to a friend in England on December 10, 1644 (printed in 1645 as *New England's Lamentations for Old England's present Errours and Divisions*), Thomas Shepard had expressed a widespread American sentiment: "To contend, and divide, and grow drunk, and stagger with novelties, and every new device of unstable minded men, while the common Enemy is in the field and the Sword of the Lord stands at every man's door almost, this argues deep distempers, close hypocrisies, and such unreasonable wantonness and abuse of liberty that the Lord Christ will not pass by without darkening the Sun and turning the Moon into blood, which will and shall continue until the Lord hath made the remnant which shall escape a poor, weak, humble, pliable-spirited people unto the good ways of grace." In comparison with conditions in England he boasted: "We wonder at God for our peace that the Lord gives us in these parts, we know not how to improve it. The reports of the divisions in *New-England* are fables; the Churches are here in peace; the common-wealth in peace; the Ministry in most sweet peace; the Magistrates (I should have named first) in peace; All our families in peace; We sleep in the woods in peace, without fear of the *Indians,* our fear is fallen upon them. When we travel abroad, we rise up, and lie down in peace; yet this peace giveth us no rest, while our dear *England* is in trouble, for which we would weep, and we wish our heads fountains in this wilderness, for our sins there as well as others."

But such peace was not easily maintained. Governor John Winthrop (whose Journals provide the best contemporary record of life in the Bay Colony) tried to keep it by judicious flexibility in the enforcement of strict laws and found himself charged with exceeding his powers as a magistrate. After his acquittal by the General Court, on July 3, 1645, he made a "little speech" on the causes of "such distempers as have arisen amongst us." They were basically questions "about the authority of the magistrates and the liberty of the people," he declared; and he made it clear that in his own opinion the magistrates, though elected by the people, derived their "authority from God, in way of an ordinance, such as hath the image of God eminently stamped upon it." They might err from lack of skill for their offices, but if they were faithful in their calling and erred in good faith the people "must bear it." Liberty, he added, was of two sorts—the natural liberty to do as one pleased and the civil or federal liberty to do "that only which is good, just, and honest"—and of the two the latter was "the proper end and object of authority," for which the people should hazard their goods and their lives.

Such was the attitude of a people who had as one of their literary spokesmen the Reverend Nathaniel Ward who called himself *The Simple Cobler of Aggawam in America* (1647) when he set out "to help 'mend' his Native Country," which he considered "lamentably tattered, both in upper-leather and sole." His "honest stitches" got him an invitation to preach before the Presbyterian Parliament, and they included an outright attack on the principle of religious toleration. Four things, he wrote, his heart naturally detested: the standing of the Apocrypha in the Bible, foreigners dwelling in his own country, alchemized or counterfeit coins, and "Tolerations of divers Religions, or of one religion in segregant shapes." As the "Herald of New England" he proclaimed in the name of the Bay Colony "that all Familists, Antinomians, Anabaptists, and other Enthusiasts, shall have free liberty to keep away from us, and such as will come to be gone as fast as they can, the sooner the better." He expressed his contempt for any colony—such as Roger Williams' Rhode Island—which would provide "free stable-room and litter for all kind of consciences, be they never so dirty or jadish," and added that if England should "either willingly tolerate or weakly connive at such course," the church would soon become "the Devil's Dancing-School" and the civil state a "Bear-garden."

Ward of course was like the English Thomas Coryate and Robert Burton in being one of the eccentric literary wits of the seventeenth century, but the resemblance between his attitude and that of the colony as a whole was revealed when the New Englanders undertook to set Old England an example of unity. They called a synod of churches in Cambridge in June 1648, to draw up *A Platform of Church-Discipline* for their own use and for the guidance of their brethren in England. They signified their desire for unity by a unanimous acceptance of the English Westminster Confession "in matters of doctrine" and confined themselves to an exposition of the New England way of church government on which they hoped the warring factions of Presbyterian and Independent might compromise. The result was accepted by the Massachusetts General

Court in August and published for "public edification"
with a Preface which made clear its intent. "The more
we discern (that which we do, and have cause to do
with incessant mourning and trembling) the unkind,
and unbrotherly, and unchristian contention of our
godly brethren and country-men in matters of church
government"; the Preface stated, "the more earnestly
do we desire to see them join together in one common
faith; and ourselves with them."

The authors of the Cambridge Platform displayed a
considerable amount of self-righteous humility when
they addressed to the English Puritans such words as
these: "And if the example of such poor outcasts as
ourselves might prevail, if not with all (for that were
too great a blessing to hope for) yet with some or other
of our brethren in *England* . . . we hope in Christ it
would not only moderate our harsh judging and con-
demning of one another in such differences of judgment as may be found in the choicest saints; but prevent (by the mercy of Christ) the peril of distraction
and destruction of all churches in both kingdoms.
Otherwise, if our brethren shall go on to bite and de-
vour one another . . . it will be to the consuming of
them, and us all; which the Lord prevent."

The example of the "poor outcasts" had no effect.
Before the Cambridge Platform could be printed,
Cromwell had declared for "union and right understanding" among all "godly people, Scots, English,
Jews, Gentiles, Presbyterians, Anabaptists, and all."
And by the end of the year Colonel Thomas Pride had
purged Parliament of its Presbyterian members, whose
understanding of union, like that of the Americans, was
not "right," and a court was being constituted to try the
King and order his execution on January 30. Only such
temporary followers of the New England way as Wil-

liam Hook and Sir Harry Vane and such dissenters from it as Hugh Peter and Roger Williams were friends of Cromwell and the new order in England. The solid builders of the Bay Colony became not only conservative but reactionary.

The reaction took a form that Roger Williams had expected—the use of civil authority and sometimes bloody punishment to enforce unity of religious belief. Taking Nathaniel Ward's position "that God doth no where in his word tolerate Christian States, to give Toleration to such adversaries of his Truth, if they have power to suppress them," the secular authorities of the Bay Colony had Obadiah Holmes publicly whipped in 1651 for being a Baptist, and two of his fellow visitors from the colony of Rhode Island were fined. Three years later, the Reverend Henry Dunster, the learned and faithful president of Harvard College, was indicted by the Grand Jury for "disturbing the ordinance of infant baptism in the Cambridge Church" and was forced to resign his office and remove to the Plymouth Colony. When the Quakers began to make their appearance in 1656, the Boston authorities were prepared to move quickly against them under laws forbidding heresy; and the first arrivals were placed under arrest before they left shipboard and had an opportunity to create a civil disturbance. When whipping, branding, and ear-cropping failed to keep others out, the united colonies of the orthodox New England Confederation threatened economic sanctions against Rhode Island for standing on liberty of conscience and thus providing a "back door" for the admission of religious enthusiasts into Zion. Massachusetts passed a law in 1658 providing for the death penalty against Quakers who returned from banishment, and two male Quakers were hanged in 1659 and a woman (a former follower of

Anne Hutchinson) in 1660. No one in the orthodox colonies of New England could any longer disclaim the
bloody tenet of persecution for cause of conscience or
attempt to wash it white. The signs of the times had
been so clear as early as 1652 that John Clarke could
say that while Old England was becoming new, "New
England is become Old."

III

The primary reaction of the New Englanders to the
events in Old England during its Puritan period was
a determination to make the law prevail even though
they had been forced to go beyond God's law in their
effort to free their society from those persons who refused to accept the sort of judicious interpretation of
the Word to which John Cotton had yielded in the
early years of the settlement. But always opposed to
the law was the land—a land which had compelled
the original Puritan immigrants to bring with them
settlers whose qualifications lay not in saintliness but
in their skills. It had thus impelled the Saints toward
a system of church government which was in itself disposed to place more reliance upon individual character
than upon institutionalized authority, and it continued
to attract great numbers of settlers whose interests
were material rather than religious. Most of them were
welcomed, for the early Saints of New England, like
the later landowners of the South, knew that neither
divine grace nor material wealth gave a man the ability
to grind corn, thatch a roof, construct a plow, or build
a boat; and they had to recognize the value of a man
who could do these things, else their own grand designs would fail because the social fabric was too weak

to sustain them. The recognition was practical rather than theoretical, but it was conscious on the part of colonial leaders who regularly protested the inflexibility of regulations sent over from England or who displayed, with John Winthrop, an apologetic feeling for not having codified their own laws for "want of sufficient experience of the nature and disposition of the people." Their ideology was rigid enough, but they knew that man did not live by ideas alone, and they were prepared to make tacit compromises with the practical demands of a new country.

In literature a quiet movement toward individuality may be seen in the differences between the early and later poetry of Mrs. Anne Bradstreet. The poems in the first edition of *The Tenth Muse Lately Sprung Up in America,* most of them written some seventeen years before their publication in 1650, were conventional and perhaps nostalgic reflections of her reading in the Elizabethan poets before she left England. The new poems that appeared in the posthumous second edition of 1678 were, with the exception of "The Four Ages of Man," reflections of her individual emotional experiences—"Contemplations" of external nature and the pleasures of the imagination, expressions of affection for her husband and children, or the display of emotions aroused by a burning home. The human experiences of daily life had come to mean more than books to her when she sat down to express herself in verse.

But other writers who occasionally produced verse during this early period were inclined to remain conventional, and it is impossible to generalize from a single case. Yet Mrs. Bradstreet's way of poetic development was the real New England way of ordinary living. The plan of settlement in self-sufficient communities required a mutual recognition of the dependence of individuals upon one another. In towns so small that a dozen individuals might undertake to form a church, every person was well known. His opinions and character were familiar to his neighbors, and his strong points and shortcomings were generally discussed and carefully estimated. The result was that no matter how he might stand in the eyes of the Lord, he had an independent standing in society. And no Puritan was so impractically pious as to deny that a good reprobate might be a useful citizen.

Such good but unsanctified citizens, in contrast to the English custom, were forbidden the privileges of the church. They were permitted and eventually required to attend divine worship, but it was the worship of a God who had turned his face away from them for all eternity; and the temporal signs of reprobation were always with them in their inability to select the minister whose word they heard, to choose the elders who supervised their conduct, or to vote for the men who represented their material interest in civil affairs. New immigrants who had been church members in England, baptized children who had grown to maturity without the experience of grace, and persons who had once been of "the poorer sort" but had found a ready means of advancement to prosperity and respectability—all were in the same outcast position. The spirit of piety was too prevalent in New England for them to demand admission to the church for selfish reasons; but hypocrites had crept into the church with unsanctified designs, and honest men on the outside were a disturbance to the conscience of honest men within.

The Puritan Saints who accepted the obligation to be their brothers' keepers, in fact, knew their brothers. Such ministers as John Cotton and Thomas Shepard,

especially, were acutely aware of the hypocrisy within
the church and were candid in admitting its existence.
Their clear-sightedness, at times, tempted them to
abandon the teachings of William Ames and other
Puritan fathers by preaching that the "gathered"
church of visible Saints was not a reality but an appearance, that formal and superficial evidences of
grace were all that should be required for admittance.
Another impulse was to compromise rather than abandon their principles, and in that spirit the Cambridge
Platform of 1648 recommended the admission into
church fellowship of "those with weak measures of
faith" and advised against "severe examinations."

But such measures could not solve the problem. The
individuals whose plight was so bothersome were not
of the sort who could be induced into the church by
easy examinations of half-hearted professions of faith.
As their numbers increased and their pressure became
genuinely insistent, the modesty of their demands became evident: those who were baptized wanted nothing for themselves, but they did want the privilege of
baptism for their children in order that they might enjoy the protection of the church while awaiting the experience of grace. An association of ministers, in 1657,
met and offered a solution to the problem, and, after
five years of discussion and debate, it was formally
adopted by a synod in 1662: the doors of the church
were opened halfway in order that baptized but unsanctified persons might claim the sacrament of baptism for their children but not the sacrament of the
Lord's Supper for themselves. Such halfway members
thereby gained the right to vote in civil elections but
not in matters of church government. The Puritan
church in America never adopted the semicatholic
principles of the Anglican and Scottish churches, nor

did it accept the principles of sectarian toleration
which flourished in Cromwell's England. It did, however, adapt its ideology to the requirements of individuals whose importance in the land was great enough to
compel a reinterpretation of divine law.

This "Half-Way Covenant," as it was sardonically
called in a later period, destroyed the unity of the Congregational churches and kept some of them apart for
more than a century. It had temporary political implications inasmuch as it gave the civil franchise to a
considerable number of respectable citizens who might
otherwise have formed an influential opposition to the
theocracy. But there is no evidence that it was adopted
for political reasons and very little indication that it was
passed under the illusion that it would strengthen
rather than weaken the church by an increase in its
membership. The synod of 1662 did not gather to dwell
upon statistics. Its members gathered to consider the
spiritual situation of the children of their friends and
neighbors and of their own grandchildren, whose
names they knew and whose rights as individuals to
the protection of the church they felt a strong compulsion to recognize. The fact that the claims of the individual were strong enough to modify a rigid and reactionary ideology without raising a rival system to
oppose it shows that the seventeenth-century Puritans,
through the force of their environment, were being impelled to follow what was later to become a characteristic pattern of American intellectual behavior.

IV

The pattern of individualism did not appear, however, in the literature of the late seventeenth century.

On the contrary, the prevailing tone of Puritan writing in America from the Restoration of 1660 to the Glorious Revolution of 1688 was one of uneasiness and strain. This tone may be perceived in the tendency of the later Puritans generally to substitute dogmatism for assurance in their expression of religious beliefs, in their emphasis upon fear rather than faith in their attitude toward the Divine Being, and in their obsessed search for evidences of God's providence, which they seemed no longer able to take for granted. For three decades and more their literature became a literature of fear, motivated by a suspicion that God had turned his face from them and directed by an effort to find symbols of evil abroad in the land.

The restoration of the ungodly Stuart dynasty was a blow which they did not formally admit but which they could not avoid feeling, especially as it soon strengthened the position of tolerant Rhode Island and brought an investigation of religious persecution in Massachusetts. Michael Wigglesworth may have been responding to it when he redirected the attention of New England from the contemporary successes of the unrighteous to the future triumph of the Saints on Judgment Day. At that dreadful time the illusions of "carnal reason" would be confounded, and those who "put away the evil day and drowned their care and fears" would be "swept away by vengeance unawares." *The Day of Doom* (1662) became one of the most popular books printed in seventeenth-century America, for its tone was peculiarly fitted to the uneasy spirit of the times. The year 1662 was also the time of the great drought, which was visited only upon New England; and Wigglesworth celebrated it too in a poem entitled *God's Controversy with New-England*, which represented God's contempt for the falling away from grace of his chosen people yet was not published—perhaps lest it inspire similar expressions of contempt from worldly men unfit to echo the divine sentiments.

At the end of the decade Wigglesworth allowed himself to become slightly more hopeful about the present state of the world in his *Meat out of the Eater or Meditations Concerning the Necessity, End, and Usefulness of Afflictions unto Gods Children* (1670); but in 1675 the Indian King Philip's war broke out, and the New Englanders had new evidence that the devil was walking abroad. Observations to that effect poured from their printing presses in the form of personal narratives, sermons, and even an epic poem by Benjamin Tompson called *New England Crisis, Or a Brief Narrative, Of New-Englands Lamentable Estate at present, compar'd with the former (but few) years of Prosperity* (1676). It is no wonder that the Reverend Urian Oakes should have felt called upon to preach vigorously on "The Sovereign Efficacy of Divine Providence" or that Increase Mather became eager to push to completion *An Essay for the Recording of Illustrious Providences,* the ambitious effort to demonstrate God's guiding hand in human affairs which was supposedly begun in England before the Restoration and was finally published in Boston in 1684. But even in their search for evidence of God's goodness they kept their eyes open for the devil's work, and the section on witchcraft which the book contained helped prepare the way for the witchcraft hysteria of 1692 and the outburst of excited literature that accompanied it. By this time, England had permanently disposed of the Stuarts with Roman inclinations, and acquired a king of unquestionable Protestantism; the prospects of Massachusetts, after an unhappy succession of royal governors, were improving; and the colony should have been psychologically ready to return to the progressive world from which it had exiled itself. But the Puritan disease had profoundly affected the New England spirit, and the malady could not be thrown off without the experience of catharsis.

The catharsis of witchcraft hysteria was, on the whole, effective. It led to the attack on the Mathers by the Boston merchant Robert Calef, whose *More Wonders of the Invisible World* (1700) bore witness to an awareness of human values, which were more important to him than were the evidences of supernatural activity. It led to a reappraisal of his attitudes by Judge Samuel Sewall, whose *Diary* records his public confession of error and whose pamphlet, *The Selling of Joseph* (1700), and a later essay against slavery were signs of a new humanitarian spirit among the Puritans. Cotton Mather, like his father Increase, tried to preserve the old attitudes; and his "providential" history of New England, the *Magnalia Christi Americana* (1702), was a monument to the Puritan belief that God took an active part in the affairs of men. Yet Cotton Mather himself was a sort of Puritan Janus, looking before and after. His primary interest was in the relationship of God to man, but his *Bonifacius* or *Essays to Do Good* (1710) and his later volume of advice to young ministers revealed the concern for human relations which was to be characteristic of the new century. Furthermore, his essays in *The Christian Philosopher* (1721), although designed to show the unity of science and religion, offered natural science as a support to religion in a way that would have profoundly shocked his grandfather Richard, who probably never thought that religion needed a support from any source. The old specialized interest in religion was dying out as the dominant and almost exclusive interest of literary minds.

Even when it survived, as it did in the private manuscripts of America's finest colonial poet, Edward Taylor, it began to take on the emotional color of a new humanism. For Taylor was one of the few poets at the turn of the century to "preach Christ" in the old-fashioned way, and in the manuscript sermons of his *Christographia* (1701–3) he was as passionately orthodox as Thomas Shepard. Yet he rejoiced in the union of human nature with God's through Christ and found in that union justification for asserting man's superiority to the angels, and he found in Christ a pattern for human imitation despite man's inability to achieve spiritual regeneration by his own efforts. His own desire to realize God had a formative effect upon his poetry—especially upon the *Sacramental Meditations*, which provided an emotional climax to the intellectual processes of his prose discourses—for he suggested in some of them the possibility of rising through thoughts and words, reason and rhetoric to the verge of comprehending the incomprehensible. And it was perhaps this effort to find in poetry a means of knowing which went beyond reason that made his poetry so suggestive of the earlier English metaphysical poets in its unexpected juxtaposition of ideas and images which strains and shocks the ordinary and familiar processes of the mind.

But Puritanism as a solid and coherent force was rapidly disappearing. The land had won over the law, and as the descendants of the Puritans spread out over the expanding country their heritage of moral Puritanism was to become dissipated in a mist of propriety which was occasionally precipitated in revivals of State Puritanism through spasmodic attempts to regulate personal morality by law. Doctrinal Puritanism was to

survive more in the catechisms of the institutionalized
Puritan churches than in the active beliefs of their
members whose independence in many instances under the Congregational system enabled them to abandon all traditional doctrine and become Unitarian. Perhaps in the final analysis the most profound effect of
the movement was to create in the American consciousness a greater trust in written law than in legislative
assemblies and a willingness to accept a judicial interpretation of the fundamental law as a final recourse
for stability and the supreme authority in government.
But before Puritanism was completely broken down
into its residual elements, American society had to go
through a major shift of interest, involving a more active preoccupation with human affairs, during which
its literature was to reflect an entirely different quality
of mind.

CHAPTER TWO

Ways of Reason

I

THE new quality of mind reflected in the literature of the eighteenth century was the distinguishing characteristic of the period some historians call "the Enlightenment" and others call "the Age of Reason." In its essence, it represented a profound cultural change, which occurred later in America than in other parts of the Western world—a shift in the focus of men's attention from the divine mind to the human mind, a new confidence in the ability of man to solve the mysteries of nature by his own efforts, an exciting disposition to follow the dictates of reason rather than those of revelation, and a belief in self-determination rather than in providence and predestination. Its immediate cause, perhaps, may be found in the great intellectual achievements of the seventeenth century, particularly those of René Descartes, Isaac Newton, and John Locke. But, because it reflected an attitude of mind rather than a generally accepted system of ideas, the Enlightenment is one of the most complex periods in intellectual history and one of the most difficult to explore.

In America, however, the Enlightenment was clearly heralded by certain changing concepts of logic. The Puritans had been followers of the impetuous French rebel against Scholasticism, Petrus Ramus. They followed a system of logic which modern philosophers are reluctant to consider logic at all. It assumed that truth had some sort of absolute existence and that the function of the human mind was merely to perceive it. The Ramean system of logic was no more than an attempt to present a systematic way of searching out the truth and making it evident to others, and the way of seeking was one of considering alternative possibilities, or "dichotomies," between which the mind could choose. Reason, therefore, was equated with choice, and formal logicians became more subtle only as they multiplied the possibilities of choice.

The most important subtlety that developed in the Ramean system, during the century of its use in England, was that which explored a multiplicity of causes, any number of which might be independently adequate or "efficient" causes of a particular effect. It was especially useful to the Puritan followers of John Calvin because it enabled them to avoid the practical difficulty of reconciling such apparently contradictory doctrines as those of predestination and moral responsibility; for, although they believed that God operated both as a first cause and through various immediate or proximate causes, they shared with John Milton the opinion that the chain of causation was a mystery with which the human mind could not profitably concern itself. Neither Puritan theology nor Ramean logic was greatly concerned with the temporal relationship of cause and effect.

The Reverend Urian Oakes had made an exhibition of characteristic Puritan logic in a sermon on "The

Sovereign Efficacy of Divine Providence," which he delivered in 1677. In it he insisted that human will and seemingly blind chance were parallel causes, either of which might operate according to God's determination. But the determining agent was always God's mysterious will and not an unbreakable sequence of causes and effects. The manuscript verses of Edward Taylor consistently illustrated the same way of thinking. His metaphysical poem "Huswifery," for example, found as many different things contributing to man's salvation as were needed for the spinning of thread and the weaving of cloth; and his most ambitious work, "God's Determinations Touching His Elect," described so many means to the realization of grace that some readers have been willing to believe that it preached universal salvation. But Taylor's logic was clear to him if not to his later readers: whatever devices He may have chosen to use, God personally wove the cloth of salvation and elected those sinners who were to be saved by such various means.

By the early part of the eighteenth century, however, a new formal logic, better adapted to the world of Newton, was becoming known to the English-speaking countries. Basically Cartesian, it was disseminated in the American colonies by the French *Port-Royal Logic*, which had been translated into English as *The Art of Thinking*. Benjamin Franklin remembered it in his old age as one of the particular books he had read in his youth, and its influence had been strong on his first ambitious literary work. For Franklin, as a young typesetter in London, was given to reflecting upon the books he set up in print, and he was offended by the old-fashioned reasoning of a book he was putting into a second edition. The book was William Wollaston's *The Religion of Nature Delineated*, which attempted to place an ethical obligation upon human beings to discover truth by the observation of "things as they are" and to act freely in accord with their discoveries. Franklin undertook to answer it according to the more modern art of thinking.

His answer took the form of a published dissertation on *Liberty and Necessity, Pleasure and Pain* (1725), in which the nineteen-year-old philosopher denied the distinction between good and evil, on the ground that both were the results of the same first cause, and denied the moral responsibility of the individual human being, on the ground that he was the predetermined product of a chain of causation. It was a strange work for a young man who had already shown in his own life so much independence and self-reliance, and he later looked back upon it as one of the serious mistakes of his youth. So it was, in fact, because it represented an intellectual denial of all the principles by which he guided his mature life, but his ability to make such an error is an indication of the grip the new mode of thinking could get on eighteenth-century minds.

The mind which fell permanently into this sort of rationalism was that of Franklin's precocious contemporary Jonathan Edwards. At the age of sixteen, when he was beginning his senior year at Yale College, Edwards wrote his father to send him *The Art of Thinking*, which he was persuaded would be as profitable as his textbooks would be necessary to his education. He had been "mightily pleased," he wrote in one of his college notes, with the study of the "Old Logicke" because it had enabled him to order his thoughts and distribute them into classes and subdivisions after what seems to have been the fashion of the Ramean system. But the sort of reasoning to which he became devoted was the new system he described in another note: "All our reasoning, with respect to Real Existence, depends upon that natural, unavoidable and invariable disposition of the mind, when it sees a thing begin to be, to conclude certainly that there is a *Cause* of it; or if it sees a thing to be in a very orderly, regular and exact manner, to conclude that some *Design* regulated and disposed it." "*Knowledge* is not the perception of the *agreement*, or *disagreement*, of ideas" (as the Ramists suggested by their system of dichotomies), he concluded, "but rather the perception of the *union*, or *disunion*, of ideas" (as in a chain of reasoning).

Edwards was to give up his early scientific and miscellaneous speculative interests and devote himself to theology for thirty-five years before he published his *magnum opus*, in 1754, as *A Careful and Strict Enquiry into the Modern Prevailing Notions of that Freedom of the Will which is supposed to be Essential to Moral Agency*. But he did not give up the method of reasoning from which he had anticipated so much profit. "The first dictate of the common and natural sense which God hath implanted in the minds of all mankind, and the main foundation of all our reasonings about the existence of things, past, present, or to come," he said, in laying the foundation of his argument, seems to be "that whatsoever begins to be, which before was not, must have a Cause why it then begins to exist." And "if this sound principle of common sense be taken away," he added, "all arguing from Effects to Causes ceaseth, and so all knowledge of any existence, besides what we have by the most direct and immediate intuition, particularly all proof of the being of God, ceases."

Edwards had asserted his own direct and immediate intuition of God in his autobiographical *Personal Narrative* and elsewhere, but he had also learned, through his connection with the evangelical movement known as the Great Awakening, how difficult it was to distinguish between a personal revelation and an emotional illusion. In his most mature work he placed his dependence upon reason. We may suppose an intuitive knowledge of God possible, "but," he wrote, "we have not that strength and extent of mind to know this certainty in this intuitive, independent manner." The true method of knowing, as he described it in a passage which was an unconscious echo of *The Art of Thinking*, was by the movement of reason backward and forward along the chain of causation: "We *first ascend* and prove . . . from effects, that there must be an eternal Cause; and then *secondly* prove by argumentation, not intuition, that this Being must be necessarily existent; and then *thirdly*, from the proved necessity of his existence, we may *descend*, and prove many of his perfections *a priori*."

How completely Cartesian Edwards was in his point of view and how utterly dependent he was upon the rational chain of causation may be illustrated by another passage in which the author became almost as eloquent over his logical system as he had been in his Northampton sermons: "Yea, if once it should be allowed that things may come to pass without a Cause, we should not only have no proof of the Being of God but we should be without evidence of the existence of any thing whatsoever but our own immediately present ideas and consciousness. For we have no way to prove anything else but by arguing from effects to Causes; from the ideas immediately in view, we argue other things not immediately in view; from sensations now excited in us, we infer the existence of things without us as the Causes of these sensations; and from the existence of these things we argue other things on which they depend as effects on Causes. We infer the past existence of ourselves, or any thing else, by memory only as we argue that the ideas which are now in our minds are the consequences of past ideas and sensations. We immediately perceive nothing else but the ideas which are this moment extant in our minds. We perceive or know other things only *by means* of these, as necessarily connected with others, and dependent on them. But if things may be without Causes, all this necessary connection and dependence is dissolved, and so all means of our knowledge is gone."

It has often been said that Edwards' logic is so good that if we grant him his premises his conclusions become inevitable. Actually, though, if we grant the logic and its applicability to theological matters, either his or Franklin's premises and conclusions would both be inevitable. But few Americans would consistently grant him his logic. He acquired a limited number of followers for his "new light" theology, but many orthodox Calvinists would have agreed with the Reverend Chauncer Whittelsey who feared that the teaching of Edwards' system at Yale would lead students into deism or atheism by substituting "necessity" for an "intelligent Moral Governor." They preferred the relics of dogma to the fine structure of the new logic. The new light of Edwards' severe rationalism struck most of his contemporaries blind.

Much of the distrust of Edwards was founded upon the natural frailties of the human mind—its resistance to systematic discipline and its limited span of attention. Yet his critics did not consider themselves antirational, for they thought within a logical framework which was older than his and considerably more respectable in New England if not in the other colonies.

It had been provided by Francis Bacon, whose name had high authority in colonial America.

Bacon's logic, in a sense, was negative rather than positive. He was severely antagonistic toward the system of classical logic (into which Descartes' method was fitted by the Messrs. de Port-Royal) because he distrusted words as vehicles of thought, and he was contemptuous of the basic Ramean assumptions. Yet he agreed with the Ramists in his belief that "a faculty of wise interrogating is half a knowledge" and in his approach to truth by their method of "invention" or exploration guided by a systematic arrangement of classifications or "topics."

The real quarrel of Bacon with the Ramists was that of a scientist with Platonic abstractions. He observed that "topics are of two sorts, general and special," and he was thoroughly impatient with people who concerned themselves with the abstract "originals of things" and rejected all thought of specific things because they were considered secondary and variable. The Ramean method was one of induction, but Bacon had thoroughly damned it in *The Advancement of Learning:* "The induction which logicians speak of, and which seemeth familiar with Plato . . . their form of induction, I say, is utterly vicious and incompetent." His own method of induction was different in that it was based upon specific observations rather than perceptions of general principles, and he emphasized his attack upon the Ramean schoolmen with the caustic opinion that "men are rather beholden to a wild goat for surgery, or to a nightingale for music, or to the ibis for some part of physic, or to the pot-lid that flew open for artillery, or generally to chance or anything else than to logic for the invention of arts and sciences." Bacon's method of thinking was not foreign to his age.

His attitude of mind was simply critical, practical, and realistic.

This attitude had made a strong appeal to the tough-minded Puritans, who might be obliged to consider general principles in their theological meditations but were concerned with specific things in their daily lives. There was no inconsistency of pattern between the Ramean approach to intellectual generalities and the Baconian approach to specific material problems, and they could admire the wisdom of the Viscount St. Albans while deploring his moral and spiritual limitations. And so, when the formal Ramean logic died out, its substantial pattern of thought lingered on as a sort of practical inductiveness which was traditionally satisfying to the mind. It was also, as a sort of everyday logic, useful in the ordinary affairs of life.

Among these ordinary affairs in America, however, religion continued to be one of the most important—not only among the sons of the Puritans but in the Dutch, Quaker, Roman Catholic, and Anglican colonies to the south. Religious belief was by no means uniform, but belief of some sort was almost universal. Often it assumed a human capacity for the direct apprehension of abstract or supernatural ideas, and although this assumption was far older than any formal system of logic, the actual transformation from an implication of logic into an explicit theory of knowledge can be traced through the writings of Samuel Johnson, who graduated from Yale four years before Jonathan Edwards and discovered the new learning of Locke and Newton before he discovered the new logic of the Port-Royal *Art of Thinking*.

Like Edwards, Johnson undertook to compose an undergraduate compendium of human knowledge in an "Encyclopedia of Philosophy," which, in its earlier version, dealt with the art of reasoning entirely in Ramean terms. After he had read Locke, shortly before graduation in 1716, he revised his consideration of the intellectual powers in order to stress the importance of "ideas" and recognize the faculties of perception and reflection, or, as he called them, "apprehension" and "reason." But he retained "judgment," or choice, as the basic intellectual process because it was a "perception of the agreement or disagreement of any two or more ideas" and consequently the only secure foundation for any knowledge other than the simplest sort, and he continued after graduation to recommend the study of Ramus as the best introduction to logic for college students. For the next three decades, while he made his way from New England to New York and from the Puritan into the Anglican church, he strove to absorb the new learning without changing the pattern of thought fixed in his undergraduate mind. By the time he published his *Elementa Philosophica* (1752), the first textbook in philosophy to be printed in America, he was sufficiently under the influence of Bacon to stress accuracy of observation and perception more than he had in his youth but still determined that this accuracy should be achieved by the use of Ramean dichotomies. He had also become acquainted with Cartesian logic and rejected it in favor of the simpler intellectual process of judgment.

But judgment upon those philosophical matters which were of more interest to him than science, he now realized, required some absolute basis which Bacon did not provide. Sensory experience was not enough. Something more was needed. To fill this need, Johnson reaffirmed the general topics that Bacon had denounced, explicitly developed the Platonic notion which was implicit in Ramean logic, and asserted the existence of "a kind of intellectual light within us" which affects our minds so strongly that "they can no more withstand the evidence of it, than they can withstand the evidence of sense." Thus the basis of judgment might be intuitive as well as sensuous. And, having given his allegiance to an intuitive "intellectual light," Johnson had less use than ever for the elaborate reasoning process he now called "demonstration" and had once called "reason." In a rhapsody entitled "Raphael," composed a decade or so later, he could epitomize his mature thought by having "the Genius of the English America" represent man as a rational being whose knowledge of truth was an apprehension of "things as they really are." He would have to apprehend them in "their beings and relations, connections, and dependencies as they stand variously situated one to another," but it was a direct apprehension rather than the acceptance of a demonstration. For a mind was not absorbed in its own true interest, he suggested, if it "must needs be continually worried in endless mazes of anxiety" and was "ever fluctuating in doubt, skepticism and uncertainty, or under a perpetual delusion,—mistaking sounds for things and grasping at shadows instead of substance." This antispeculative character of his logic was strongly opposed to both the old Scholastic and the new Cartesian method, but it brought Bacon into accord with Ramus by explicitly affirming a new means of perception which balanced the light of sense with the light of intuition and thus anticipated the nineteenth-century notions of a sensory understanding and a Transcendental reason.

There had developed, in short, two patterns of logic which provided quite separate ways for the human mind to follow into the Age of Reason. The new method which Descartes systematized had proved invaluable in the development of a new cosmology and a new mathematics—and Jonathan Edwards tried to use it as an instrument for the creation of a new theology. It was primarily deductive and concerned with general principles. The other method, as Bacon had presented it, provided a sound basis for the solution of practical problems relating to the architecture of fortune and the relief of man's estate. It was primarily inductive and concerned with specifics. But it permitted the inclusion and development of an intuitional heritage from the older Ramean system which enabled men's minds to accept simply and readily certain general ideas—especially those relating to religion and morals—which were actually beyond Cartesian demonstration. All of the major ideas and attitudes of the later Enlightenment and the self-conscious Age of Reason were to appear within these two logical frameworks, and the American inclination toward one or the other—an inclination which gave lasting character to the national way of thinking—was to be determined by certain qualities that developed under the influence of the American environment.

II

If there was any single predominant impulse which led men to seek out the American environment it was a concern for the architecture of fortune. The leaders of the Puritan colonies had come to New England for religious reasons, and there were many other religious refugees among the thousands who followed them across the Atlantic—especially to such tolerant settlements as Rhode Island, Pennsylvania, and Maryland. But the vast majority of the immigrants, as the tenor of the promotion literature (designed to encourage their settlement) has shown, were seeking a land of opportunity where they could get a new start in life and enjoy a new sort of existence. They were a self-selected lot of people who were willing to take a chance for their own betterment; and even their idealistic leaders and encouragers, from John Winthrop of Massachusetts Bay to James Edward Oglethorpe of Georgia, would have been willing to admit that their leadership and encouragement was directed toward the relief of man's estate. The Baconian impulse was overwhelming, and neither the static system of Puritan morality nor the inherent laziness of the gentlemen adventurers in Jamestown could resist it for long.

The desire to improve one's place in the world achieved its most spectacular success in the southern colonies, especially among those settlers who had enough capital to invest in substantial areas of wilderness and to import bound servants to develop their estates. They were the sons of goldsmiths and woolen drapers and the offshoots of gentry who were forbidden English land by the laws of primogeniture but who had a consuming ambition to be landed gentlemen in the tobacco country. Many of them achieved their desires, and the great plantations of the Fitzhughs, the Carters, and the Byrds developed a pattern of civilization which was also realized in the rice and indigo plantations of South Carolina and the manorial estates of New York. The entire seaboard south of New England and the river country which adjoined it became dotted with the holdings of a gentry who were mostly self-made.

These new gentlemen of the new world differed from their English brethren. The American tended to be expansive rather than conservative. However large his possessions were, he wanted to increase them; and he was, by necessity, the steward of his own estate with an active interest in trade. He could not despise commerce and live upon rents derived from well-established tenants. Instead, he marketed his own produce through his English agent and was constantly engaged in purchasing laborers—bound servants, who had to be replaced every five years, and Negro slaves. If he speculated in lands distant from his home plantation, as most of the gentry did, he had to recruit settlers to make them profitable. Money was always necessary for his many expenses, and to obtain it he was not above playing the part of the tradesman himself, importing rum and manufactured goods for the yeoman farmers in his neighborhood and sometimes sending out deputies to trade with the Indians. He watched the expenditures of his trans-Atlantic agent, collected fees for his services to the colony, and kept a close eye on the rulings of the English Board of Trade, which controlled the tobacco monopoly and tried to control all colonial commerce. Every successful planter had to be a merchant of sorts, and his sons, who were generally sent to England for a gentlemanly education, normally spent some time in an English commercial house before coming home to look after their many affairs.

The literature which reflects their lives provides a revealing record of gentlemanly leisure and business-like activity. The *Secret Diary* of the second William Byrd of Westover, kept in his own private shorthand, is a copious and intimate account of everyday activity which reveals the dual nature of the eighteenth-century Virginia gentleman. The son of a large land-holder, Byrd was educated in England, where he acquired a proficiency in learning and a taste for

literature which he carefully cultivated after his return
to America. Each morning before breakfast he devoted
an hour or more to reading Latin, Greek, or Hebrew—
or, on rare occasions when a ship arrived from England, to reading the latest books in English or French.
Afterward he entered into a busy round of plantation
activities, as a supervisor of agriculture and handi-
crafts and as doctor and judge to his bond servants and
slaves. He was a rollicking host to his many friends and
a colonial politician of considerable eminence. He said
his prayers, kept a record of his diet, and devised
schemes for exploring and settling the western regions.
But above all things he was the architect of the family
fortune, scheming for advantages over enterprising
rivals and increasing his large inheritance fivefold. His
one major ambition was to die in a position greater
than that to which he had been born.

There were variations, of course, from the gentlemanly pattern revealed by William Byrd. His brother-
in-law, Robert Beverly, author of the *History and
Present State of Virginia* (1705), was more aggressively American, furnishing his house with articles of
home manufacture and showing as much interest in
the Indians as Byrd had shown in the white back-
woodsmen in his *History of the Dividing Line* between
Virginia and North Carolina. In Puritan New England,
properly enough, the pattern was more Spartan, if it
can be judged by the Reverend John Adams' poetic
representation of "The Contented Man" or Benjamin
Church's "The Choice." New Jersey's William Living-
ston professed a desire for a life of "philosophic solitude" in a retreat full of good books rather than costly
furniture, and he was content to grow his own grapes
rather than import Madeira; but the dream of a private
estate with a well-filled cellar was widespread, and the

surviving colonial homes of New York, Pennsylvania, and Maryland bear witness to the fulfillment of the dream by many persons who did not give it expression in writing. The common quality of these dreams, however, was that they were of a position to be achieved rather than of one in which the dreamer could settle.

The dream of individual progress toward some higher estate, of course, was far more widespread than the gentlemanly ideal. The majority of colonial Americans either were or aspired to be yeoman farmers, and the small estate, held through a nominal quitrent or in fee simple, represented the most common aim of colonial ambitions. George Alsop had been its spokesman in the seventeenth century. *A Character of the Province of Maryland* (1666) described a poor man's paradise, in which the equity of the laws made even bondage agreeable and every bound servant could look forward to the early achievement of fifty private acres and the possibility of their increase. These could be improved and passed on to children who, by virtue of their property, would proudly call themselves free men and enjoy all the rights and opportunities of freedom. The aspirations of the small farmers rarely found such direct expression in literature, but they lay back of such social ferment as that represented by the manuscript accounts of Bacon's Rebellion in seventeenth-century Virginia and the published protests against Oglethorpe's excessive paternalism in eighteenth-century Georgia; and they paralleled, in a modest but more pervasive way, the ambitions of the landed gentry.

The mechanics and artisans of the small but flourishing towns did not find a literary spokesman until the eighteenth century, but when they did, theirs was the clearest voice in colonial America. It came from Benjamin Franklin, who, while a mere boy, wrote a series of "Dogood Papers" for the Boston *Courant* which satirized the pretensions of the gentry and attacked the obstacles that the Puritan conception of a static society placed in the way of a mechanic's aspiration to higher education. After his settlement in Philadelphia and his brief period of logical intellectuality—a period which extended from his London *Dissertation on Liberty and Necessity* through his *Articles of Belief and Acts of Religion* in 1728—Franklin became the persistent and articulate opponent of all forms of deterministic philosophy and especially of that precept of the Puritan ethic which taught that a man's duty was to labor contentedly in a humble calling unless he found a ready and easy entrance to another. When he ran away from his apprenticeship and deserted the colony of Massachusetts, Franklin abandoned the static implications of the Puritan ethical system; and his action was not an uncommon one, if we can believe the observations of Ebenezer Cook, author of *The Sot-Weed Factor*, in Maryland, at the beginning of the century. His distinction lies in the fact that he made a career of discreet opportunism, achieved fame by the exercise of a practical inductiveness, and expressed on a high literary level the devotion of a humbly born individual to material ambition.

Franklin quickly learned "the Way to Wealth" as a printer and publisher and expounded its simpler aspects in Poor Richard's widely read *Almanack*. The practical results of his observations concerning ordinary life and the possibility of improving it were soon evident in his own city: a street lighting and sewage system, warmer homes with fewer smoking chimneys, the first circulating library in America, a philosophical society for the advancement of learning, and an academy for its dissemination which was to become a college and eventually a great university. His broader observations and inferences from them led to the publication of his *Experiments and Observations on Electricity* in 1751 and to European fame as America's first scientist. When he became involved in international politics, in England on the eve of the American Revolution and in France during the actual war, he acquired a notable reputation for ironic good sense and developed the pose of sophisticated simplicity which made him a successful negotiator in the French court; and his last service to his country was that of the wise and witty compromiser of differences in the Constitutional Convention. More than any other single person he became the new world's representative of the Enlightenment.

It was enlightenment, however, in the Baconian rather than the Cartesian sense. Franklin's interest was in immediate causes and immediate effects, not in the chain of causation. There is little speculative reasoning in Franklin's writings, and, after the philosophical *errata* of his youth, almost nothing that could be equated with logical demonstration. His method of reasoning was that of observation, classification, and judgment. Perhaps this is nowhere more evident than in his *Autobiography,* a book dedicated to that belief in "the truth of things as they are" which had so offended him in his youth but to which he had become as devoted in practice as Samuel Johnson was in theory. For the private benefit of his son, he showed how closely the architecture of his fortune was related to the ways of the world and how practical and immediate was his concern for the relief of man's estate. It is a narrative of shrewd perception and generally shrewd choice.

And one of the most interesting sections in the

Autobiography, from the point of view of American intellectual history, is that in which he explains his scheme for attaining moral perfection. His was no speculative plan directed toward the perfectibility of mankind. Instead, it was a down-to-earth system of individual improvement. To achieve it, Franklin drew up a list of accepted virtues—a systematic group of "topics"—scrutinized, one by one, his week-long efforts to practice them, and passed judgment upon his success. The virtues themselves were either identical with or subdivisions of those found in the Puritan system of ethics. The only thing lacking was the Puritan dependence upon God and the sense of piety which pervaded the whole Puritan system. In its empirical concern for improvement by the light of "sense" it was the sort of scheme that Bacon might logically have drawn up had he been interested in moral advancement, but in its failure to admit any other light it went only partially along the intellectual way which Americans were to follow during the latter part of the eighteenth century.

For Franklin's mind was a secular mind, public-spirited and progressive but lacking in that peculiar quality sometimes called "American idealism" and often associated with such of his younger contemporaries as Thomas Jefferson. It was a quality which might be described as a sort of religious perception brought to bear on human affairs, but the weight of evidence seems to be against any theory that it represents a transfer of religious training into secular thought. Instead, it represents a pattern of thought which could be used alike by the Puritans of the seventeenth century and the skeptics of the eighteenth—equally adaptable to a belief in the depravity or in the perfectibility of man.

III

An independent United States of America, in fact, might never have come into existence during the eighteenth century had the colonists not shown a widespread willingness to follow, along political as well as religious lines, what Samuel Johnson called "a kind of intellectual light within us"—an intuitive light which began to dawn long before Johnson formally defined it in his *Elementa Philosophica.* Identified as the light of nature, it may be recognized as a reflection of many aspects of seventeenth-century thought in Europe; and in America it seems to have made its first literary appearance in *A Vindication of the Government of New England Churches* by the Reverend John Wise in 1717.

In such a religious context the light of nature might easily be confused with the supernatural light Jonathan Edwards saw when he became aware of his regeneracy, for Wise was indeed writing about a church made up of God's elected Saints. But he actually professed to have discovered it in the works of the German jurist, Samuel von Pufendorf, and he specifically disregarded the question of man's moral turpitude while assuming a close relationship between man's "natural" and "civil" being and asserting his subjection to the "law of nature" in both civil and church government. This law he described as "the Dictate of Right Reason founded in the Soul of Man"—a dictate apparently revealed by the same "light of nature" which made self-evident man's inherent liberty and equality and which did "highly value" democracy as a form of government. It was not a law hypothesized by the sort of speculations which led Locke to assume a state of nature preceding the social compact but a law which was intuitively perceived.

The mystery surrounding this concept of natural law in eighteenth-century American thought is that it was so rarely used. The colonial architects of fortune were aggressively concerned with their "rights," but they obviously preferred to defend their rights as "freeborn Englishmen," whose immunities and privileges were solidly founded on precedents identifiable by the light of sense rather than that of intuition. Such is the attitude, at any rate, found in such early landmarks of American political thought as the Maryland resolution of 1722, the Connecticut election sermon by Jared Eliot in 1738, and the 1747 sermon by Charles Chauncy which the Massachusetts General Court tried in vain to suppress. It was also the attitude taken by the great colonial lawyer, Andrew Hamilton, in his famous defense of the freedom of the press during the trial of John Peter Zenger who was being prosecuted with all the power of the New York colonial government. The English constitution, unwritten but firmly incorporated in legal precedent, provided a more solid basis for judgment than anything to be found in an intuitively perceived law of nature.

Yet when constitutional law failed to achieve some practical end, the law of nature found its advocates. As a last resort in the Maryland controversy, for example, Daniel Dulaney used it as the basis of a pamphlet insisting upon *The Right of the Inhabitants of Maryland to the Benefits of English Law* in 1728, and an anonymous New England clergyman who called himself Philalethes asserted it in behalf of the Church of England in a pamphlet on *The Essential Rights and Liberties of Protestants* in 1744. But both founded their arguments upon John Locke, and it is doubtful whether they considered this law spontaneously perceptible to all men. The person who left no room for doubt was the Reverend Jonathan Mayhew whose *Discourse on Unlimited Submission,* on the centennial anniversary of the beheading of Charles I, called it "treason" manifold "to say that subjects in general are not proper judges when their governors oppress them and play the tyrant." To Mayhew the powers or rulers were not so much limited by English law as by "the eternal laws of truth, wisdom, and equity, and the everlasting tables of right reason—tables that cannot be repealed, or thrown down and broken like those of Moses." In placing the dictates of natural reason not only above legislative acts but above the Ten Commandments, Mayhew elevated the law of nature to the highest position it had yet achieved in the American colonies.

Nevertheless, English common law held its superior place in the minds of most Americans until the very eve of the Revolution. It dominated John Dickinson's *Letters from a Farmer in Pennsylvania to the Inhabitants of the British Colonies* (1768), which vigorously defended the constitutional right to representative government and proved to be the most popular expression of American political thought during the decade. Yet the concept of intuitively perceived natural law was lurking in the background, and Dickinson himself had alluded to it in a pamphlet of 1766. Accordingly, when the First Continental Congress met in Philadelphia in September 1774, its members were in practical agreement concerning their attitude toward the regulatory powers of the British Parliament—but were not in agreement concerning the ideological grounds for their attitude. John Adams later recalled that he wanted to insert into the declaration of principles "an appeal to those general ideas of natural right so clearly and broadly laid down not long afterward in the Declaration of Independence" but that his desires had been opposed by the delegates from Pennsylvania, Virginia, and Maryland. This restrictive attitude, however, was soon to change. At some time during that same year the Philadelphia lawyer James Wilson decided that the times required the publication of his earlier manuscript *Considerations on the Nature and Extent of the Legislative Authority of the British Parliament* and so publicly announced his conclusion from "the law of nature" that "all men are, by nature, equal and free." In the fall, when the "Westchester Farmer" began to address his *Free Thoughts on the Proceedings of the Continental Congress* successively to the farmers, the merchants, and the members of the legislature of New York, the young Alexander Hamilton took his quill in hand to refute him with "a more comprehensive view of the dispute." To the citizens as a whole he recommended an application without delay to the study of the law of nature as expounded by Hugo Grotius, Samuel von Pufendorf, John Locke, the Baron de Montesquieu, and Burlamaqui; and in a later pamphlet he insisted that "the sacred rights of mankind . . . are written, as with a sunbeam, in the whole volume of human nature, by the hand of divinity itself, and can never be erased or obscured by mortal power." There is a strange irony in the fact that Alexander Hamilton should have preceded Thomas Jefferson in a public expression of inviolable attachment "to the essential rights of mankind" and of a conviction that "the whole human race is entitled to" the blessings of liberty. But the political writers of the time were dipping their pens in the ink of human interests rather than of abstract philosophy, and Hamilton, as later events were to show, had a quicker eye for interests than Jefferson ever did.

For the fact seems to be that the light of nature had little inherent appeal to Americans, who were inclined to accept its guidance only toward some material end and only after the light of sense had failed. They preferred to be empirically progressive and chose to think their way forward by other means only when they became impatient with their rate of progress. Accordingly, when hostilities had broken out with England and the American cause was failing to progress, it was perhaps natural that they should leap toward independence under the guidance of an Englishman who had not arrived in America until the latter part of 1774 when the appeals to legal precedents had failed and the expediency of the law of nature was becoming widely recognized. Thomas Paine's argument for independence as a "natural right" was supported by a combination of realistic observations and false analogies, but in January 1776 it was an almost inevitable expression of the "common sense" of a people who were in a desperate state of transition from civil war to revolution. In any case, Paine's *Thoughts on the Present State of American Affairs* was a pamphlet which cleared the way for a document which was remarkably in part what its authors intended it to be— an expression of "the American mind."

The greater part of the Declaration of Independence is, of course, a piece of temporary political propaganda designed to divert American antagonism from the British parliamentary government to the king and so destroy the sentimental basis of colonial loyalty. But its whole argument provides the best illustration to be found in literature of an emergent American way of thinking. It opens with an appeal to Cartesian logic in a subordinate clause—a reference to that progressive "course of human events" in which a certain action "becomes necessary" in order to reach an end made legitimate by "the laws of Nature and of Nature's God." But the "causes" which were declared to "impel" that action bear no relation to the linked Cartesian pattern of ratiocination. The logic of the Declaration was of a quite different sort. One efficient cause of the action was that "all men are created equal," and operating with it as additional efficient causes were the "certain unalienable Rights" with which men "are endowed by their Creator." Of these Rights, the principal ones were "Life, Liberty, and the pursuit of Happiness"; and the cause helping men to secure these rights was the institution of "Government," which derived its inner impulse from "the consent of the governed," who possessed a further inherent "Right" to change the government if it did not perform its proper function. The occasion or pretext for change was a cause operating from without—here described in the elaborate bill of particulars drawn up against George III, listing the acts of tyranny which formed the greater part of the document—and the instrument of change was the solemn publication and declaration contained in the concluding paragraph.

The formal logical structure of the Declaration (which happens to correspond with John Milton's analysis of the "Efficient Cause" operating "singly and with others") was probably uncalculated and is relatively unimportant. What is important in American intellectual history is, first, that the Declaration avoids any attempt at elaborate reasoning or mathematical demonstration and follows a pattern of simple inferences from basic truths. Second, and equally important, these "truths" are held to be "self-evident"—

immediately perceptible by some light which was obviously not the light of sense or experience but the intellectual light of intuition. The Declaration of Independence is not only a milestone in American political history; it is a milestone in American intellectual history as well. For it reflects a calculated judgment upon what was called "the American mind" by three temperamentally different but extraordinarily shrewd eighteenth-century observers: Thomas Jefferson, John Adams, and Benjamin Franklin. And their judgment is clear. If "the American mind" was compelled to abandon the solid ground of experience, it would take off on a leap of intuition rather than along a chain of ratiocination.

With the framing of the federal Constitution, twelve years later, the American mind returned to things as they were and to the perception of the light of sense. The Constitution was an ingenious compromise of material interests and working methods, designed to meet the need for a "more perfect union" which had been made self-evident by years of experience with instability and civil unrest. The *Federalist* essays (1787–88) which argued for its ratification followed a pattern of drawing simple inferences from observable conditions or from possibilities readily conceived on the basis of recent experience. The chain of argument occasionally found in the essays rarely contained many links, and their authors—Alexander Hamilton, James Madison, and John Jay—made few appeals to abstract principles intuitively perceived. The new form of federal republican government was experimental but not speculative in its conception, expedient rather than inspired.

During all the violent controversies that marked the concluding decade of the eighteenth century in Amer-

ica, the pattern of thought revealed both in the bold-
ness of the Declaration and in the conservatism of the
Constitution was never seriously challenged. The speculative rationalism of revolutionary France created
panic among many Americans, especially after 1792,
and such literary men as the Reverend Timothy
Dwight thundered against philosophy and vain deceit.
Dwight himself retreated—in the verse of *Greenfield
Hill* (1794) and the prose of *The True Means of Es-
tablishing Public Happiness* (1795) or *The Duty of
Americans at the Present Crisis* (1798)—into an almost
hysterical defense of things as they are. But he was
actually able to discover in America few speculative
philosophers of the Continental sort.

Joel Barlow, poet, promoter, and pamphleteer, perhaps came nearer than any other American to being a
thinker after the French fashion. In his *Advice to the
Privileged Orders* (1792–93) he assumed that a "necessary" effect of the French Revolution would be the
spread of the revolutionary movement throughout
Europe, and he undertook, from France and England,
to persuade the privileged classes to face this fact
rationally. He had absorbed enough of the Continental
rationalism to trace the evils of contemporary society
through a chain of causation to their origin, but he was
too American to project his chain of argument into the
future. Of the three ways of knowing which he described in the introductory part of his *Advice,* one was
by experience and another by intuition; the other
method was by collateral experience or analogy. It was
less absolute but more applicable to politics than the
others, and in his various political pamphlets addressed to European readers Barlow tended to draw
more upon the American experience than upon de-
monstrative logic for the reforms he advocated.

The most intellectually interesting of Barlow's writings was the long philosophical poem *The Columbiad*, which was a revision of his earlier *The Vision of Columbus* (1787) made mostly in France in 1802 and published in America in 1807. For in it the American who for thirteen years had been intensely exposed to French thought surveyed the intellectual progress of the human race and made his own choice between the Continental and the Anglo-American ways of reason: Nicolaus Copernicus and René Descartes represented two great milestones in the progress of thought, but it was Francis Bacon who had most effectively taught men "what to learn, and how to know." The "moral science" of the future—which included the science of government—would be an inductive science, and the state of nature which mankind would eventually achieve would be a world-wide utilitarian state politically organized after the pattern of the federated states of America.

By the close of the Revolutionary era, then, that intangible cultural quality which Jefferson and his colleagues had called "the American mind" had settled upon the way of reason by which it would move toward enlightenment. It had rejected Cartesian logic, and, with it, the probability of any profound intellectual achievement in such fields as mathematics, theoretical science, and philosophy. Instead, it had chosen the logic of Bacon with its practical emphasis upon observation, inference, and judgment and with its bias toward such material and humane concerns as the architecture of fortune and the relief of man's estate. But it persisted in holding on to some of the "general topics" that Bacon had rejected—in considering "good" some of the abstract ideas which the English philosopher had called intellectually "vicious"—and so turned away from his cold conception of the New Atlantis. In religion and morals some of these abstract ideas were widely accepted, fervently by the devout and the conventional but only tolerantly by men like Franklin who privately considered them "impractical" and hardly worth arguing about. In political thought they were frequently useful for the purpose of achieving ends which experience could not justify and dialectic might obscure. They freed the ordinary mind from complete bondage to materialism and introduced into it that quality of idealism which was to puzzle European intellectuals for generations to come.

The result was an intellectual disposition which was usually stubbornly practical, often erratic, and sometimes extraordinarily flexible. The ordinary man was habitually given to following his own judgment, and if he suffered from the illusion that one man's judgment was as good as another's, he was also able and willing to grapple experimentally with questions beyond the range of his formal intellectual training. Occasionally he found the answers. But in any case he was probably inclined to feel a certain pride rather than shame in his awareness that his notion of what was "reasonable" differed somewhat from that of his fellows, for by the end of the eighteenth century intellectual authority seems to have become as abhorrent to most Americans as institutionalized religious authority had become at the end of the seventeenth.

CHAPTER THREE

The Naturalization of Symbols

I

In his two-volume *Brief Retrospect of the Eighteenth Century*, published in 1803, the Reverend Samuel Miller of New Jersey wrote of the United States—along with Russia and Germany—as one of "the nations lately become literary." He paid his respects to the religious literature of New England and to the political literature of the late colonies and the new nation, and he tried to explain why poetry and fiction languished in a country where popular education and newspapers flourished. The impoverishment and inadequacy of the American colleges was one reason he offered, and the scarcity of books throughout the country was another. But both of these conditions might be improved with an increase in wealth. The desire to increase wealth, however, offered obstacles of its own. The pressure of business allowed little leisure for the cultivation of literature, and the commercial spirit of the American people offered no encouragement to learning in the form of academic fellowships and other rewards. Booksellers in the small American cities were too poor to serve as patrons of native writers, especially when they could reprint freely the established authors of Great Britain. Yet he "confidently predicted" that in time to come the United States would achieve cultural conditions comparable to those of Europe and "letters will flourish as much in America as in any part of the world."

But in the meantime the new country would have to go through a literary revolution which Miller could neither imagine nor anticipate. It had already achieved its basic freedom from religious institutional authority by the very efforts of the Puritans to establish their own peculiar institution in a land which gave people more freedom than they consciously sought. It had acquired freedom from intellectual authority through the same environmental compulsion toward direct and simple thinking leading to individual judgments. And, finally, it used these slowly developed and yet undefined attitudes of mind in gaining a political freedom from Great Britain which enabled it to incorporate in a written Constitution assurances of permanent freedom from religious establishments and from governmental interference with fundamental human rights. But these underlying attitudes of mind had not yet been generally brought to bear upon the more subtle and tenuous problems of literary expression.

For the art of literature is the art of communication by symbols that are rarely defined explicitly in the minds of either writers or readers. In their larger and grosser forms these symbols are subjects, themes, or interests which have some special value at a particular time and therefore help inspire linguistic symbols with the living vitality that is the essence of literature. During the late eighteenth century and early nineteenth century the values found in the new subjects of pop-

ular interest tended to be emotional rather than intellectual, eccentric and personal rather than traditional
and social—in short, Romantic—and the most popular
themes were the attractions of external nature, the
fascinations of the past, and the rebellion against
tyranny. Like most people in the process of escaping
narrow provincial interests and acquiring an international literary consciousness, the Americans of this
period were acutely sensitive to what was grossly
"new" on the literary horizon, and the country "became
literary" in terms of the English Romantic movement.

Aside from a newborn nation's enthusiasm for politics, in fact, an interest in nature was one of the most
widespread qualities exhibited in late eighteenth-
century American verse. At the end of the Revolution,
Colonel David Humphreys, in *A Poem Addressed to
the Armies of America* (1780), had tried to cheer and
quiet the continental soldiers by describing the beauty
and productivity of the Ohio lands which had been
promised them and in which they were assured that
the "golden years" would "anew begin their reigns."
But usually, as in his poem "On the Happiness of
America," Humphreys was less practical: nature was
simply a fashionable symbol for the poet to use, and,
like most of his contemporaries, he followed the fashion. Philip Freneau had already dwelt proudly upon
the subject of natural abundance in "The American
Village" in 1772, had written enthusiastically about the
natural beauties of Santa Cruz in the West Indies, and
was engaged in writing a variety of nature poems ranging from the grandeur of "The Hurricane" to the simplicity of "The Wild Honey Suckle." These poems grew
out of the poet's own experience. But the attractions
of a popular symbol led other writers far afield, and
in 1788 Richard Alsop completed but did not publish

a long poem *The Charms of Fancy* which "rang'd o'er
nature's wide domain" from the Atlantic seaboard to
the Ohio country and crossed the seas, through the
medium of travel books, to dwell upon the charms of
Tahiti, the peculiar animal life of Australia and Africa,
the fireflies and upas trees of Siam, and the gardens
of Shiraz.

Such poems as these dealt with nature in an appre-
ciative way rather than in the meditative way which
was to become a Romantic fashion. At most the
external scene refreshed the American poet, as it had
James Thomson in earlier eighteenth-century England,
or gave the same pleasure to his imagination that it
had given to Mark Akenside's. But a more philosophical consideration was already beginning to emerge. As
early as 1772, Timothy Dwight, a young tutor at Yale
College who had recently published a poem on America in the manner of Alexander Pope's *Windsor Forest*,
began to think of nature as a means of escape from
literary tradition. In "A Dissertation on the History,
Eloquence, and Poetry of the Bible," delivered at a
public commencement of the college, he attacked the
neoclassical rules and praised the biblical writers for
allowing "their imaginations an unlimited range," giving "life to the whole inanimate creation," and thereby
finding "the shortest passage to the human soul."
During the years that followed, Dwight studied and
taught the *Elements of Criticism* by Henry Home,
Lord Kames, and found in it a systematic esthetic,
which he used in his biblical epic *The Conquest of
Canäan* (1785). From Kames he learned to make his
images "distinct," "complete," and "lively" by having
the reader stand as "a real spectator" at "the very place"
from which the scene was to be described and to
achieve his effects by following the "course of nature"

in his descriptions. The results were pedantic, for Dwight was more of a schoolteacher than a poet, but he persisted in what was at least a theoretical revolt against pedantry. "Nature ought to be consulted in reference to Aristotle," he wrote in an anonymous series of critical essays called *The Friend* (1786), for "on this plan the wings of genius would be no longer clipped, and . . . the writer who produced pleasing selections of images and sentiments from the widely extended and endlessly diversified paradise of nature, would be assured of regaling the taste of his readers." Two years later, in the locodescriptive poem afterward published as *Greenfield Hill*, he put his critical theories to practice in what was perhaps his most varied and successful poetic work.

The most interesting of the meditative writers on nature, however, was Thomas Odiorne, who attempted to treat the subject philosophically in a blank verse poem unhappily called *The Progress of Refinement* (1792). Believing that the human mind was formed to bear a delicate relationship to "external things," which were, in turn, admirably formed "the mind to amuse and raise the bliss of thought," he anticipated his slightly younger contemporary William Wordsworth in an attempt to explain this mutual adjustment in terms of the associationist psychology of David Hartley. Accordingly, he carefully portrayed the development of the mind, under the influence of external nature, from its state of sensory perception through its acquisition of imaginative ideas into the increasingly complex region of ideas of ambition, self-interest, sympathy, God, and morality. Furthermore, in a true Hartleyan and Wordsworthian fashion, he dwelt upon the reciprocal influence of these complex ideas upon simple sensation, holding that a man not only grew intellectually under the influence of nature but learned by his growth to find a greater and more mature pleasure in the natural scenes that stimulated his development. Two years before this, in the Preface to the ninth edition of his poem on the happiness of America, David Humphreys had also made the Wordsworthian suggestion that the minds of American poets were "imperceptibly impressed with the novelty, beauty or sublimity of surrounding objects," which thus "gave energy to the language which expressed our sensations." But neither Humphreys nor Odiorne became a Wordsworth. In fact, the one quality they had in common with Freneau, Dwight, Alsop, and their other nature-loving contemporaries was that their language distinctly lacked the living energy of poetry.

Had they been right in their assumptions concerning the direct connection between objects and words —either by Platonic correspondence or Hartley's material vibrations—they might have shown, even within the range of their limited talents, a bit of the life they fondly hoped for. But they fooled themselves by overestimating the specious values of a fashionable subject. However poetic or philosophical they may have felt in the contemplation of natural surroundings, they could not have been stirred—even had they possessed the capacity—to the depths of the great English poets who found in nature a purer font of inspiration. For nature meant escape, peace, and a restoration of nervous energy to the troubled Wordsworth, the persecuted Shelley, and the world-weary Byron; and, no matter how they may have attempted to rationalize their relation to it, the experience of escaping from the haunts of men provided them with a release of creative energy which did vitalize their language with new qualities of sensitivity and suggestiveness. But to country-bred Americans, for whom the lowing kine were often reminders of their daily chores, nature offered no such psychological values. It was a popular symbol, large enough for them to grasp and use with no appreciation of the way it was beginning to revitalize the verbal symbols of English Romanticism. While crossing the Atlantic into a new cultural environment it suffered a sea change and became something artificial rather than alive.

Among the other gross symbols of Romanticism, the fascination of the past had little to offer Americans during the first flush of their incipient nationalism. They knew little of their own history at the time of the Revolution, for the period of historical investigation was just beginning and that of popular myth-making was to come a generation later. Yet they strove to grasp and use the past as they were using nature. As an undergraduate at the College of New Jersey Philip Freneau contemplated "The Pyramids of Egypt" with poetic awe and made efforts at an epic and a descriptive poem on Christopher Columbus. But for his public commencement poem he turned toward the future and in collaboration with a classmate, Hugh Henry Brackenridge, wrote on "The Rising Glory of America." He set the precedent for other young poets who made commencement programs ring with prophecies of the achievements of the new country, and the idea of progress became far more prevalent than pictures of the past in late eighteenth-century American verse. Poets were acutely aware, however, of the popular symbol. They versified such events from the French and Indian Wars as the capture of Louisburg and Arthur St. Clair's defeat, and stories of the ancient mound builders of the Ohio country attracted the *Anarchiad* poets, who called themselves "the Wicked

Wits" of Hartford and fascinated the anonymous author of *The Returned Captive* (1787). But only Timothy Dwight, in "The Destruction of the Pequods" in *Greenfield Hill,* succeeded in achieving anything like a Romantic tone in a treatment of the American past. Their difficulty was that progress was a part of their experience. The past was not. And in dealing with this Romantic symbol they were beginning to realize that something which made sense in terms of their own experience was a more valid source of poetic inspiration than something which did not.

The best representation of this conflict between the attractions of the past and the future, symbol and belief, is Joel Barlow's philosophical poem *The Vision of Columbus* (1787), which he was later to revise into *The Columbiad.* The actual experiences of Columbus did not interest him, and so he made his poem principally a "vision" of American colonial and Revolutionary history. But to it he added a survey of the pre-Columbian civilization of the Incas in Peru and a prophetic survey of the future when the nations of the world would be brought together by improvements in transportation and peoples would be united by the progress of thought toward the discovery of those "general laws in every breast, Where ethics, faith, and politics may rest." One survey was designed to display the highest achievements of human society under the direction of "the laws of Nature and Reason." The other foretold the future for a people who had the benefit of revelation and were following the divine plan. Each, at the time, had a genuine intellectual value for Barlow as a Romantic symbol; but each, in these insecure days of his ambitious youth, was relatively cold in its attractions. The significance of the conflict did not appear until he began to revise the poem fifteen years later. By then he was ready to leave the pre-Columbian past as he had originally described it and devote his greatest effort to a revision of his idea of progress and incorporation into it of his mature belief in the power of human effort and the self-determination of mankind.

If the symbolic value of the past was translated into a dream of the future when it crossed the Atlantic, the symbol of rebellion against tyranny suffered a more drastic change. For the tyrannical monarch—who, as exemplified by Percy Bysshe Shelley's Jove, was to become the climactic symbol of this sort in English Romanticism—had been placed in contempt before the American people by the authors of the Declaration of Independence and squeezed dry of its emotional force within a decade. By the time the federal government was being formed, the mob had a more powerful effect than the monarch as a moving symbol of tyranny. Yet the sensitiveness to new fashions was strong, and the antidemocratic young poet Richard Alsop, while reading Claude Étienne Savary's *Letters on Egypt* the year after its publication in English, was as impressed as the yet unborn Shelley was to be by the irony of the ruined statue of the tyrant Ozymandias. Alsop, too, in *The Charms of Fancy*, versified his impression. But instead of holding the monarch up for execration as Shelley did, he merely treated his "pompous claim" to unlimited power as a curious irony. The emotional value of the symbol had almost completely disappeared.

II

The decay in value which marked the passage of the grosser symbols of Romanticism did not cause them to disappear from American literature. On the contrary, they flourished on its surface as fashionable manifestations of interests which the writing of the new world reflected from that of the old. Even the least valuable among them—that of rebellion against tyranny—became commonplace in the political satire which was so characteristic of the era. In the first installment (1775) of his Revolutionary satire *M'Fingal* John Trumbull had undertaken to mock the Tories, but in the last, composed at the end of the war, he became more indignant at the tyrant mob and eventually joined the Wicked Wits of Hartford in a concerted attack upon the rule of Anarch, which they saw foreshadowed by the pre-Constitutional turmoil. Philip Freneau moved in the opposite direction politically and in the last decade of the century sacrificed most of his early Romantic promise to satiric journalism in which he versified his opposition to the aristocratic tyranny implicit in the Federalist policies as he saw them from a Jeffersonian point of view. Descriptions of nature became increasingly evident in American verse as the symbol acquired greater depth in the poetry of England, and the past was being brought into everyday consciousness by a dozen state historians and by such myth-making biographies as Parson Mason Locke Weems's of George Washington, David Humphreys' of Israel Putnam, and John Filson's less pretentious biography of Daniel Boone.

But the basic problem of the American writer remained unsolved. Unable to resist the current of influences from abroad, he could not adapt his borrowed symbols to the attitude of mind which had become his native heritage. The deepest and most original values of the symbols did not make sense in terms of his own experience. Empirical and practical by adjustment to the environment in which he lived, he was frustrated by his inability to find a practical meaning in the material which so evidently had a profound significance for authors abroad. The nature of his dilemma can perhaps be best illustrated by Charles Brockden Brown, for three years the most prolific of early American novelists. In his effort to achieve popular success, Brown turned to the Gothic tradition, generally neglected or scoffed at in matter-of-fact America, and in *Wieland* (1798) produced a tale of terror which included death by spontaneous combustion, mysterious voices, and a multiplicity of senseless murders. He tried to adapt his sensationalism to a new environment by offering a rational explanation of his mysteries, but it was not a successful attempt, for there was evidently no union of sensationalism and reason in Brown's mind as he composed the novel. With more preparatory awareness, he attempted such a union in *Arthur Mervyn* (1799) and *Edgar Huntley* (1799) by drawing upon the terrors of the yellow-fever epidemic in Philadelphia in the one and upon the dangers of the American forest in the other, but his effects were those of absurdity. That he had too little talent and too much fluency is obvious, but *Ormond* (1799) reveals a deeper reason for his failure. Here he followed William Godwin in an attempt to present an unvillainous villain, but he could not, as Godwin did in *Caleb Williams*, hold society responsible for the evil he was unwilling to attribute to an individual. The society he saw around him was not the society of classes and pressures which Godwin observed in England, and, as a result, Brown's novel was a motiveless imitation which was like Godwin in everything except the strength of belief.

A more successful writer of prose fiction was Hugh Henry Brackenridge, the classmate and collaborator of Philip Freneau, who eventually found himself observing the rising glory of America from the vantage ground of the western Pennsylvania frontier. American democracy rose, he discovered, only to heights of demagoguery and pretentious ignorance, and he sought to boost it higher by satire in the manner of *Don Quixote* and Henry Fielding's *Tom Jones*. His long-continued *Modern Chivalry* (1792–1815) outrambled its earliest prototype and outdid *Tom Jones* in its essays in explanation. But it is more alive than the writings of Brown or of the many sentimental novelists of the period, partly because of its interest as social history and partly because Brackenridge almost succeeded in mastering his material by his point of view. He found an inspiring symbol in the national scene and in his dream of a national future. But he found the reality of the scene disillusioning and his dream apparently frustrated. So he laughed—somewhat in bitterness, somewhat for relief, and somewhat in the hope that his satiric laughter might help his dream come true.

The unconscious escape into laughter and the conscious desire to achieve an idealistic aim through satire may, in fact, be one of the reasons why the mocking spirit was so strong in American literature during the late eighteenth and early nineteenth centuries—in the later essays of Benjamin Franklin, in the verses of the Wicked Wits, the political poems of Philip

Freneau, the essays and allegories of Francis Hopkinson, such novels as Royall Tyler's *The Algerine Captive* (1797), and such dramas as Tyler's *The Contrast* (1790). In any event the mockery of the early Knickerbocker group in New York—William and Peter Irving, James K. Paulding, and others—prepared the way for the first successful solution of the American writer's problem of dealing with the native past in a way which enabled him to adapt a conventional symbol to a new sense of values and thereby in effect find a literary advantage in his own apologetic self-consciousness.

Washington Irving, who was to become one of the most conventionally Romantic of American writers, began as a somewhat old-fashioned satiric humorist with contributions in the manner of Joseph Addison and of Oliver Goldsmith to New York newspapers under the signature of Jonathan Oldstyle (1802–3). A few years later he was associated with his older brother William and James K. Paulding in the composition of the *Salmagundi* papers, professedly designed to "instruct the young, reform the old, correct the town, and castigate the age." In the same spirit, he and William undertook to parody a contemporary guidebook to the city. But when the older brother gave up the project, Washington Irving, affected by a personal grief at the death of his fiancée, allowed his mind to escape into the past and produced a *History of New York* (1809) which was primarily concerned with the Dutch rule of the colony and was purportedly composed by a queer Dutch character named Diedrich Knickerbocker. Through at least one book of it ran a strong strain of contemporary satire, but on the whole it was a humorous treatment of a Romantic subject which Irving could not handle in a grave or earnest vein. He undoubtedly found in the past a means of escape from the weary weight of an unintelligible world, but the associations formed in his mind were neither lofty nor sober. His native past was something that he could take seriously but not solemnly.

Much of the humor in the Knickerbocker *History*, of course, reflected the cultivated character of Irving's youthful mind. Yet his later writings were to show that his basic temper was not that of a humorist, that the primary charm of the past to him was Romantic, and that his humor was mostly evident in his treatment of contemporary subjects and American history and legend. In *The Sketch-Book* (1819–20) his humorous cast remained evident in his observations on the English scene but was most obvious in the two American stories, "Rip Van Winkle" and "The Legend of Sleepy Hollow," attributed to Diedrich Knickerbocker. In *Bracebridge Hall* (1822) he began to mellow, and in the *Tales of a Traveller* (1824) he tended toward the serious treatment of the Gothic and the grotesque except in the American setting of "The Devil and Tom Walker." After he had become seriously interested in Spanish history and turned to Spanish legendary material for fiction, in *The Alhambra* (1832), there was little in his writing to suggest that he had ever made his reputation as a humorist. Successive revisions of the Knickerbocker *History* gradually eliminated many of the passages which had provoked laughter in the first edition, and an examination of his later writings on the American West shows that he tended to cut the comedy out of his actual experiences as he recorded them in his Journal and remove it entirely from his published *Tour of the Prairies* (1835). It took him a quarter of a century to learn to contemplate his own country without concealing his mixed emotions behind the mask of laughter.

His friend and former collaborator, James K. Paulding, was also slow to learn, and back of them both lay not only the conflict between a borrowed Romantic symbolism and an inbred attitude of mind but a theory of esthetics which exaggerated the American literary dilemma. This was the belief that literary quality depended upon the natural associations which existed in the author's mind as he wrote and which he shared with his prospective readers. It was based upon John Locke's notion that all ideas were the products of sensation and reflection and upon David Hartley's exposition of the psychological processes by which these simple ideas were combined by association. Thomas Odiorne had used this psychology in his philosophical poem on *The Progress of Refinement,* but it did not have any great effect upon literary practice until it had been systematized into esthetic doctrine by Sir Archibald Alison in 1790 and spread abroad in the early nineteenth century. Its most unhappy effect upon the American writer was to make him feel self-consciously limited, in comparison with the European, by his own nationality. Since America had no familiar past, he could either stay at home and make shift with the humdrum associations of his natural surroundings, or he could go abroad and make a belated attempt to acquire associations with a past which American readers could not share and into which he himself could not fit as naturally as could a European. Such intimate friends as the minor poets Joseph Rodman Drake and Fitz-Greene Halleck parted company over this problem—Drake to write artificially about "The Culprit Fay" in Hudson River surroundings and Halleck to go abroad and become a second-rate Byron in "Marco Bozzaris."

Irving, of course, found his serious literary inspiration abroad. But William Cullen Bryant, who was America's first successful writer in verse as Washington Irving was in prose, kept his at home. Like Irving, Bryant's first endeavors were in the field of contemporary satire, and his poem *The Embargo*, published in 1808 when the author was only fourteen, was an attack upon the Jeffersonian administration comparable to the one Irving was preparing for the fourth book of his Knickerbocker *History*. But Bryant struck his most congenial note a few years later in "Thanatopsis," a poem which in its first version represented the melancholy outpourings of a young man brooding upon an early death, when he would lie down with the wise and good of ages past and all nature would be his sepulcher. Bryant was fascinated by both of the major and by now well-established Romantic symbols, but he could find little in the American past which moved him deeply. He was to search for Romantic associations in Indian legends, in the events of the American Revolution, and in the fancies he wove about the ancient mound builders in "The Prairies," after he had paid tribute to the abstraction of "The Past" in 1828. The identifiable wise and good of ages past, however, were not buried on American soil, and there were few spontaneous associations with this theme that he could share with his fellow countrymen.

Nature, perforce, was the subject best suited to the solemn chords he had learned to strike so successfully in "Thanatopsis." He approached it in the manner of James Thomson in an "Inscription for the Entrance to a Wood" (1817), learned the art of suggestive description in "Green River" (1820), moralized it in numerous poems, and eventually pantheized it in "A Forest Hymn" (1825). He seems to have reached his greatest maturity about 1820 when he began to realize the constructive rather than the limiting implications of the associationist esthetic and, as in "A Winter Piece," allowed his descriptive verses to flow along trains of thought like those of Wordsworth with a coherence which appeared spontaneous rather than predetermined. Soon afterward he put "Thanatopsis" in its final form by giving it a framework of sixteen and a half new lines at the beginning and fifteen and a half at the end, making the sonorous lines of the original poem represent "the still voice" of Nature rather than the melancholy outpourings of youth and thereby giving them more dignified and philosophical associations. Four years later, in a lecture "On the Nature of Poetry" (1825), he distinguished between the imitative arts of painting and sculpture and the "suggestive art" of poetry, which dealt in words as arbitrary symbols and appealed to "the mind" rather than to "the senses." The success of a poem depended upon the capacity of its reader's imagination to pursue "a path which the poet only points out, and shape its visions from the scenes and allusions which he gives. It fills up his sketches of beauty with what suits its own highest conceptions of the beautiful, and completes his outline of grandeur with the noblest images its own stores can furnish." In practice and in theory, Bryant succeeded in naturalizing one of the great symbols of Romanticism by insisting that nature poetry make sense in terms of the American writer's and reader's mutual experience.

Through Irving and Bryant American literature began to move toward the solution of one of its greatest problems in achieving a character of its own. As a subordinate part of a much greater literature in English, it was inevitably subject to the dominance of the interests and fashions which developed across the Atlantic—those great and readily recognizable symbols

which had the power to stir new depths in creative
spirits and at the same time give some assurance of
communication. Provincial Americans needed this assurance badly and grasped at the means of getting it
without realizing that these symbols lost much of their
power when transferred to a different cultural environment. But Irving discovered that the American past
actually did possess vitality if he adapted his treatment
of it to the temper of his own mind and reassured himself and his readers, during his early years, with the
knowledge that he did not take it very seriously.
Bryant discovered that he could make serious use of
external nature if he adapted his treatment of it to the
stream of associations he found in his own mind and
could normally anticipate in the minds of his readers.
Both conscientiously referred their borrowed symbolism to their own individualities instead of accepting it
superficially at its face value, and neither stirred any
considerable depths in their personal reference. But
they gave the lesser symbols of their language a greater
vitality than can be found in their predecessors and
marked the way for the eventual triumphs of their
successors. It remains to be seen, however, what could
be done seriously with the American past.

III

James Fenimore Cooper became a novelist almost
by inadvertence. A landed gentleman by inheritance
and a former naval officer whose energies could not be
absorbed by farming and business, he wrote and published *Precaution* (1820) at the age of thirty-one in a
burst of irritation over an English novel on manners
on which he thought he could improve. Its Jane

Austen-like portrayal of life in an English vicarage, however, was foreign to his experience and temperament, and he turned almost immediately to a story of the country he knew and in *The Spy* (1821) told a tale of border activity in the American Revolution in the manner of Sir Walter Scott which is memorable for its yeoman hero, Harvey Birch, who was much more alive than the major historical figures who stalked its pages. Neither book wholly satisfied him, however, and so with some qualms but considerable ambition he combined the method of one with the material of the other and undertook a novel of distinctively American manners representing a typical aspect of the American past. The result was *The Pioneers* (1823), a story of frontier settlement in the Otsego country of central New York state. Its substance was drawn from the periphery of Cooper's own childhood memories, for his father had founded such a community, represented it in the federal Congress, served as its judge, and reared his family there. Young James had known its geography and inhabitants intimately and its early history by vivid hearsay.

The book, then, was the closest that American fiction had yet come to the reality of personal experience. Through it ran a romantic plot, which created a background of mystery and ended with the reconciliation of two old friends through the marriage of a recognized and a missing heir, but most of its characters were realistic representatives of frontier types—the substantial but venturesome promoter and his dependents, the shrewd and opinionated Yankees who formed the great body of settlers, the emigré French storekeeper and the wandering German, the retired soldier whose wife kept the tavern, the minister and the schoolteacher, the former British sailor who had gone into service, the humble Negro, and the professional wood chopper. On the outskirts of the settlement Cooper placed two other representative types—the "Indian John" hanger-on, Chingachgook, last of the once-great tribe of Mohicans, who died in a forest fire bravely singing his death song; and the hunter in buckskin jacket and leather stockings, Natty Bumppo, scrawny and old and wise in Indian ways, whose unfailing rifle saved the heroine from a wild panther and accompanied him on his solitary flight into the western forest after he had fought his battle with civilization and resolved the plot. From the lives and mannerisms of these people and from the opportunities for construction and entertainment on the frontier Cooper drew the real substance of his tale.

But the life of the story was not entirely of his determination. For he wrote and published at a fortunate time, when the mythology of America was just coming into being. A score of historians had by now made the American past and the American scene more familiar to the general public, and many of them had followed the example of St. John de Crèvecoeur's *Letters from an American Farmer* (1782) and of Thomas Jefferson's *Notes on Virginia* (1784–85) by struggling consciously against the European myth of the "degenerative effects" of the American climate. The "man of America," settler and savage, was being ennobled in reaction to the theories of the Comte de Buffon, Abbé Guillaume Raynal, and others in France and England. Chauvinism was growing more widespread after the successful conclusion, in 1815, of a second war with England. The war itself had discovered a new type of hero, quite unlike the gentlemanly generals George Washington and Nathanael Greene of the Revolution, in "Old Hickory" Andrew Jackson and his hunters of

Kentucky, who were credited with winning the dramatic Battle of New Orleans. The buckskin-clad hunter, in fact, had already begun to emerge in literature as the distinctive man of America. John Filson's *The Discovery, Settlement, and Present State of Kentucke* (1784) had attracted wide attention to its supposed author, Daniel Boone, as the prototype of the pioneer who opened up the wilderness west of the Appalachians, and Boone had been made the hero of an epic poem in Daniel Bryan's *The Mountain Muse* (1813). The poem had been too poor to catch the public fancy, but the public fancy was ready for a self-sufficient frontiersman who seemed at the same time both real and wonderful.

Cooper caught the wave of readiness. Natty Bumppo in his original appearance might have been too uncouth for the prepared pattern of a hero myth, but he was introduced to the public in the panther-killing episode, which was published in advance of the book and which helped sell the entire first edition in a single day and establish its author as America's first successful professional novelist. A primitivistic symbol, growing out of the national past, had finally developed in the new world.

Yet Cooper may not have been aware, at the moment, of what he had created. Natty Bumppo (or Leatherstocking, as he came more frequently to be called as the irony gradually disappeared from his characterization) certainly grew upon his creator in the course of the story and acquired dignity in *The Pioneers*. But Cooper's next book was another tale of the American Revolution, *The Pilot* (1823), built around one of the most daring ventures of John Paul Jones and centered upon the character of Long Tom Coffin as a sort of Leatherstocking of the ocean. The self-sufficient sailor, however, was not a part of the common consciousness of the American people, and it was in Natty Bumppo that Cooper found the symbol of communication as well as power. Before he left for Europe in 1826 he wrote and published *The Last of the Mohicans*—an exciting adventure story rather than a novel of manners, dealing with Natty and Chingachgook's maturity—and in Europe he completed *The Prairie* (1827), which dealt with the beginning of the westward migration and Natty's death on the Nebraska plains. Later he was to involve Natty in a self-sacrificing love affair in *The Pathfinder* (1840) and fill out the complete series of the Leatherstocking Tales with an account of Natty's youth in *The Deerslayer* (1841). With the noble young Hawkeye of that book his portrait of Natty Bumppo was complete.

As one follows the evolution of Natty's character through these books, in the order in which they were written, it becomes evident that he did not spring full-blown from Cooper's mind. His first appearance in *The Pioneers* is almost comic—a scrawny, snaggle-toothed fellow who is so absurdly dressed that his name is obviously ironic. He is more closely akin to Irving's Ichabod Crane than to Daniel Boone, as though Cooper shared Irving's inability to take seriously an American type. As he develops in the course of the book, however, his ridiculous appearance is forgotten, and he becomes a self-reliant individualist in rational rebellion against society and its rules, regulations, inflexibility, and waste. In *The Last of the Mohicans* he is a very glorification of the empiricist, the alert and accurate observer whose ready inferences are immediately translated into actions and whose self-reliant individualism is the salvation of those representatives of society who are in his charge;

and in *The Prairie* he becomes the somewhat senti-
mentalized symbol of the past, the follower of a way
of life which has no place in the modern world. It is
only in the last two books that his intuitive qualities
are greatly emphasized and the reader becomes
acutely conscious of his natural goodness. The development of Natty Bumppo's character, in fact, paral-
lels the development of American literature during the
early part of the nineteenth century and provides a
romanticized but rather extraordinary reflection of
what the authors of the Declaration of Independence
called "the American Mind."

It is for that reason, perhaps, that the character
of Natty Bumppo has remained Cooper's crowning
achievement in fiction despite the fact that he was to
write richer and more thoughtful novels than any of
the Leatherstocking Tales. In Europe he took offense
at Scott's failure to deal with social progress in his historical novels and attempted to improve on his master
in a trilogy—*The Bravo, The Heidenmauer,* and *The
Headsman* (1831–33)—which presented an American
democrat's view of the shortcomings of the Venetian
republic, the effects of the reformation in Germany,
and a fantastic survival of primogeniture in Switzer-
land. After his return to his own country in 1833 he
found that his beloved democracy had changed character in the age of Andrew Jackson, and he became
involved in bitter quarrels while devoting himself
mostly to the social criticism of such novels as *Homeward Bound* and *Home as Found* (1838) and the in-
structive essays of *The American Democrat,* of the
same year. Out of his antagonism toward the proletarian revolt of the early forties, which found expression in the reform movements, the breakup of political
parties, and the rent wars of New York state, grew

his finest novels of social history—particularly *Satanstoe* (1845), which provided the eighteenth-century background of the settlement described in *The Chainbearer* (1845) and brought the background up to date with the anti-rent violence in *The Redskins* (1846). He also wrote other novels of the American frontier, such as *Wyandotté* (1843), and dealt with the sea in many stories, of which *The Red Rover* (1828) and *Wing-and-Wing* (1842) are perhaps the best; and by the time his prolific career was brought to a close by his death in 1851 the American scene and the American past had become thoroughly absorbed in the main stream of American literature.

In his later years Cooper was joined by a host of writers who pursued similar themes in fiction. John Neal, in *Logan* (1822), had actually preceded him in an elaborate treatment of the Indian; and James K. Paulding's *Koningsmarke: the Long Finne* (1823) discovered the frontiersman simultaneously with *The Pioneers*. But it was not until the middle of the next decade that historical and frontier fiction began to flourish: Robert Montgomery Bird of Philadelphia created the most horrific of Indian fighters in *Nick of the Woods* (1837), and John Pendleton Kennedy of Baltimore turned from the nostalgic local color of *Swallow Barn* (1832) to an effective treatment of the Revolution in *Horse-Shoe Robinson* (1835). By the time Charles Fenno Hoffman produced *Greyslaer* and Daniel Pierce Thompson achieved a perennial popularity with *The Green Mountain Boys*, in 1839, novels and stories of the American past had become a fad.

Among the many writers in the new fashion, however, Cooper's only serious rival was the South Carolinian William Gilmore Simms. Beginning with *Guy Rivers* (1834) and *The Yemassee* (1835), Simms pub-

lished a large number of exciting border tales, which
included a series on the American Revolution running
from *The Partisan* (1835) to *Eutaw* (1856) and the
sensational *Beauchampe* (1842) based upon a recent
Kentucky tragedy which Poe had tried to dramatize.
But Simms's virtue was that of a storyteller rather
than that of the serious artist whose driving compulsion is to make literary symbols come to terms with
those inbred qualities of mind of which he might not
be fully aware but upon which he depends for coherence and depth of communication. An ardent south-
erner who was never completely accepted by his native
Charleston, Simms was sectional rather than national
and somewhat superficially sectional at that. He
neither created nor captured a national or a regional
myth, and despite his success in creating exciting plots
and vivid scenes his literary style is less vital than even
Cooper's.

For James Fenimore Cooper, successful though he
was in transferring the Romantic symbol of the past
into the American forest, did not triumph over all the
difficulties in the way of developing a national literature. His lesser symbols, his actual words, never
achieved the life which attracts the sensibilities of
later readers and stimulates them to search for deeper
meanings than lie on the surface of literature. Although
many of the faults which Mark Twain was later to
list as his "literary offenses" were the faults of his time,
Twain was right in his attribution of insensitivity to a
man who did not, while writing, live his material, however much of it he may have drawn from his own past
experience. What Cooper did—most evidently in the
hero of the Leatherstocking Tales—was to incorporate
in fiction the underlying and almost undefinable results of two centuries of American experience. He ob-

served the law of organized society moving into a new land and focused the sympathies of his readers upon a representative American who followed the impulses of his own individuality. He gave his representative American a rare degree of reason in making him a complete observer, acute in his inferences, sound in his judgments, and inclined to follow intuition rather than argument in matters that could not be settled by sensory perception. And he represented him as the natural product of his own environment rather than as a borrowed type placed in a new setting. Such accomplishments represent successive stages in the trial of American literature to see whether it was ready for a genuinely independent development. But Cooper realized all this within the character of Natty Bumppo rather than within himself. It was not until the writer incorporated within himself the results of this slow growth of "the American mind" that his verbal symbols became alive and American literature reached its period of triumph.

PART TWO

The Achievement
1829-1867

CHAPTER FOUR

The Empirical Attitude

I

IF any single author epitomizes the American literary experience of the second quarter of the nineteenth century he is Edgar Allan Poe. Born in Boston of strolling players, he was orphaned at the age of three and taken into the home of John Allan in Richmond, Virginia, and educated in private schools in England and Richmond in preparation for the University of Virginia. After a financially catastrophic year at the university he quarreled with his foster father and ran away to his native Boston where, at the age of eighteen, he enlisted under an assumed name as a private in the United States Army and left with a printer his first volume of verse, *Tamerlane and Other Poems*, which appeared in 1827 with no other signature than "By a Bostonian" on its title page. When a year and a half of successful soldiering found him stationed near Richmond, he renewed his relationships with John Allan and gained his assistance in getting a discharge from the ranks and an appointment to the United States Military Academy at West Point. He was not again accepted into the Allan household, however, and

while awaiting his long-delayed appointment sought
out his paternal relatives in Baltimore, where he made
his home with his inadequately pensioned grandfather, his aunt, Maria Clemm, and her small daughter Virginia. There he published a second volume
of *Poems* in 1829, under his own name, and entered the academy in the autumn of 1830. He had
been a good enlisted man, but he was now writing
poetry and was rebellious against the discipline used
to turn him into an officer and gentleman. As a result,
he tried in vain to get an honorable discharge, committed a record number of disciplinary offenses, and
left for New York with the permission of the authorities, who court-martialed and officially dismissed him
in absentia. He took with him enough manuscripts to
justify a new edition of his *Poems* and enough subscrip-
tions from his fellow cadets to enable him to print it a
few months later in 1831.

This brief personal history is important because it
helps explain why Poe, in four short years, made his
own peculiar way through the whole literary experience of the preceding generation. He was a socially
displaced person—a man who called himself a Bostonian in Virginia accents, who had been reared as an
orphan in a city which judged a person by his family
background, and brought up to be a gentleman without the funds to sustain his gentility. Both proud and
weak, he had no sustaining background which he
could proudly call his own; and in his weakness, as
his poems show, he was inclined to project himself by
his imagination into other backgrounds and take on
the protective coloring he found there. His experience
resembled that of the earlier generation because he
borrowed the symbols of English Romanticism, but it
was peculiar in that Poe's symbols were not so much

the major subjects and themes of the Romantics as the personalities of the Romantic poets themselves. He apparently tried to be—not simply to write like—Lord Byron and Samuel Taylor Coleridge and, to a lesser extent, John Keats and Percy Bysshe Shelley.

Poe's deeper inclination toward personal rather than toward thematic symbols was not the result of indifference toward the latter. For the title poem of his first volume, *Tamerlane*, was a consciously associationist poem dealing with the influence of nature upon the human spirit in terms of the psychological theories of David Hartley. Under the influence of his natural surroundings its hero developed ideas of sensation, imagination, ambition, and self-interest, and was seduced by a "fickle star within" himself to leave his native mountains and conquer the world before he acquired the higher and more complex ideas of sympathy, God, and morality, for which he eventually returned. But the returned hero is Byronic—old in deeds but not in years, the proud outlaw of his own dark mind, self-exiled from his own success—and attention is focused so intensely, through the device of the confessional monologue, upon the character of the hero that the theme of the poem is generally overlooked. Writing in the first person with many suggestions of self-revelation, Poe identified himself with the Byron of the later *Childe Harold* and *Manfred* and confirmed the identification in his revisions of the poem by excising some of the associationist language and transforming the "fickle star" which led him astray into a Byronic inner "fire."

Such Byronism was not at all unusual, of course, in a time when a majority of young American poets were adopting a "pale but interesting" pose, and it seems natural enough to discover it in "Dreams," "Spirits of the Dead," "Stanzas," and various other poems in the 1827 volume. The peculiar quality of Poe's imagination only becomes evident when he abandoned his Byronism and adopted the personality of Keats for his "Sonnet—To Science" in 1829 and to a certain extent for "Al Aaraaf" in the same volume. In 1831 he became Shelley for a while in his Platonic conception of "Israfel," and both Shelley and Byron entered for a moment into the composition of the otherwise Coleridgean poem "The Sleeper." He had evidently discovered and been captivated by the Galignani pirated edition of Coleridge, Shelley, and Keats; and of the three the personality of Coleridge made the deepest impression upon him. It was to last for a long time, but among his early writings it is most apparent in "The City in the Sea" (1831), where he followed the dreamy imagination of the author of "Kubla Khan" down through the "caverns measureless to man into a sunless sea," where he found a city which may have been designed for pleasure but was inhabited by Death.

The literary evidences of a tendency toward borrowed personality are hard to separate from evidences of imitation and even parody, and Poe's first ventures into prose fiction, in his plan for a collection of "Tales of the Folio Club," show that he actually depended upon imitation and parody for his literary inspiration. The only practical distinction between the two processes, perhaps, must be made in terms of depth. When Poe wrote "The Scythe of Time" (later called "The Predicament"), for example, he was obviously writing a parody of the kind of magazine fiction he had satirized in "How to Write a Blackwood Article"; but when he used the same formula and the same conceit of the scythe of time in "The Pit and the Pendulum" he gave the impression of a personal sense of terror rather than that of the commercialized sensationalism which he had once satirized. Poe's success in creating this sort of illusion was first evident in the early horror story "Berenice," which he sent to the editor of the *Southern Literary Messenger* in 1834 with a letter of apology and explanation. The story might be considered a violation of good taste, he wrote, but it was of the kind that increased the circulation of the popular British magazines; and he cited numerous examples, including the serialized *Confessions of an English Opium Eater,* which was then thought to be the composition of Coleridge. The knowing references to opium dreams and other dissipations in such successive stories as "Ligeia" and "The Fall of the House of Usher" show that Poe was building his own Romantic personality out of elements of Coleridge and Byron and, as a writer at least, living this role convincingly.

This Romantic personality reached its most perfect development in "The Raven" in 1845, in which the Byronic hero was struggling, like Coleridge in the "Ode to Dejection," to find surcease from sorrow by abstruse research in strange and curious volumes of forgotten lore; and in the recitations he delivered as "the author of 'The Raven'" Poe seems to have played this role to the limit by making the most of his pale but interesting countenance and his threadbare suggestion of a proud past. But the role could have been satisfactory to him only in occasional creative moments. For Poe's normal life was anything but romantic. He had married his cousin Virginia when she had reached the age of thirteen, and by doing so had acquired a mother in Mrs. Clemm and the obligation to support a family in the hard world of commerical journalism. As editor of the *Southern Literary Messenger,* Burton's *Gentle-*

man's Magazine, and *Graham's,* as free-lance writer
and eventually as proprietor of his own *Broadway
Journal,* he fought off poverty from 1835 to 1845 with
copyreading, criticism, reviewing, and creative work
in a profession where competition was stiff and ruthless and he himself was handicapped by susceptibility
to alcohol. To survive and maintain his pathetic pride
in such an environment he had to play an empirical
as well as a Romantic role.

His earliest approaches to commercial fiction were
in themselves indicative of an empirical strain of mind,
and this strain found a public outlet in his early criticism. But this anti-Romantic attitude became a role
about 1841 when he began to write such calculated
"tales of ratiocination" as "The Murders in the Rue
Morgue," "A Descent into the Maelström," "The Mystery of Marie Rogêt," and "The Gold Bug." At about
the same time, in 1842, he systematized his critical
formula for the short story in a review of Nathaniel
Hawthorne's *Twice-Told Tales* which stressed the
need for "unity of effect" through an appeal to some
single intellectual faculty comparable to faculties identified by the pseudoscientific theories of phrenology.
In his detailed account of M. Dupin's methods of observation and inference in "The Murders in the Rue
Morgue" Poe had identified and described the sort of
ratiocination used in these stories and in much of his
criticism, but he did not lay claim to it as the dominant quality of his own mind until he published "The
Philosophy of Composition" (1846) in a gesture of
rebellion against any identification of himself with the
hero of "The Raven." For the hero of this fantastic
account of how he wrote the poem is the complete
opposite of the Romantic—a coldly calculating emotional engineer whose approach to poetry is rational

rather than emotional, empirical rather than intuitive
—a kind of Benjamin Franklin among poets who could
pass himself off as a Byron whenever he put his mind
to it. The personal implications of the poem and the
essay are almost schizophrenic.

But Poe, however morbid he might appear in the
pages of biographers who were overimpressed by his
Romantic past, was not a mental case. He was an
American, striving to find a successful way to adapt
borrowed literary symbols to an inbred attitude of
mind. He had obscurely felt, as Cooper had not, that
the adaptation should be made within himself; and
his unfortunate personal circumstances had enabled
him first to project himself into his symbols. But his
whole cultural environment was against this experiment, and he reacted by professing to be a sort of
architect of composition who was as practical and
materialistic as the world in which he moved. Yet he
knew that his reaction was extreme, and even before
writing "The Philosophy of Composition" he had
sought a middle ground of intellectuality on which he
could stand firmly. He defined it in a revised characterization of M. Dupin in "The Purloined Letter" of
1845. In this story Dupin developed into a man of intuition as well as a man of reasoning, a poet as well as
a mathematician, whose imagination provided him
with a hypothesis, whose reason controlled its application in terms of probability, and whose observation
merely verified it. He reversed the procedure he had
followed in "The Murders in the Rue Morgue" and
"The Mystery of Marie Rogêt" by first solving the
mystery and then looking over the situation. In the
language of eighteenth-century American intellectual
history, he followed "an intellectual light within him"
when the "light of sense" (as represented by such a

highly trained observer as the prefect of police) had failed.

This was the intellectual pattern that Poe himself, in his later years, was determined to follow and by which he was to reconcile the two extremes of his affected personalities. He was to write like the introspective hero of "The Raven" in such later poems as "Ulalume" and "Annabel Lee," like the calculating author of "The Philosophy of Composition" in "The Bells," and perhaps like a combination of the two in the technically magnificent short story "The Cask of Amontillado"; but the work he took most seriously and by which he expected to be known to posterity was his prose poem *Eureka*, published in 1848, the year before his death. In it he attempted to solve the mystery of the universe, its creation and destruction, and he began by a grotesque satire upon traditional modes of reasoning and an intensely serious description of the intellectual path that he himself would pursue. The reasoning processes he satirized were the "creeping and crawling" methods of deductive logic from Aristotle to Immanuel Kant and of inductive logic from Francis Bacon to John Stuart Mill. The true advancement of learning, he maintained, came through leaps of intuition, which produced theories that could be called truths when they were corrected and cleared of their inconsistencies. By this method he developed his highly imaginative conception of a universe which had been created by an explosion of "unparticled matter" and which was falling rapidly toward its own center and would eventually collapse into the nothingness of unparticled matter again.

Such a grandiose theory, of course, was unlike M. Dupin's theory of the purloined letter in that it could not be verified by observation; and Poe's last mad gesture of escape was to spurn all solid ground while allowing his imagination to take off into infinity under the exclusive control of his phrenological bump of comparison. Yet in his own peculiar way he discovered the method of bringing life into the verbal symbols of American literature by striving intensely within himself to bring into adjustment the larger symbols of popular communication in English and the basic attitude of mind absorbed from his American environment. He was pursuing what Nathaniel Hawthorne, in a favorite phrase, called "wisdom tested by the tenor of a life." The inadequacy and pretentiousness of his wisdom and the waywardness and perversity of his life limit his greatness but not his vitality. His words live to be read—with pleasure, fascination, and often distaste, but with an inner value that cannot be denied. With him American literature passed through its trial and entered its period of triumph.

II

The tenor of Nathaniel Hawthorne's life was as different from that of Poe's as was his background. For Hawthorne was a firmly settled New Englander, born and bred in the oldest of Massachusetts Bay towns, Salem, where until the age of thirty-four he lived with his widowed mother and older sisters with only such ventures abroad as were required by summer vacations, a college education in Bowdoin, and a brief interval of magazine editorship in Boston. Three years after his graduation from college he published his first novel, *Fanshawe* (1828), which started out as an imitation and ended up as a synopsis of the manner of Sir Walter Scott—a performance which evidently shocked its author as soon as he saw it in print, for he immediately withdrew it from circulation and attempted to destroy the existing copies. When he recovered he began the slow process of learning to write, and the rest of his life was devoted to the two severely practical activities of writing and earning a living. He rarely mixed the two—never, after his first early experience, attempted to become a journalist like Poe. He earned very little from his short stories, and before he became a novelist he lived by working in the Boston Customs House from 1838 to 1840, by acting as the unpaid treasurer for Brook Farm (in the vain hope of finding in that Transcendental community a place to live cheaply, write, and bring his wife-to-be during the following year), and by serving as surveyor of customs in his native Salem from 1847 to 1849. Eight years later he was appointed American consul in Liverpool by a classmate who had been elected president of the United States, and after four fairly remunerative years he turned again to writing, in Italy and England, before coming home to die in 1863.

From intensive reading in the secluded atmosphere of old Salem and from the folklore he picked up on his vacations, Hawthorne acquired a richer knowledge of the New England past than was possessed by most writers of his generation, and he was closely associated with it through the traditions of his own family, which included a judge in the notorious Salem witchcraft trials of the seventeenth century and the popular hero of a Revolutionary sea ballad. *Fanshawe,* though its scene was a college town very much like the one he knew, had shown how much he had been attracted by the historical romance; and it was only natural, when he began to write more seriously, that he should have accepted the popular symbol of the past as his medium of communication. He was also attracted, like Poe, by the Gothic element in English Romanticism and was to make frequent use of the supernatural and the occult. He was not, however, a sensationalist by nature or by affectation. By cultural tradition he was a moralist and by disposition an observer, and his creative imagination was compact of Romantic symbols and realistic observations leading to some moral conclusion. The tenor of his own life was detached, matter-of-fact almost to the point of skepticism, and judicious; and the wisdom which passed its test was mildly speculative and largely empirical.

The story of Hawthorne's development as a literary artist is the story of a growing firmness of confidence in his own wisdom and of a gradual shift of emphasis from symbol to substance until Romantic material became a flexible medium of realistic self-expression. One of the earliest of his published short stories, a mere sketch called "The Hollow of the Three Hills" (1830), is interesting chiefly as an illustration of his starting point. Its time is the colonial period, its setting something like Poe's later "misty mid-region of Wier," and its characters a witch and her client who wants a supernatural vision of the effects of her elopement upon her abandoned husband and family. She learns that the effects have been devastating and dies in an illustration of the moral, so conventional to the triangle story in sentimental fiction, that the wages of sin is death. From such an unpromising beginning Hawthorne developed a richness of intellectual and artistic interests which can only be sampled in terms of certain questions which he posed to himself and answered as he grew in assurance. The most important of these, perhaps, concerned the validity of empirical observations—the trustworthiness of those appearances from which the senses collected material for judgment. Hawthorne posed the question in the story of "Young Goodman Brown" (1835) who either attended or dreamed that he had attended a witches' Sabbath and saw there all the good people of his seventeenth-century New England village. Was his experience real or imaginary? Were the good people hiding hearts of evil or were they what they seemed? Young Goodman Brown was never allowed to know because Hawthorne himself had not yet made up his mind. He offered a tentative opinion almost immediately in the allegory of "The Minister's Black Veil" (1836) in which the veil was a symbol of the minister's conviction that every man's heart was obscure to his fellows, but it was not until 1843, in "Egotism, or The Bosom Serpent" that he expressed his own belief in the ubiquity of secret sin. The questioning skepticism apparent in these stories, however, was a permanent quality of his mind.

Such skepticism posed another question for the artist who had to deal in appearances but had to go beneath them in order to avoid the superficial and the commonplace. Could he do so? He could, Hawthorne decided, but only at a cost to himself. If he dug into his material with an inner wisdom, Hawthorne suggested in "Drowne's Wooden Image" (1844), he might, in "a brief period of excitement, kindled by love," find the touch of genius necessary to the life of his own images. But the price, he added in "The Artist of the Beautiful" (published in the same month), was isolation from the common affairs of humanity through a predominating "sense of moral cold," which placed ordinary human love in competition with his art. Even if he succeeded in the supreme act of creation, the practical attitude of the world might rob his work of its life, or carelessness might destroy it. The artist was a lonely man whose greatest accomplishment had to be realized entirely within himself.

Most of Hawthorne's American contemporaries felt that the writer's place was on the world's great field of battle—that he should be up and doing—and Hawthorne himself found a resemblance between the isolation of the poet and that of such active types as the prophet, the reformer, and the criminal. So, in the years of his development, he had to face a final question concerning the responsibilities of a man whose pursuits placed him "either in advance of mankind, or apart from it." He had already expressed the opinion, in "Dr. Heidegger's Experiment" (1837), that it was vain to interfere with the normal course of natural events, and in "The Birth Mark" (1843) he concluded that the effort to do so would lead only to tragedy. His world was the everyday world, and his role in it was that of a penetrating observer who brought forth wisdom and expressed it in a form designed for delight. Such was the wisdom he had tested by the tenor of his own life and brought to literary perfection in the last and finest of his short stories from this period— "Rappaccini's Daughter" (1844), the Gothic folk tale of a poison maiden whose beautiful appearance concealed the death within and whose innocent love affair demonstrated the tragedy of cold-blooded interference with the course of nature. Hawthorne's use of Romantic material to express his realistic view of the world reached its climax in that story.

But he was to continue to develop as an artist, and the short stories also reveal the influence of his intellect upon his art. For Hawthorne's compulsion to observe beneath the surface of human appearances pushed him into the realm of psychology. An impulse in that direction may be seen in one of the earliest of his tales, "Roger Malvin's Burial" (1832), in which he shows an interest in the effects of a broken promise upon a young man's later life and his tragic release from its burden. The impulse is stronger in "Young Goodman Brown," where the question of the actuality of Brown's experience is irrelevant to the author's concern with the question raised by its effect upon him. "The Minister's Black Veil" often puzzles readers by its subtitle "A Parable" because the parable is in the minister's act of donning the veil and the story is mostly about the psychological effects of the act upon the puzzled parishioners. What was happening in these and other stories was that Hawthorne's artistic interest was developing in two directions—one the direction of meditating upon the questions posed in his tales and eventually expressing his opinions in the form of conclusive moral allegories, and the other the direction of pursuing his answers through the minds of his characters. "Rappaccini's Daughter" owes much of its effectiveness to the fact that it avoided these extremes and is neither a psychological story nor an allegory but a fantasy which includes motive and meaning, and it was in this state of balance between two artistic directions that Hawthorne escaped from the pressure of constant writing and gathered his forces for a return to the longer form of fiction.

In the two decades after *Fanshawe* Hawthorne's total publication amounted to only three volumes of short stories: *Twice-Told Tales* in 1837, a second edition with an added volume in 1842, and *Mosses from an Old Manse* in 1846. The last took its title from the house in Concord, Massachusetts, to which he had taken his bride, Sophia Peabody, and in which he lived until his savings were exhausted and he was in desperate need to stop writing and work for a living. A new political administration enabled him to receive an appointment as surveyor of customs in Salem, and he laid aside his pen and returned home in 1847. He was approaching the peak of his creative development, however, and his major intellectual preoccupations with secret sin and the evils of interfering with nature seem to have been pushing him toward some story which would be longer and more clearly moral than "Rappaccini's Daughter." What was going on in his mind and in the privacy of his office or study is not a matter of record, but we can infer from the results that he was at the crossroads of his development. He could either invent a story which had a meaning and thus continue with his parables or moral allegories, or he could make a story out of his own search for its meaning by exploring the effects of some significant action upon the inner lives of his characters and thus become a psychological novelist. Although he could not have seen his alternatives so clearly, it is probable that he considered the novel as an art form and rejected it because he did not trust himself to deal with the common affairs of everyday life as he thought a formal novelist must. Instead he settled upon the "romance"—something off the beaten paths of normal existence—which would give him the freedom of intellectual realism without the restraints of actuality. But his dilemma existed even within the bounds of this compromise.

The result, in 1849, was the "fragment" of an "abortive" moral romance and a completed historical one. The first was published in the *Boston Magazine* for January of the following year under the title "Ethan Brand." It took its origin from a suggestion contained in "Egotism, or The Bosom Serpent" that there was some wanderer abroad in the world whose secret sin was worse than egotism, and it identified this "unpardonable sin" as an abstract "hardness of heart." But a reference within the published story was more specific; for Ethan Brand, in his wandering search for the unpardonable sin, had at one time performed a "psychological experiment upon a young girl," and this violation of another personality was his most severe offense against human sympathy. The published story was another Gothic fantasy, but back of it lay some of Hawthorne's very real preoccupations and worries—his feeling that an artist's inquisitive observations estranged him from humanity, his agitated fears concerning his wife's interest in mesmerism as a possible psychological cure for her frequent headaches, his conscience-ridden notion that his own professional curiosity about the human mind somehow identified him with hypnotic charlatans of the stage and couch and categorized artists as passive brethren of criminals and reformers.

But Hawthorne was finding human beings too complex to be presented as figures in moral allegory. He had read the psychological writings of his old college professor Thomas Upham and had found in Upham's simplified theories a framework for analyzing individuals without risking the pitfalls of actuality. His finished romance, in consequence, was analytic rather than allegorical in its conception, deterministic rather than parabolic in its plot. *The Scarlet Letter* (1850) was a story of the three major characters in a conventional triangle plot: Hester Prynne, who was married to an elderly physician, Roger Chillingworth, and her lover, the brilliant young Puritan minister, Arthur Dimmesdale. The hackneyed love story so familiar to readers of the sentimental novel, however, was entirely in the background. Hawthorne began his tale with Hester's release from the colonial New England prison, where she had served the first part of her sentence for adultery; she was beginning her additional sentence, to wear forever in public the scarlet letter "A" as a sign of her sin. He could not have written the book had not two decades of observation, since "The Hollow of the Three Hills," taught him that the wages of sin might be life instead of death. For the story was about Hester's growth and her lover's and husband's decay —a growth and decay determined by the effects of her adultery upon three characters of distinctly different psychological composition.

In the terms used by Upham for his threefold analysis of personality—intellect, affections, and will—all three characters were of high intellectual capacity, although Hester's capacities were undeveloped. Her primary characteristic at the beginning of the story is the strength of will which enables her to endure her punishment, remain in her own community with her illegitimate child, and wear her symbol of adultery boldly while stubbornly concealing the identity of her lover. The first part of the book deals with her intellectual growth until "her life had turned, in a great measure, from passion and feeling, to thought," and she had assumed "a freedom of speculation" almost unknown in colonial America. But "the scarlet letter," Hawthorne said, "had not yet done its office." Her passion and feeling had been self-centered, and the remaining part of the story reveals the development of her social affections as her peculiar circumstances brought her into broader sympathy with humankind. She became, at the end, a completely developed person. In contrast, Roger Chillingworth's lack of sympathy destroyed him. Rich in his intellectual endowments, strong in will, he devoted himself to the purpose of discovering and destroying the man who had wronged him. His was the hardness of heart attributed to Ethan Brand, and he demonstrated it by the psychological experiment he performed on Arthur Dimmesdale while serving as a physician to his body as he tried to destroy his soul. What he actually accomplished was his own spiritual destruction. Between the two stood Arthur Dimmesdale, intellectual and compassionate, who was too weak to confess and pay the social penalty for his crime and whose weakness made him the battleground for the conflicting wills of Hester and Roger. He died physically of the strain but was saved spiritually when, with Hester's assistance, he found the strength of will necessary to gasp out his confession. This psychological plot was worked out in little more than outline, for Hawthorne was an expositor rather than an illustrator of the inner lives of his characters; but this was the plot determined by that "dark necessity" of which Roger Chillingworth spoke with "gloomy sternness" when he referred to "fate" in terms of a chain of causation beginning with Hester's first sin.

The Scarlet Letter is thus the first deterministic novel in English, but Hawthorne was a moralist rather than a logician, and the intellectual substance of the story is to be found in its anti-Puritan morality rather than in the Edwardsian or Cartesian logic of its plot. Unlike Alfred Tennyson in the contemporary *Idylls of the King,* Hawthorne had looked at the world rather than its conventions for the truth he would express in his art. He had discovered that empirical truth and proverbial morality did not always correspond and had merely chosen to rationalize his empirical observations in terms of psychological determinism. That his deterministic method was an artistic device rather than a serious intellectual quality is revealed by his next book, *The House of the Seven Gables* (1851), in which the determinism was purely romantic and the morality conventional—the working out of an old curse which visited the sins of the fathers upon the children of several generations. He came closer to the conventional novel in this story of contemporary Salem, which included among its characters a leading politician of the town, than he ever came in his other books; but he reversed his usual method by making the plot romantic and its trappings real and sacrificed his greatest strength in the change.

For Hawthorne's peculiar attraction for critics who are too sophisticated for the sensationalism of Poe is to be found in his use of Romantic symbols to express the thoughtful conclusions of a realistic mind. From that came the quality of ambiguity, ambivalence, or irony which many critics love faithfully despite their inconstant terminology; and the weakness of his later novels came from his efforts to escape or subordinate the Romantic symbols he had learned to use so well. His next book, *The Blithedale Romance* (1852), had as its working title the name of its central character, Hollingsworth, and was evidently designed as a realistic case study of a type prevalent on the American scene —the reformer, a man so obsessed with philanthropy that his natural human sympathies were perverted to the brink of madness. Its setting was partly in a Transcendental community like Brook Farm, which was "a little removed from the highway of ordinary travel," he said in the Preface, and was therefore a theater in which his characters could act out their parts "without exposing them to too close a comparison with the actual events of real lives." But he seems to have felt insecure without his Gothic symbols and so introduced into the book an unnecessary secondary villain, the mesmerist Westervelt, who performed a psychological experiment upon a young girl and brought with him an atmosphere of mystery but made no real contribution to the major plot. This was to be Hawthorne's last work of fiction for eight years. It represented a broadening of his psychological interests from the individuals he had examined in *The Scarlet Letter* to the types he had approached in *The House of the Seven Gables* and handled more firmly here. But it also represented a tendency toward speculative psychology which took him off the solid ground of observation, weakened his control over Romantic symbols, and made him use them for sensational rather than intellectual effects.

When Hawthorne had written his campaign biography of Franklin Pierce, served out his consular appointment at Liverpool, traveled in Italy, and returned to fiction with *The Marble Faun* (1860) his tendency toward speculation had increased and his interests broadened from the psychology of types to the philosophy of human nature. This was his most ambitious novel, for in it he attempted to sketch the Italy of monuments, art galleries, and expatriate Americans and to deal with the philosophical problem of evil as he had dealt with the individual problem in *The Scarlet Letter*. Its central character was the faunlike Donatello, Count of Monte Beni, who has the natural innocence and graceful simplicity of an animal until he commits a murder at the subtle instigation of a female character and is brought by punishment and remorse to a state of moral consciousness which makes him human. The story is a modern version of the Garden of Eden with the Miltonic thesis of the fortunate Fall through which humankind can be elevated to a new and greater estate than that of innocence. An American sculptor, Kenyon, makes its implications specific when he confesses to his "perplexity": "Sin has educated Donatello, and elevated him. Is sin, then,—which we deem such a dreadful blackness in the universe,—is it, like sorrow, merely an element of human education, through which we struggle to a higher and purer state than we could otherwise have attained? Did Adam fall, that we might ultimately rise to a far loftier paradise than his?" With Hester Prynne, Hawthorne had been able to give a clearly affirmative answer to a comparable question because he had seen enough of the world to imagine an individual who could be improved by experiencing sin and suffering its consequences. Logically he could extend his imagination backward to the realization of such a character in a state of innocence comparable to that of the original Adam. But did he have any empirical evidence for the universal application of his particular observations? Could the Baconian method support a great philosophical truth?

In Hawthorne's mind it could not. The sculptor could only ask forgiveness of the shocked Hilda who protested that his speculations made mockery "not only of all religious sentiments, but of moral law." Hawthorne himself had the same limitations as Matthew Arnold in "Dover Beach"; he could merely say, in effect, "Ah, love, let us be true to one another," as the sea of his empirical wisdom withdrew over the drear and naked shingles of a world beyond his powers of observation. His wisdom was that of his own life—observant, questioning, perceptive, and assured only when his speculations could be supported by his individual perceptions. Like Poe, he was tempted to speculate beyond the limits of his individual wisdom; but, unlike the wayward author of *Eureka,* he held onto the light of the senses rather than discard it in favor of some intellectual light within. In doing so he sacrificed breadth and failed to master the great philosophical theme with which his fancy played in *The Marble Faun,* but he brought the symbols of Romanticism down to American earth and in *The Scarlet Letter* completely mastered them. He and Poe each illustrates in his own way the lesson that the American writer had been obliged to learn—that he had to find within himself the means of adapting the popular materials of a literature in English to the attitudes of mind characteristic of people who were not English but who were sharing with the English a cultural heritage which had begun to diverge into separate ways. He differed from Poe in that his life and mind were more firmly rooted in the prevailing empiricism of the American tradition, and in that difference lay Hawthorne's greatest strength and his greatest limitation.

III

The lesson illustrated by Poe and Hawthorne is one that American writers found hard to learn, and the external forces that encouraged a talented man to take the easy way of avoiding it are best revealed in the career of Henry Wadsworth Longfellow. A younger classmate of Hawthorne's at Bowdoin College, Longfellow was a more brilliant man to whom success came early. At the time of his graduation at the age of seventeen he was offered a position as instructor in modern languages at his college and went abroad to improve his knowledge of French, Spanish, and Italian. By the time he reached the age at which Hawthorne began his apprenticeship to the art of the short story, Longfellow had proved himself a competent poet and essayist and so able a teacher and scholar that he was offered the Smith Professorship of Modern Languages at Harvard on condition that he make another trip abroad in order to perfect himself in "the German." On this trip his young wife died in Rotterdam, and the bereaved husband threw himself into the study of modern German literature, escaping, somewhat as Poe did, into symbols created by other writers and especially by the young Johann Wolfgang von Goethe. He also met the stately young Frances Appleton, daughter of a prominent Boston banker, and spelled his grief by long private periods of Romantic passion.

When he returned to take up his duties at Harvard, he continued to pursue Frances, proposed marriage and was rejected, and exposed his pursuit and passion most romantically in two books published in 1839— *Hyperion: A Romance*, strongly influenced by Goethe's *The Sorrows of Young Werther*, and a volume of poems appropriately called *Voices of the Night*. The two books revealed enough to contemporary Boston to cause something of a scandal, and the second reveals enough to the historian to show that Longfellow had learned early and consciously the lesson that Poe and Hawthorne illustrate. For the collection of poems included some of his early nature verse in the manner of English Romanticism, and in the "Proem" to the volume he referred to them and declared that he should put aside such childish things and look into his heart and write. He resolved to do so, expressing his passionate distress in such verses as those of the title poem and indicating his determination to overcome it in "The

Psalm of Life," which he had written to illustrate and grasp the mature wisdom of the Goethe who composed the articles of indenture for the conclusion of *Wilhelm Meister's Apprenticeship*. But the public reaction to his attempt to wear a German heart on a Boston sleeve evidently made him review his lesson and discard it. Instead of developing a greater emotional maturity in his verse, he suppressed the dictates of his heart, produced a collection of popular *Ballads and Other Poems* in 1842, and never again exposed his inner life to the public although he worried himself to the verge of a nervous breakdown and made another trip abroad to recover.

The rewards for his discretion were many and great. He quickly became the most popular and most highly paid magazine poet in America, Frances married him in 1843, and he settled down to a widely admired family life in Craigie House as a scholar-poet whose adaptations of foreign meters to English words made him one of the most versatile poetic technicians in the language. The shorter poems collected in such volumes as *The Belfrey of Bruges and Other Poems* (1846) and *The Seaside and the Fireside* (1850), the narrative *Tales of a Wayside Inn* (1863, 1872, 1873), and the long single poems *Evangeline* (1847), *Hiawatha* (1855), and *The Courtship of Miles Standish* (1858) were all enormously popular and made him the best known of all American writers abroad. But he had his secret disappointments. The posthumously published sonnet, "Mezzo Cammin," written on his thirty-fifth birthday during his third trip abroad, reflects his regret at having spent half his life without accomplishing some great work; and he evidently tried to force such an accomplishment by finding some great subject. He experimented unsuccessfully with the major reform movement of his time in some *Poems on Slavery* (1842) but eventually settled upon a poetic history of Christianity in the form of a dramatic trilogy. He began with a considerable amount of energy by a treatment of Christianity in the Middle Ages in *The Golden Legend* (1851) but had to force himself to the continuation in *The New England Tragedies* (1868)—one of them, *John Endicott*, actually written in prose and translated into blank verse—and to the first drama of the trilogy, *The Divine Tragedy* (1871). Published all together as *Christus: A Mystery*, they sold well but represented no great literary achievement: Longfellow never succeeded in erecting that "lofty parapet of song" of which he dreamed in his youth.

Yet running through the great amount of his work is a thin strain of memorable poetry which stands out in impressive contrast to the wordy hexameters of the sentimental *Evangeline* and the even wordier trochees of the Indian epic *Hiawatha*. And most of it shows that he had ignored rather than forgotten the lesson summarized in the "Proem" for his first collection of verse. For Longfellow's best poems were formed by the union of some detached image with a deep emotion which he was able only obliquely to express. "The Arsenal at Springfield" (1844) is a magnificent exercise in metaphor comparing the massed guns to an organ, but it is vitalized by a passion for peace under the threat of imminent war; and "The Building of the Ship" (1849) gathers force from the concluding intensity of the poet's demand for union at a time when the sentiment for disunion was strong in New England. Such poems as "My Lost Youth" (which adapted Johann von Herder's translation of a Lapland song to Longfellow's nostalgia for Portland, Maine) or "Jugurtha" and other poems on old age may be exceptions to the rule in that they are direct expressions of conventional emotions, but Longfellow's finest poetic achievement was a direct outgrowth of his deepest and most carefully controlled feeling.

The six sonnets of the "Divina Commèdia" sequence were written and used as introductions and conclusions to Longfellow's translation of the three parts of Dante Alighieri's poem. But they bear reference to the tragic occasion which forced him into the labor of translation—the death of Frances, by fire from an exploding lamp, in the spring of 1861. As he had done after the death of his first wife, Longfellow sought to escape from personal sorrow by entering into another literature in another language; but this time he was able to blend his greater grief with a work of art more intellectually and emotionally mature than the products of German Romanticism. The first sonnet, used to introduce the *Inferno*, is the most directly personal. In it Longfellow compares Dante's "medieval miracle of song" to a great Gothic cathedral into which he can enter, "not ashamed to pray," and escape "the loud reverberations of the street" while "the eternal ages watch and wait." The allusion, however, is to the turmoil accompanying the outbreak of the American Civil War in that year, and it is only by indirection that the reader can follow the author in this and successive sonnets through the stages of his private grief for which the stages of Dante's poem serve as a device which some modern critics would call an "objective correlative." Yet the fifth sonnet, introducing the *Paradiso*, is deeply moving in its imagery of Beatrice "clothed in a garment as of flame" and of the rose; and the sixth, with its great tribute to the poet whose words provided "the pathway of thought for all Italy," may have acquired dignity from the author's own determination to continue building, almost immediately, his own lofty parapet of song. Longfellow was to pay fine and discriminating tribute to other poets in other sonnets during the years that followed, and he may have been at his best in recognizing in others those qualities that he had not been able to achieve.

In some respects the most happy of American writers were those who faced the conditions faced by Longfellow—the rich rewards of conformity to the public taste and the condemnation of all deviation into European manners—and found within themselves the qualities which a superficial public liked. Such a person, at any rate, was Oliver Wendell Holmes—a wit and man of sentiment who blended his two characteristics into a light charm from which he rarely deviated in his poems or essays. From the time he brought together the sentiment of "Old Ironsides" and the wit and humor of "The Ballad of the Oysterman" in "The Last Leaf" (1831) to the time he composed "Dorothy Q" (1871) in his declining years, he preserved an astonishing unity of poetic tone which is perhaps best exemplified in the perfection of "On Lending a Punch Bowl" (1849). The secret of his success, perhaps, may be found in his earliest essays written for the *New England Magazine* in 1832, for they are obvious imitations of Laurence Sterne and readily caught the fancy of a public which had a long and happy acquaintance with Shandyism. Yet Holmes was his own Yorick and his own Mr. Shandy, and when he began his essays again, after a twenty-five year interruption, for the *Atlantic* in 1857, "The Autocrat of the Breakfast Table" could no longer be classed as an imitator of anybody. His sentiments and his prejudices, his wit and his passion for punning (which he humorously denounced as a form of "verbicide") had become so characteristically

Holmesian that he could sustain them through a long series of "breakfast table" papers attributed to "the Autocrat," "the Poet," and "the Professor" until he moved them into the twilight of "Over the Teacups" (1890) at the age of eighty-one.

As a scientist, surgeon, and distinguished physician, he was profoundly serious about some things—carelessness and quackery in his own profession, which he attacked in such essays as "The Contagiousness of Puerperal Fever" (1843) and "Homoeopathy and Its Kindred Delusions"; the notion of conflict between science and religion, which he denied implicitly in "The Chambered Nautilus" (1858) and explicitly in "The Secret of the Stars"; and the Calvinistic dogma of predestination, which he bitterly opposed in his essay "Jonathan Edwards" (1880) and in the first of his "medicated novels" Elsie Venner (1861). But he was at his best when he was taking even serious matters lightly, as in the veiled satire on the logic of Jonathan Edwards in "The Deacon's Masterpiece; or, The Wonderful 'One-Hoss Shay'" among the verses included in the Autocrat of the Breakfast Table (1858). Rarely in his literary writings did he lose his temper—as he did when he felt pushed around by too many reformers and wrote the biting verses of "The Moral Bully" (1862)—but, instead, kept the equanimity of a man who was sure of himself within a small but popularly acceptable range of feeling and who was therefore one of the most consistently successful minor writers of his time.

These men—Poe, Hawthorne, Longfellow, and Holmes—represent the empirical strain in American literature of the mid-nineteenth century. They indulged in various fancies and experienced varying degrees of emotion, but they followed reason in the

Baconian sense of what John Locke had called the "human understanding" and tested wisdom by the tenor of individual lives that fell within the two patterns set by the flighty Poe and the solid Hawthorne. None of them (except Poe, perhaps, in his last mad fling) tried to magnify the intuitive light within them into an absolute guiding principle, and none of them, in consequence, brought the whole pattern of American thought to bear on the problem of literature. Their shortcomings left a vacuum into which another school of writers, usually called Transcendentalists, were all too eager to rush.

CHAPTER FIVE

Transcendentalism

I

RALPH WALDO EMERSON received an extraordinarily good if completely uncalculated training to become the leader of the Transcendental movement in America. Like Hawthorne, he lost his father at an early age, but he was not brought up in the atmosphere of seclusion which characterized the Hawthorne home. Mrs. William Emerson had four sons to rear, practically no financial resources, and a rugged sister-in-law who was determined that the boys would not only be reared but educated in the expectation that some if not all of them would enter the Congregational or at the worst the Unitarian ministry in which their father had been prominent. So the boys were brought up in the penny-pinching atmosphere of a boardinghouse— many boardinghouses, in fact, for Mrs. Emerson rarely made enough from her boarders to keep up with her rent—while the boys struggled through preparatory school and helped themselves and each other through Harvard College. Waldo graduated in 1821, made a trip south for his health, taught school for a while, passed through the Harvard Divinity School, and in

1829 was ordained as the assistant to the pastor of his
father's old church in Boston. He was married in the
same year to Ellen Tucker, who died in 1832.

Such an early background would normally tend to
keep a young man's feet on the ground and turn him
into a plodder after he achieved a position of security.
But within it Emerson found certain impulses toward
the clouds. In the first place, he possessed a considerable amount of private literary ambition, which found
expression in the copious verses he was scribbling
throughout his youth. In the second, he had instilled in
him a driving self-reliance by the determination of his
aunt, Mary Moody Emerson, and by the obstacles he
had to overcome in his efforts to get an education. And
in the third, he was caught by a rising tide of ideas that
carried him forward on its crest. The tide had risen on
the other side of the Atlantic and consisted of a body of
intellectual symbols which were as important to the
development of American literature as were the material symbols of Romanticism. They were ideas which
were supposed to transcend those that John Locke attributed to sensation and reflection and were therefore
eventually to be called Transcendental.

They began to elevate Emerson's mind so unobtru-
sively that he could hardly have thought of himself as
doing more than drifting along on the stream of conformity. For Harvard College had developed in the
American tradition and continued to reflect the prevailing American attitudes of mind. It placed great
emphasis upon the philosophical training of its students
and brought their training to a climax in their senior
year by careful instruction in the empirical philosophy
of Locke's *Essay on the Human Understanding*. But
its authorities, like the good Americans they were, distrusted the elaborately rationalistic empiricists who

followed Locke—Bishop George Berkeley, whose reasoning cast doubt on one's ability to know the real existence of the physical universe; David Hume, whose skepticism extended to ideas themselves; David Hartley, whose psychological theories were wholly material; and Bishop William Paley, whose observations and reflections had led him to a cold-blooded utilitarian morality and whose rationalism had to be balanced by the analogical reasoning of Bishop Butler before his religious theories could be made fit for undergraduates. Accordingly, every student who was tutored on the *Human Understanding* was formally required to write an essay criticizing Locke with respect to "certain controverted points."

The most essential of these points was Locke's use of the *tabula rasa*, or blank tablet on which ideas were engraved by experience and reflection, as an image of the human mind and its implicit denial of the existence of innate ideas. It violated the well-established American belief in self-evident truths, and Harvard would have none of it as an absolute principle. The hard-headed New Englanders were quite willing to assume that the external world was self-evidently real, most of them were quite willing to accept God on the same basis, and they had found a school of kindred souls in Scotland who were willing to assert as much in an aggressive philosophical system. Under the leadership of Thomas Reid, they had been called the Scottish "Common-Sense" school of philosophy because they insisted that all human beings, in all times and places, had a common sense of reality, morality, and beauty. They had modernized the residual Platonism in Puritan thought, put it in opposition to the empiricism of Locke, and used it to attack the new skepticism. The Harvard students of Emerson's generation were required to study Reid's *Inquiry into the Human Mind* before they were allowed to approach Locke. At the personal suggestion of Harvard's president, Emerson also read Dugald Stewart, Reid's most important follower, and prepared an undergraduate prize essay which showed his acquaintance with the Scottish modifications of empiricism.

These modifications, however, were not very exciting to a young mind. They simply loosened the grip that Locke might otherwise have held on it. The excitement came when Emerson read Coleridge's *Aids to Reflection* in the edition issued by President James Marsh, of the University of Vermont, in 1829. There he found a dramatic distinction between Locke's ordinary human "understanding" and the transcendent intuitive "reason" as well as an exposition of the importance of the latter. He had been finding support for an anti-empirical theory of knowledge in his other reading, he had found no inspiration in the Divinity School, and he was perhaps already dissatisfied with the "pale negations of Unitarianism." At any rate, he was ready for a wave of inspiration to look within himself for some sort of guidance that he had not received from the forces that beat upon him from outside. In his first sermon, three years before his ordination, he had announced that man was the architect of his own fortunes and that his spiritual guide was his inner conscience— and after three years of formal ministry he found his conscience, now a rational faculty which transcended the ordinary "understanding"—at variance with his material fortunes. He resigned his pulpit in 1832 and, a lonely widower threatened with tuberculosis, set sail for the Mediterranean. In the course of his travels through Italy and back by England he met the great men of English literature, Walter Savage Landor, Wil-

liam Wordsworth, and Samuel Taylor Coleridge, and
was disappointed by them all. Traveling itself had no
intellectual appeal for him, and by the time he reached
Scotland and drove out to Craigenputtock to see
Thomas Carlyle he was ready for a new wave of influence.

He got it with a rush from a man who was lonelier
than himself and with whom he spent a night in order
to talk and lay the foundation for a lifelong friendship. He returned home to Concord, Massachusetts,
where he had decided to settle, with an agreement to
reprint the first volume of Carlyle's *Miscellanies* and
to publish the strange novel *Sartor Resartus*, which was
then running serially in *Frazer's Magazine*. The latter,
at once hard-bitten and intensely inspirational, had a
powerful effect upon him. Germanic rather than native
in its background, it detached the lingering elements
of Scottish philosophy from the defense of material
reality (to which Emerson was indifferent) and devoted its enormous energy to an attack on empiricism
which was sardonic, evangelical, autobiographical,
and as moving as some great moral force. To Carlyle,
the whole material universe and time itself was either
an emblem or a means of concealing some nonmaterial
reality—a "garment of the Spirit," he said in the figure
of speech around which the book was constructed—
and the question of its absolute existence was relatively unimportant. What did matter was that man
should recognize the existence of spiritual force, accept
it as the ultimate good, and follow its dictates at the
expense of all material desires. He was a lay preacher,
whose doctrine Emerson could accept as an expression
of his own independent ethical impulses but with
whose dogmas he could disagree because they were
personal rather than authoritative. The Scot's words

and ideas were to echo long in the American's mind as he took to the lecture platform for his pulpit and living and as he sat down in his study to write.

But Emerson did not become a slavish follower of Carlyle. The aristocratic social pattern into which Carlyle unconsciously fitted his thought, the excessive self-abnegation of an arrogant spirit, the harshness of phrase and the bitter humor—all these were foreign to Emerson's make-up. And he had learned the lesson of the American writer before he began to write: "Every man's condition is a solution in hieroglyphic," he said in the Introduction to his first book, "to those inquiries he would put. He acts it as life, before he apprehends it as truth." He had to look within himself and find a solution for various inquiries before he could become an effective evangelist for what he had already begun to call "human culture." Furthermore, despite his intense interest in the new symbols of an intellectual Romanticism, he was as fully exposed as any of his contemporaries to the older symbols of Romantic material. His first and most important problem was a reconciliation of their conflicting claims. His first and most important inquiry would be into the hieroglyphic of "nature"—the material world of "not me." Why is it? What is it? Where did it come from? To what will it lead? These were the questions—undreamed of in Hawthorne's philosophy—which Emerson felt obliged to put.

The most important of these inquiries was the first: Why is nature? For Emerson, despite what he was to say in his lecture on "The Transcendentalist" in 1841, was never a philosophical idealist except in occasional moments of poetic fancy. The universe he set out to explore in the little book called *Nature* (1836) was clearly a dualistic one, consisting of matter and spirit with man standing between the two, composed of both, and having direct knowledge of the material world through his human "understanding" and of the world of spirit through his Transcendental "reason." One value of the material world Emerson derived directly from the tradition of English literary Romanticism: The open air and unspoiled landscape put one in tune with the infinite—"In the woods, we return to reason and faith. . . . all mean egotism vanishes . . . the currents of Universal Being circulate through me; I am part or parcel of God." Another value was commonplace: Nature provided the commodities required to sustain life and work. A third, beauty, was more complex, for Emerson conceived of beauty in a threefold sense: natural beauty, perceptible to the sense; spiritual beauty, made evident to the understanding by acts of heroism and virtue; and, finally, beauty as an "object of the intellect," which "searches out the absolute order of things as they stand in the mind of God" and attempts to re-create it through the active powers in the forms of art. "Thus is Art," he said, "a nature passed through the alembic of man." And in this final concept of beauty may be found the distinctive doctrine of American Transcendentalism—a gospel of practical activity based upon an intuitive perception of ideal order, a perception which was and must be that of each individual person. The alembic of one man's genius could do no more than distill something which would stimulate the perceptions of others, and the responsibility of the American Transcendentalist was not to command but to inspire.

At the time he was writing *Nature*, however, Emerson was not prepared to develop the implications of his distinctive point of view. He was still forming his ideas, reading his inner hieroglyphic; and the influence of

Carlyle was still strong upon him. His fourth justification for the existence of the material world, in the chapter on "language," seems to have been directly inspired by Carlyle's notion of the emblematic nature of the universe; and his fifth, in terms of "Discipline," is a gentler version of Carlyle's stern inspirationalism. Nature disciplines the understanding to the material world and also disciplines the reason by an emblematic verification of its premonitions. The contrast between brute nature and the potentialities of mankind suggests the final reason for the existence of unconscious matter—to make injured, marred, and defective human beings realize that they "all rest like fountain-pipes on the unfathomed sea of thought and virtue whereto they alone, of all organizations, are the entrances."

After his creative and inspirational justification of the existence of nature, Emerson was relatively indifferent to the philosophical question of what it was, whether it was a reality or an illusion. "Idealism" was "a noble doubt" of the outward existence of nature, he said in his chapter on that subject, for which he found certain empirical justifications but which he rejected out of an intuition which hardly seems to be more than pure sentiment. The origin of the material world was of even less concern, for in a discursive chapter on "Spirit," he did no more than offer casually the Miltonic notion that it was the "remoter and inferior incarnation of God, a projection of God in the unconscious" —an affirmation which denied the popular pantheism of William Cullen Bryant and casts more light upon Emerson's theology than upon his philosophical inquisitiveness. His own interests were primarily ethical and were revealed in the enthusiasm of his final chapter, "Prospects." His inquiry into nature had demonstrated the inadequacy of the understanding and had so excited him over the value of reason that he could declare "that a dream may let us deeper into the secret of nature than a hundred concerted experiments." "At present, man applies to nature but half his force. . . . his power over it is through the understanding, as by manure; the economic use of fire, wind, water, and the mariner's needle; steam, coal, chemical agriculture; the repairs of the human body by the dentist and the surgeon. This is such a resumption of power as if a banished king should buy his territories inch by inch, instead of vaulting at once into his throne." His own call was clear. He would teach man to use his entire force, his reason as well as his understanding, and trust that the march of the intellect toward a universal perception of absolute order would produce its own genius for other types of action. In any event, he would have nothing to do with inch by inch reforms: "The problem of restoring to the world original and eternal beauty is solved by the redemption of the soul."

At the time that Emerson was writing *Nature* the United States was entering into an era of passionate reforms, which ranged from violent attacks on Negro slavery to the advocacy of Graham's whole-wheat bread as a moral substitute for meat. Emerson himself had been subject to successful pressure to raise his voice against the removal of American Indians to western reservations and to a much more intense but so far unsuccessful pressure to join the abolitionist movement. His own inbred compulsion to minister to the ills of the world made him sensitive to the spirit of the times, and for that reason perhaps the most significant inquiry he made in *Nature* was not an explicit one but rather the implicit search he made within himself for his proper place in the America of his day—for a wisdom of speech and action which conformed to the tenor of his own life. His decision to preach inspiration made him seem slightly mad to even so good a friend as Hawthorne (who distrusted all reformers but was particularly sardonic about a man who, like Hollingsworth in *The Blithedale Romance*, undertook a "grand project" of "reforming criminals by appealing to their higher instincts") and a laggard or skulker to the many good people for whom the evils of slavery were more vivid than the vision of "original and eternal beauty." But he had found in his own condition the only adjustment possible between the foreign symbols of a new intellectual Romanticism and the prevailing attitudes of mind in his own country, and the words with which he expressed this adjustment were so vitally alive that they made him the most controversial and the most important American literary figure in the first half of the nineteenth century.

II

The literary importance of Emerson is to be seen less in his individual and rather chaotic philosophy than in the way he expressed it in comparison with America's two other leading Transcendentalists—Amos Bronson Alcott and Henry David Thoreau. Alcott was Emerson's older contemporary, his Concord friend and neighbor, and to a certain extent his mentor. Without a formal education, he had formed his Transcendental ideas out of his efforts to digest his miscellaneous reading under the probable influence of doctrines of the mystical "inner light" taught by the Society of Friends, or Quakers, for he had been exposed to them during his wanderings as a Yankee peddler in North Carolina. While Emerson was forming his ideas, Alcott was in

Boston spreading his by formal "conversations" with adults on Friday evenings and Sunday mornings and with the children of the Temple School from whose unspoiled intuitions he hoped to derive a new harmony of the Gospels. Although nominally an Episcopalian, Alcott was a radical in religion who went far beyond the Unitarians in denying the peculiar divinity of Jesus and in insisting upon the divine nature of all mankind. He was also interested in the progress of literature and the arts, and for their encouragement he instigated, in the autumn of 1836, a plan for less formal conversations among the intellectual leaders of Boston and its environs. Ralph Waldo Emerson, George Ripley, Frederick H. Hedge, James Freeman Clarke, Orestes A. Brownson, Convers Francis, Theodore Parker, John Sullivan Dwight, C. A. Bartol, W. H. Channing, Henry David Thoreau, Elizabeth Peabody, and Margaret Fuller were among those who eventually participated in these gatherings of what came to be called the Transcendental Club, and through them the influence of the new movement spread from Maine to New York and as far west as Cincinnati, Ohio.

But Alcott was a thoroughly impractical man. The publication of his *Conversations on the Gospel* with the Temple School children brought down the wrath of Boston upon his head and almost provoked a riot against his person. Yet he never learned discretion. When the group of Transcendentalists established their ideal community at Brook Farm (1840–44) with its relatively sound attempts at profit sharing and production and its progressive experiments in education and the encouragement of music and literature, Alcott was not a participant. Instead he sowed his own extravagant crop of "Transcendental wild oats" (as his daughter, Louisa, put it) at Fruitlands, where he not only undertook to keep his group of "Pythagoreans" free from all animal matter in food and dress but limited them to "aspiring" vegetables whose fruits grew upward and forbade them cotton because it was produced by slaves. Pure linen and beans, however, offered a poor defense against the rigors of a New England winter, and the experiment failed. His "Orphic Sayings," published in the Transcendental periodical *The Dial* (1840–44), had none of the inspirational quality which people seem to have found in his conversations; and, although he was to live long and in his old age preside over the Concord School of Philosophy, his achievement survives as a fantastic story rather than a substantial record. Emerson may have had him in mind when he asked the question: "Of what use is genius, if the organ is too convex or too concave and cannot find a focal distance within the actual horizon of human life?"

At any rate, Emerson kept the focal point of his own genius upon everyday human life. Most of his writings represent a practical application of the ideas he had developed in *Nature*. His first major opportunity occurred in 1837 when he was invited to address the Phi Beta Kappa society at Harvard to whose undergraduate membership he had not been entitled by his own academic record. Taking as his subject "The American Scholar," he spoke formally on education by nature, books, and action. But his plea was for the young scholar to vault into his intellectual throne by making use of that universal reason which the understanding too often corrupts into eccentricity. With reference to books, this called for "creative reading"—the bold rejection of scholarly and literary authority unless the reader's own heart flamed with awareness of "the authentic utterances of the oracles."

For "in yourself," he concluded, "slumbers the whole of Reason; it is for you to know all; it is for you to dare all." Such a line of discourse was enormously stimulating to young men who for years had been "meek young men in libraries" and were now ready to strike out for themselves without quite knowing what problems they would face. But when Emerson used it again the following year in his Divinity School Address he ran into trouble. Even the most liberal of theological professors could not allow him to attack the authority of historical revelation and advise each fledgling minister: "Yourself a newborn bard of the Holy Ghost, cast behind you all conformity, and acquaint men at first hand with Deity." This "latest form of infidelity," as it was called in a pamphlet issued by Professor Andrews Norton, aroused a storm of opposition which kept Emerson off the Harvard lecture platform for almost three decades.

But the lyceum platform welcomed him all over the United States, and out of his various lectures he composed the aphoristic *Essays* (first series), which he published in 1841. They ranged in subject from "History" to "Art" and included practical applications of the ideas developed in *Nature* to such matters as "Compensation," "Friendship," "Prudence," and "Heroism." Two of them, however, were of especial importance. His essay on "Self-Reliance" is the best epitome of his philosophy. Inclinations toward social conformity and intellectual consistency were the greatest obstacles to self-reliance, he declared, and the major faults of the age were its reliance upon such props as a belief in an external God, upon the "superstition of Travelling," upon faith in the cultural influence of literature and art, and upon the hope for social progress and reform. "Whoso would be a man, must be a nonconformist," he exclaimed. "Nothing is at last sacred but the integrity of your own mind." This integrity depended upon absolute allegiance to "the aboriginal Self on which a universal reliance may be founded"—an "immense intelligence" in which all men lie and from which they receive intuitions of truth and justice. In another essay, "The Over-Soul," he tried to define this intelligence, or at least separate it from all the anthropomorphic connotations of God, by identifying it with such terms as Platonic "unity," the Quaker "light," the metaphysical "divine mind," mystic "fire," and psychological "energy." He seems to have been almost completely indifferent to the theoretical identification of the source of knowledge so long as it was recognized as knowledge which transcended that gained from the experience of the senses and the ordinary reflections of the mind.

These early addresses and essays reveal Emerson's Transcendental gospel at its evangelical height. In the *Essays, Second Series* (1844) he brought the oversoul into closer contact with the earth, writing on more specific subjects ranging from "The Poet" to "New-England Reformers" and including discussions of "Character," "Manners," "Gifts," "Nature," "Nominalist and Realist," and "Politics." The most significant essay in this series is perhaps that on "Experience" in which he divided "the Lords of Life"—the intellectual inclinations by which men lived—into two equal groups, transcendental and empirical, and identified them with moods of varying value according to each individual's temperament. "The mid-world is best," he wrote, returning to his concept of intellectual beauty, which combined the genius for intuitive perception with that for practical expression, a balance between "power and form." In a series of lectures composed shortly afterward and published in 1850 under the title *Representative Men*, he preserved this ideal of the balanced intellect, standing apart from the extremes of the mystic as represented by Emanuel Swedenborg and the man of the world as represented by Napoleon Bonaparte. His ideal philosopher was Plato because he was "a balanced soul" who combined the intuitive genius of the East with the empirical genius of the West and "could see two sides of a thing." In *Representative Men*, too, he demonstrated the basic difference between the democratic individualism of his own pattern of thought and the aristocratic absolutism of Carlyle's. For although his choice of a subject was obviously influenced by Carlyle's *Heroes and Hero-Worship*, Emerson did not present his great men as the godlike embodiments of some social ideal which captured the best instincts of the masses. His great men were representative of types, not of an archetype, and greatness itself was a kind of eyewash —"a collyrium," he said in his lecture on "The Uses of Great Men," "to clear our eyes from egotism, and enable us to see other people and their works." Yet "every hero becomes a bore at last," for "no man, in all the procession of famous men, is reason or illumination, or that essence we were looking for; but is an exhibition, in some quarter, of new possibilities."

Emerson was to depart from his democratic inspirationalism in his use of popular racial ideas in his otherwise shrewd analysis of *English Traits* (1856). But in general he was to preserve rather than modify or develop these basic attitudes in the essays collected in *The Conduct of Life* (1860), *Society and Solitude* (1870), and *Letters and Social Aims* (1876) before his death in 1882. The secret of his literary success lay not in the consistency of his ideas, however, but in his ability to deny worldly values in the language of worldly wisdom. His stylistic method was the opposite of Hawthorne's. For while Hawthorne was a man who used Romantic symbols to express the conclusions of a realistic mind, Emerson made his intellectual Romanticism sound like Franklin's Poor Richard leading people along "The Way to Wealth." Few of his readers and even fewer of his hearers understood the philosophical implications of his theory of the universe or of knowledge, but all could thrill to the words of his essay on "Self-Reliance." "To believe your own thought, to believe that what is true for you in your private heart is true for all men—that is genius" is an observation which might be variously interpreted, but in any interpretation it is one which appealed strongly to the attitude of mind that had become characteristic of Americans during the eighteenth century; and so was the suggestion that we are often "forced with shame to take our own opinion from another." The notion that "society everywhere is in conspiracy against the manhood of every one of its members" probably lurked in the mind of the worst failure ever driven to make a desperate new start on the frontier, and the lowest of stay-at-home rebels would agree that "the only right is what is after my constitution; the only wrong what is against it." Everyone can at some time or another take consolation from the belief that "a foolish consistency is the hobgoblin of little minds," just as every weary way-worn wanderer is sometimes prepared to agree that "travelling is a fool's paradise." The verbal garment of Emerson's Transcendental spirit was of traditional homespun.

This homespun quality of Emerson's aphorisms was the essence of what his admirers called his "wit," and it was often cryptic. "Art is a nature passed through the alembic of man," "Books are for a scholar's idle times," "Men descend to meet," "Poetry was all written before time was," "Let us treat men and women . . . as if they were real; perhaps they are"—such remarks as these contain the essence of all Emerson had to say, but their meaning is rarely obvious. Wit of this sort is especially characteristic of his poetry, which is often more cryptic, searching, and intimate than his prose, and is generally more admired by sophisticated modern readers. Written at various times and collected in two small volumes, *Poems* (1847) and *May-Day and Other Poems* (1867), it contains the record of profound personal experience and philosophical speculation which is controlled by the sort of wry humor and personal modesty that brought Emerson's intellectual pretentiousness down to earth and enabled him to dwell on common ground instead of in Alcott's clouds. "The Problem" analyzes his attitude toward the pulpit, "Uriel" is a light allegory giving his version of the Divinity School Address and its aftermath, and the "Ode" to W. H. Channing is a wry but soul-searching response to the pressure brought to bear upon him by the abolitionists. The basic personal explanation for the change in tone between the first and second series of *Essays* may perhaps be found in the reference to the loss of his "larger" optimism in his "less" grief found in the "Threnody" on the death of his son Waldo in 1842, and the popular little poem "Days" is his personal apology for not having been a better follower of his own doctrines.

His speculative poems are generally bolder and more searching than his prose. Although "Each and All" and "Give All to Love" are relatively simple, the light summary verses with which he frequently prefaced his essays suggest deeper thought than do the essays themselves—particularly in the case of "Compensation" and "Experience." But the most haunting of all his verses are those in which he attempted to express philosophical doctrines which fascinated him without gaining his acquiescence. "Hamatreya," asserting the permanence of the earth and the mortality of man, stands at one extreme among these; and "Brahma," denying the reality of the material world and of Lockean ideas, stands at the other. But perhaps the most teasing of all is "The Sphinx," which he wrote for the Transcendental periodical *The Dial* and insisted, to the distress of his friends and the discouragement of his readers, upon using as the introduction to all his collections of poems. In it he gave, through the person of "the poet," his customary answer to the question of what was wrong with man—a summary of his prose evangel, on the platform and through the press—and then denied it all in terms of the philosophical idealism he had specifically rejected in *Nature*. It provides the ultimate evidence of his refusal to take himself solemnly—of the focus of his genius in a life whose intellectual activities could transcend the understanding but whose sympathies were with it.

III

By the middle of the nineteenth century the American attitude toward European literary symbols—the insistence upon modifying them until they made sense in terms of the individual's own experience—had become so deeply rooted that it was ready to flower into some sort of symbolic expression of its own; and, among the Transcendentalists, Henry David Thoreau was the writer who gave it this sort of expression. Like

Emerson, he had been prepared for the new thought before he was exposed to German philosophy, either directly or at second hand through Coleridge and Carlyle, and before he developed a fancy for Oriental literature. But his preparation had been more indigenous and radical, for he was brought up in a Concord household which was devoted to the doctrines of radical abolitionism—the doctrines of William Lloyd Garrison and his followers who believed in the moral obligation of the individual to follow the dictates of an intuitively perceived, ideal, and absolute moral law. He seems to have been not greatly influenced by his studies at Harvard, from which he was a rebellious graduate in the class of 1837, but he was prepared to be affected by Emerson's *Nature* when he received an advance copy of that little book a few days before its formal publication. Accordingly, when he returned home to Concord he was ready for a meeting of minds with his older neighbor, which resulted in a relationship of mutual influence rather than that of teacher and disciple.

In Concord, Thoreau was as much a rebel as he had been in Harvard. A sometime schoolteacher, pencil maker, and surveyor, he was primarily an independent Yankee odd-jobs man who could do Emerson's household chores for hire without having his judgment in any way affected by his menial position when he collaborated in the editorship of *The Dial*. He wrote poetry and published some of the best of it in *The Dial*, and, like so many of his contemporaries, he kept a copious private Journal. From his Journal, his verse manuscripts, and even from his college essays came his first book, *A Week on the Concord and Merrimac Rivers* (1849), which was a miscellany of observations on abstract subjects and external nature, given a semblance of form by the incidents of a trip that he had made with his brother John. Its reception was discouraging, for he was obliged to publish it at his own expense, and about four-fifths of the edition was returned to him unsold. In the same year he also published, in Elizabeth Peabody's collection of *Aesthetic Papers,* his famous essay "On the Duty of Civil Disobedience"; but that, too, left the contemporary public cold because it seemed to be little more than a belated expression of the antigovernment sentiment which the radical abolitionists had made commonplace five years before. With the help of America's foremost newspaper editor, Horace Greeley, and with the loyal support of the editors of *Putnam's Magazine,* he was more successful in the periodicals and published accounts of various walking trips under the titles of "The Maine Woods," "Cape Cod," and "A Yankee in Canada," which appeared in book form after his death. Posthumous collections were also made from his Journals and published under the titles *Excursions* (1863), *Early Spring in Massachusetts* (1881), *Summer* (1884), *Winter* (1888), and *Autumn* (1892); and his *Collected Poems* appeared in 1943. But the only book after the *Week* which he himself prepared for the press was the gradually evolved *Walden* (1854), which purportedly deals with his personal experiences as a hermit on the shores of Walden Pond from July 4, 1845, to September 6, 1847, but is actually a symbolic expression of his whole life.

Thoreau went into retirement for the same reasons that had led several of his friends to find huts in the woods and many of his contemporaries to join in the establishment of such Utopian colonies as Brook Farm. He wanted to live economically, escape distractions, and find leisure to read and think and perhaps to

write. The experience was by no means unique, but
the book which grew out of it was. For *Walden* is not
a simple record of life in the woods. It is a testimonial
of what that episode in life had come to mean to him
after almost a decade of reflection during which the
original manuscript record grew greatly in size and
deepened in implication. His purpose is suggested in
a sentence near the beginning of the book: "When one
man has reduced a fact of the imagination to be a
fact to his understanding," he wrote, "I foresee that all
men will at length establish their lives on that basis."
Like Emerson, he wanted to reform the world by
opening men's eyes to their own potentialities rather
than by changing social conditions; but his method
was by example rather than by evangelism. He had
a less sublime faith in the currents of Universal Being,
comparing them to the vegetable juices or sap of a
plant, and believed that the mass of men could escape
the quiet desperation of their lives more readily by
the light of common understanding than by that of
Transcendental reason. He was trying to bring the
oversoul down to earth by action rather than by
words, an empirical Transcendentalist who wanted to
make his own life a factual emblem of the imaginative
doctrines of "Self-Reliance."

The result was a book which in some respects succeeded better than anything Emerson ever wrote in
adapting the Transcendental theory of knowledge to
the pattern of logic that had already formed a characteristically American attitude of mind. It was practical
in that it was a report on an experiment designed to
show that the economic problems of living could be
easily solved by a simplification of life and that man
was a self-sufficient creature who could find infinite
entertainment in the solitude of the woods. It admit-

ted the importance of intuitive knowledge and insisted that, in times of crisis, a man had to stand on
his principles even if he went to jail for them; but its
stress was upon the material activities of daily living.
Man could live by higher laws, Thoreau maintained,
but could not change the animal nature within him—
although, upon second thought, he recognized a moral
obligation to overcome it. This high-minded approach
to practical life—or the practical approach to the
high-minded life—produced some of the most lumi-
nous prose in nineteenth-century literature, and especially in the sections dealing with his observations,
such as "Brute Neighbors" and "The Pond in Winter,"
Thoreau wrote with a clarity and suggestiveness which
none of his American contemporaries could rival.

Yet *Walden* was not nearly so well adapted to contemporary readers as were Emerson's essays. For
Emerson addressed himself to readers who still felt
that they could assert their individual manhood within
the framework of society however much it might be
in conspiracy against them. Thoreau seems to have
assumed that the conspiracy had succeeded—that he
could maintain the integrity of his own soul only by
withdrawal, either in spirit or body or both. "Civil
Disobedience" had been his testament of spiritual
withdrawal, a declaration that "I, Henry Thoreau, do
not wish to be regarded as a member of any incorporated society which I have not joined" and "am not
responsible for the successful working of the machinery of society." In *Walden* he simply withdrew a little
bit further into the symbol of the hermitage. The
withdrawal itself was to become a successful revolutionary tactic with Mahatma Gandhi and his Indian
followers—and "Civil Disobedience" was to be used to
advocate it—but first the symbol had to acquire a new

emotional value in later generations, when the conflict between the individual and society became more pronounced. For Thoreau's sensitivity was ahead of his times, and it took the form of excessive aggressiveness. He revealed it in his own version of what had now become the American writer's conventional scheme of reference within himself: "I should not talk so much about myself," he announced in the second paragraph of *Walden*, "if there were anybody else whom I knew so well." Such an attitude is indicative of something more than an advanced sensitivity, and Thoreau's writing often suggests personal frustration by giving the impression that he would rather show up the world than improve it. His early poems had revealed a tendency toward hero worship which was to continue through and perhaps partially explain his later essays on John Brown, and it may be that he was always affected by a personal ambition to play the hero in patched breeches. At any rate, he addressed *Walden* particularly to "poor students" and to such other readers as would "accept such portions as apply to them." Whatever he may have been when he went into the woods, rebel, escapist, or genuine experimenter, he used himself in his book as Emerson said a great man should be used—as a "collyrium" to clear men's eyes and suggest to them their own potentialities if they would follow the bent of their individual geniuses. The hero of *Walden* is a "representative" common man.

Such a contemporary as James Russell Lowell was utterly incapable of understanding this role. For Lowell, although only two years younger and a year behind Thoreau at Harvard, was the product of a different intellectual atmosphere. Born a member of what Oliver Wendell Holmes was to call "the Brahmin caste of New England," Lowell had had a well-established place in society and a tendency to accept a considerable amount of responsibility for the successful operation of its machinery. Furthermore, the academic influences upon his mind were different from those which supported Emerson and Thoreau. An age of sentiment was approaching in America, dominated in popular literature by women and women's magazines; and Harvard, as usual, had its corporate ear to the ground. Had Lowell completed his studies with his class he might have escaped some of its worst effects, but he was a careless student who was "rusticated" to Concord for a summer of new philosophical study before he was allowed to take his degree. Harvard's new philosophy, as presented in a textbook by Sir James Mackintosh, resembled the old in that it was opposed to Locke's empiricism, but it based its opposition upon a belief in innate sentiments rather than innate ideas. A basic moral feeling frequently referred to as "sympathy" was common to all mankind in all ages, it held, and out of this active and universal sentiment all moral ideas were formed. As a young man Lowell was almost as wayward and impressionable as Poe, and, although he resented Harvard, his alma mater's endorsement of feeling as a guide to thought and action enabled him in later years to justify his erratic and sometimes violent literary career on moral grounds.

Lowell's anger at being sent to Concord kept him from becoming closely associated with the Transcendentalists there, and, although he published in *The Dial* and the Brook Farm *Harbinger*, he was never to admit any formal allegiance with that school. Yet he fell under direct Transcendental influence through the person of Maria White, the young woman he mar-

ried in 1844, who taught him to admire Carlyle and
see physical objects as the emblems of some spiritual
reality. Through Maria, too, he came in contact with
the radical abolitionist thought which had helped
prepare Thoreau for Transcendentalism and with the
Platonism in which she took refuge from her fear of
sensual experience. The result was that a person of
intense emotional disposition refused to conceal his
emotion, as did Longfellow, but forced it outward toward all humanity. "That love for one, from which
there doth not spring Wide love for all," he wrote in
the best of the sonnets to Maria published in *A Year's
Life* (1841), "is but a worthless thing"; and his whole
early attitude was that his personal emotion should
bear the "goodly fruit" of humanitarianism. Accordingly he became active in every reform movement into
which Maria directed him, especially the abolitionist
movement with which her family was associated and
which provided Lowell, after their marriage, with employment on the editorial staffs of the *Pennsylvania
Freeman* and the *National Anti-Slavery Standard*.

Yet Lowell was not, by temperament, the insensitive and violent radical that many of his antislavery
poems and most of his editorials suggest. He considered himself primarily a poet, and in an early "Ode"
(originally published in 1842 and revised for the 1844
Poems) he attempted to define the role of the poet in
the modern world as an old-fashioned prophet and
teacher brought up-to-date by a feeling of love and
kinship for common humanity. But he was not a man
of action, as Lowell made clear in "An Incident in a
Railway Car," which described the effect of Burns's
poetry upon a group: the poet might be something of
a philosopher in his effort to translate feeling into
thought, but his proper function was to translate this

thought into words sufficiently stirring to make ordinary men conscious of their basic moral feelings. His own problem, since he was committed to exclusive reliance upon some aboriginal self of intellectually undirected feeling, was that of remaining stable long enough to find and be himself—for he was as firmly convinced as any of his contemporaries that a man's writings were closely identified with his own individuality. The problem was one he never solved. He was a man of natural wit who strove earnestly for high seriousness. His impulses were convivial and social, but he was involved in the bitterest controversy of his generation. He had a sensuous interest in material objects and an almost Keatsian genius for expressing it, but he had been persuaded by Maria and Poe (under whose editorial influence he fell for a time) that the proper aim of poetry was a vague "ideality." All his qualities and commitments were, in the emotional sense of the word, honest. But they could be neither reconciled nor accepted as the momentarily inconsistent dictates of a wise oversoul. As a result, he worried and never acquired much vital assurance except in occasional moments of escape from self-consciousness.

In these moments, however, he produced some of the most brilliant verse of his time. He was freest when he wrote under the pseudonym of the shrewd but semiliterate Yankee, Hosea Biglow, and the first of the Biglow "papers" is not only a fine example of Lowell's wit but the best succinct summary of radical abolitionist sentiment—for its earthy shrewdness, nagging irritability, humanitarian faith, and political disunionism—to be found in American literature. The collected first series of *Biglow Papers* (1848) reveal the inconsistency of Lowell's political thought (for some of them were as conservatively Whig as others were radical), but Hosea remained the best part of Lowell as a poet, and the happiest combination of his sensuousness and his wit is the quietly personal "Sunthin' in the Pastoral Line" in the *Biglow Papers, Second Series* of 1867. His wit also broke through his cultivated seriousness in the anonymous poem *A Fable for Critics* (1848), which was an extraordinarily clever and generally acute survey of contemporary American writers, including himself with his "bale of isms," vainly attempting to climb Parnassus. But to balance and perhaps compensate for these he published, in the same year, *The Vision of Sir Launfal* as an exhibition of the vague "ideality" which was his most consistent aim and his greatest curse. In later years he was to display his remarkable technical virtuosity in the Harvard "Commemoration Ode" (1865) for the Civil War dead and his capacity for meditative verse in *The Cathedral* (1870), but he was never able to direct all his powers into a single channel. His talents were greater and more varied than those of most of his contemporaries, but he failed as a poet because he could not find in the tenor of his own life a sound test for his wisdom. His inner light was too flickering to read by with steady vision.

When Lowell faced the fact that his poetic ambitions were vain he settled down as a literary critic, and his later reputation was based upon the essays written while he was Smith Professor of Modern Languages at Harvard and editor of the *Atlantic Monthly* and the *North American Review* and the addresses he gave while serving as the American minister to Great Britain. Collected under such titles as *Fireside Travels* (1864), *Among My Books* (1870, 1876), *My Study Windows* (1871), *Democracy and*

Other Addresses (1887), and *Political Essays* (1888),
they reveal a mind which could range widely over
literature with a capacity for meticulous observation
and an intuitive perception which found something
fresh and new in the most hackneyed subject. He had
been forced, while delivering a series of Lowell In-
stitute Lectures in Boston in 1855, to work out a series
of categories or commonplaces—ranging from a Transcendental imagination to a sound understanding
—through which he sought out the essential characteristic of an author and his work; and this system served
him, as a scholarly critic, instead of the character he
failed to achieve as a poet. In one of his essays he
called Thoreau "a skulker" for taking his high-minded-
ness into the woods rather than onto the battlefield
and exercising his sympathetic imagination upon fish
rather than directing it toward mankind. Despite all
his acumen he could not learn that a writer—at least
an American writer—must achieve lasting respect by
individual integrity rather than by good intentions or
by good social works. Nor could he guess that posterity would accept almost any system of professed
values in literature provided they were focused in the
depths of a coherent personality, which he himself
lacked but which is required to give words a vital relationship that makes them endure and perhaps say
more to one generation than they do to another.

CHAPTER SIX

The Time of Tension

I

AT the halfway point in the nineteenth century there was no American writer who could be considered fully "representative" of that intangible generality which may be called, with purely figurative succinctness, the American mind. Authors had learned that they could not borrow literary symbols without giving them a life from within themselves which had some relationship to the prevailing attitudes of life around them. But none had captured completely within himself the prevailing attitude of mind which had developed during the eighteenth century. Poe had shown an impulse to do so but had abandoned the solid ground of American thought in the desperate egotism of *Eureka*. Hawthorne was holding the empirical line in *The Scarlet Letter* after having satirized Transcendentalism in various short stories which anticipated the attitude he was to display in *The Blithedale Romance*. Emerson's early addresses and essays were providing an evangelical complement to the empiricism of Hawthorne and his fellows but were extravagantly overestimating the power of Transcendental reason, while

Thoreau was in the process of struggling to achieve a balance upon an instrument too sensitive for its task, and Lowell was illustrating the vagaries of something like a Transcendental impulse which was outwardly directed. The period was one of tension and conflict between the forces of empiricism and Transcendentalism, skepticism and faith, foreshadowing the later conflict between the symbols of science and religion. America had not yet developed, in short, a theory of knowledge which would fit into its well-established pattern of logic.

It was perhaps too early to expect any single author to absorb—much less to reconcile—the conflicts of American thought which were securely within the tradition of literature. For, after all, the major problem of the new American literature had been that of finding its own national character within such a great and firmly established tradition of writing in English that it might well have been overwhelming. A literary American had to absorb a great deal of the conscious thought of Great Britain and the Continent before he could absorb that of his own country, and, from one point of view, it was triumph enough that one generation could be sufficiently united by the undercurrents of national thought to find a characteristically American way of handling the international substance of literature and give it a subtly independent tone. In any case, the writers of the mid-century who most nearly caught the tensions of the whole country were all self-educated, relatively unaffected by academic ties with Europe and the esthetic allegiance that accompanied these, and therefore as free to be influenced by American writing as by that from abroad.

The youngest of these at the time of his greatest success was Herman Melville. Born in New York City, he was one of eight children left by their father's early death without means for much formal education, and he grew up during a financial depression which gave him a strong feeling of responsibility for his family's support. After various attempts at employment in commerce and engineering he shipped as a common sailor across the Atlantic in the summer of 1839, returned to a poorly paid job as a schoolteacher, and tried his fortunes in western Illinois before becoming desperate enough to sign up for a Pacific whaling voyage at Christmastime in 1840. The whaling ship, he was to say later, became his Yale and his Harvard. It and other kinds of ships certainly provided him with the material for his writing and made him independent of most of the literary symbols with which his contemporaries were compelled to deal. He deserted his first ship, the *Acushnet* of New Bedford, in the Marquesas in the summer of 1842, spent a month as a nervous refugee among the cannibal tribe of native Typees, and was rescued by an Australian whaler on which conditions were so bad that he refused service in the harbor of Tahiti and spent some time under arrest in the local open-air calaboose. After escaping to the neighboring island of Morea, he was on the beach for a couple of weeks before finding another whaler which would take him on for a voyage and discharge him in the Hawaiian Islands. There he obtained a job with a respectable but antimissionary merchant and planned to stay for at least a year. But he became homesick and enlisted in the United States Navy for transportation back to Boston, which did not materialize until he had spent fourteen months at sea, mostly off the coast of South America, where he was bored by inaction and upset by the severity of naval discipline. Eventually he received his discharge in October 1844 and made his way back home to the village of Lansingburgh on the upper Hudson River, where he began to tell the tales that formed the substance of his first book.

He called the book *Typee, or a Peep at Polynesian Life* (1846), and it was a titillating narrative of hardship and escape, fears of being eaten, fascination with primitive life, and friendly relations with dusky maidens. It was first published in England, however, as one of a series of travel books guaranteed to be factually true but as exciting as fiction; and to satisfy his publisher Melville may have included in it more anthropological detail than he otherwise might have thought of—more than he could remember, anyway, for *Typee* marked the beginning of his lifelong practice of telling a story and amplifying it with technical and circumstantial details based upon later research. The book was a popular success both in England and in his own country, and he followed it immediately with an account of his adventures in Tahiti, which he called *Omoo* (1847). It was not as exciting as *Typee,* but it contained more humor and a greater air of authenticity; and its success persuaded Melville that he was so well launched as an author that he could propose marriage to Elizabeth Shaw, daughter of the Chief Justice of Massachusetts, and move with his whole family (his mother, four sisters, and two younger brothers) to the better literary atmosphere of New York City. His next book would be a continuation of his adventures, but this time in his imagination rather than in fact—a work of fiction rather than semifictionalized autobiography. He began it before his marriage and removal.

The elements of external autobiography in his first two books, however, had made it unnecessary for him to learn the lesson that had been compulsory for other American writers of his generation—that art was no substitute for integrity, that even a work of pure fiction had to come to a focus within an author's individual experience in order to acquire form and life. And Melville's experience had hitherto been of the body and not the mind. Furthermore, in New York his mind was in a chaos of belated stimulation. He was discovering the literature of the Renaissance and of the English seventeenth century in the rich library of his new friends, Evert and George Duyckinck, and was enormously stimulated by the robust vigor of François Rabelais, the allegorical meanings of Edmund Spenser, the eccentricities of Robert Burton, and the rhetoric of Sir Thomas Browne. He may have given some thought to the differences between formality and essential belief as he made the transition from the Dutch Reformed church in which he had been reared into the Episcopal church favored by Elizabeth. He was learning about politics at a time when the old parties were breaking up under the pressure of the antislavery and other reform movements and tensions were particularly great in the Democratic circles in which he moved. Under those influences his book kept changing character. It changed from an adventure story to a pilgrimage of talkers and storytellers who found themselves on a quest which resembled the Rabelaisian quest for the Holy Bottle modified by the softness of Spenserian allegory and the sentimentality of Victorian flower symbolism.

Mardi, as it was called when it was published in March 1849, was purportedly a satiric allegory of a voyage through the world, but actually there was little intellectual coherence in it except in those chapters which were introduced as an afterthought—after Melville had become interested in the French Revolution of 1848, brought together his political ideas, and expressed them in an easily interpreted commentary on revolution in Europe, imperialism and reform in England, and social conditions in the United States. He took a strong stand against slavery, satirized American democracy, and attributed the individual freedom of Americans to the existence of an open frontier rather than to the democratic institutions which had existed and passed away in other countries in earlier days. Although the chapters of religious allegory in *Mardi* indicate a belief in some intuitive light within and an inclination to identify "reason" with it, the dominant intellectual tone of the book is empirical, skeptical, and often sardonic; and it concluded with the suggestion that although some men may accept religion or resignation as a substitute for happiness, the hero must pursue it and be pursued by fate forever and in vain. The book failed both at home and in England, but it had opened Melville's mind to a new sensitivity and a new growth. When economic pressures forced him to the hasty composition of books based upon the tried method of exploiting personal experiences—*Redburn* (1849), dealing with his first voyage on a merchant vessel, and *White-Jacket* (1850), describing his life on a man-of-war with a combination of humor and bitterness—he was more contemptuous of them than they deserved. For they both reflected a remarkable development in literary art—in the power to focus the thoughts and emotions of the moment upon his recollections of the past and, by doing so, re-create characters with an imagination that made them more real in fiction than they may have appeared to be in fact. Without realizing it, Melville became a novelist.

If it had not been for the experience of imagining

and writing these two books, Melville could not have produced *Moby Dick*, which came into being almost unplanned during the year and nine months which followed a trip abroad in the winter of 1849–50. He wrote one version of it rapidly—"a romantic and fanciful account of the whale fishery," as it was described by a friend in early August 1850—but the published book was painfully composed during the prolonged process of revision which normally required only the insertion of technical details. And back of the pain lay a major struggle with the conflicts of American thought—the influence of Emerson, Coleridge, and Carlyle as opposed to that of Hawthorne and Melville's own intellectual predilections as revealed in his earlier books, passionate enthusiasm as opposed to everyday common sense. It was a struggle intensified on paper by Melville's own ambition, curiously acquired during the summer of 1850, to prove that the dramatic heights of Shakespeare could be reached in an American novel. Out of the struggle and the ambition came Captain Ahab, the grandest tragic hero in American fiction, the sensible First Mate Starbuck, the meditative narrator Ishmael, and the strange members of a crew which included four pagan harpooners whose primitive souls were easily stirred by passion. Ahab and Starbuck might easily be taken as representing enthusiasm and common sense, and Melville may have originally based his plot on their antagonism. But the final struggle is not between them, for Starbuck is too easily subdued, and as the revision of the book progressed, Melville increasingly referred to it as a story of "the whale," rather than "the whale fishery," indicating his growing interest in the great white whale—Moby Dick himself—as Ahab's more than worthy antagonist.

In a narrative and dramatic sense, the obvious struggle was between Ahab and the whale, a fabulous whale whose teeth had sheared off Ahab's leg in a previous encounter and to whose discovery and destruction Ahab had dedicated all his calculating cunning and fierce passion. The whale is the only character in the book known to have been drawn directly from life, and to the account of his systematic pursuit Melville brings to bear all the realistic knowledge of whaling he had gained from experience and research. The human actors in the drama—with the exception of the Parsi crew of Ahab's boat—are all individual examples of real types, however fancifully gathered together in a single ship; and the book as a whole might be described as a literary effort to balance romance and reality, enrich both with allusiveness and symbolism, and bring a novel to the high pitch of intensity found in tragic drama. The composition of it was, for Melville, a genuine catharsis. "I have written a wicked book," he told Hawthorne, to whom it was dedicated, "and I feel as innocent as a lamb."

Yet for all its suggestiveness and symbolism, there is a gross underestimation of the final depth and power of *Moby Dick* implicit in the common tendency to make the two antagonists, the captain and the whale, symbolic of anything in Melville's own mind. He conceived of them as realities and, as a dramatist, gave them emblematic qualities only in the minds of others. The "part and parcel allegoricalness of the whole" book, which Hawthorne immediately recognized and Melville admitted with some surprise, is a result of the fact that its tragic plot was essentially a fable so deeply moving to the author that it apparently colored his unconscious imagination and gave the story an uncalculated emotional and intellectual coherence.

The literal fable may be easily followed by any reader who will keep his own quirks of personality out of the book and assume that Melville was a deeply imaginative creator rather than a craftsman, crank, or critic: Ahab was a man who arbitrarily assumed that a single brute creature was the emblem of all the evil and malice of the universe and made a heroic but tragic attempt to destroy it by striking at and through its mask. Its essential meaning is to be found in the fact that the drama is a tragedy and that Melville constantly reminds his readers of his hero's biblical prototype—King Ahab of old who had "done evil in the sight of the Lord" and was led by "a lying spirit" to a bad but somewhat accidental end. No one can err greatly in his interpretation of *Moby Dick* if he simply recognizes Ahab as a tragic hero whose arbitrary assumption is his tragic flaw.

A great tragedy, however, has the seductive power of inducing readers to identify themselves with its hero, and the existence of this power in Melville's book has produced innumerable "interpretations" by critics who have made the white whale emblematic of their own frustrations rather than of Ahab's and have attributed their own obsessions to the author of the fable. Melville invites this, to be sure, by his dramatic sympathy for Ahab and his admiration for the captain's intensity, power, and defiant spirit. Yet this sort of emotional relationship to a character of one's own creation does not imply intellectual approval of his attitudes or actions, and the calculated meaning of the fable is fairly plain in the light of its literary relationships. For Ahab's emblematic theory of the universe—his conviction that "all visible objects" were but "pasteboard masks" for some spiritual reality—is strikingly like the Transcendentalism of Carlyle, and Ahab bears a close resemblance to the hero of *Sartor Resartus* in his defiant state of what Carlyle called "the Everlasting No." The implications of the fable, though, suggest the intellectual attitude of the empirical Hawthorne in whose stories Melville had recently discovered what he called the "black" truth that illusion led to destruction, and evil was engendered by the heart of man.

Melville's psychological analysis of Ahab, through the narrator Ishmael, is therefore his most rational expression of opinion concerning the philosophical theories of his own day. Crazy Ahab was suffering from an obsession which caused him to transfer his inner frustrations to some outer object, and his vision of Transcendental reality was actually but a morbid disease. Yet Ishmael's meditations on evidences of non-empirical knowledge, in the chapter on "The Whiteness of the Whale," suggest that Melville was not entirely convinced that his rational fable was a genuinely true one; and much of the tension found in the book comes from the intellectual reservations of Melville's rationality as well as from the conflict between the emotional sympathy and the intellectual disapproval he displays toward his hero. All of this, complex though it may be, is a reflection of the prevailing attitude of mind in mid-nineteenth-century America—a rational commitment to empiricism as a philosophy but with enough doubts and reservations to admit the possibility of intuition and inspiration and permit admiration for those bold spirits who, like Emerson and Thoreau in literature, would follow their own genius to whatever crazy lengths it might lead. Melville was the first American author to realize within himself his whole intellectual heritage and give it expression in the underlying pattern which controlled the composition of a single book. *Moby Dick* is the "representative" American novel of its time, and it is a great novel because it brings a broad cultural heritage to focus within a single individual's capacity for realization and thus transmits it, with a new emotional power, to posterity.

II

The greatness of a book like *Moby Dick*—at least, in what we broadly call a "Romantic" era in literature —is the product of a deep and largely unconscious sensitivity rather than of deliberate planning, and most of the writers of Melville's generation possessed a sensitivity which reflected the dominant moods of the times. Melville himself, in his later writings, was more restricted than he had been in *Moby Dick*. The novel which immediately followed, *Pierre; or, The Ambiguities* (1852), seems to have been planned as a lighter handling of the same theme, in which a younger and less heroic hero than Ahab would be allowed to follow his own inexpedient notions of absolute morality while the author dwelt upon the ambiguities of human actions and motives. The action, however, turned into that of a grotesque tragedy as Melville subordinated any concern for plausibility of plot to his increasing concern for the plausibility of motives— exploring "the cavern of man," as he put it, to its inmost depths in an effort to distinguish between intuitive impulse and hidden neurosis. Because the suggested neurosis, in this case, was incestuous the book was a failure in its own day and attracted favorable attention only after the spread of Freudian theories enabled the public to realize that Melville was actually pioneering the psychoanalytical novel.

But Melville of course could neither realize the artistic significance of his pioneering nor resist the public pressure always exerted upon a writer who uses his pen as a means of support. Consequently he turned to the ready market for magazine fiction and the discreet judgment of its editors, producing the short stories collected in the *Piazza Tales* (1856) and *The Apple-Tree Table and Other Stories* (1922) and the novel *Israel Potter* (1855). One group of his stories and sketches, "The Encantadas" (1853), may have formed the basis for a planned novel on tortoise hunting in the Galápagos Islands for which he had signed a contract shortly before his publishing house was destroyed by fire in 1853; and the most haunting of his longer stories, "Benito Cereno," may have actually been an abortive novel which was discouraged by the injudicious caution of a magazine editor. Both of them, like such complete short stories as "Bartleby the Scrivener" (1853) and "The Bell Tower" (1855), are rich in suggestiveness and in the revelation of a meditative imagination profoundly at work, but none has the far-ranging implications of *Moby Dick* or the psychological depths of *Pierre*. The nearest Melville came to recapturing his earlier breadth and depth during this period was in *The Confidence Man* (1857), a loosely constructed fantasy based upon his experiences on a Mississippi River steamer, in which he satirized both the gullibility and lack of faith found in mankind. It was the least coherent of all Melville's novels, however, and he had difficulty in arranging for its publication before he left home in 1856 on a new voyage of sight-seeing and refreshment, physical and spiritual, to Europe, Egypt, and the Holy Land.

After his return in 1857 he turned to public lecturing for three seasons and to poetry, giving up fiction

entirely for more than thirty years. Throughout the
bitter American Civil War, from 1861 to 1865, he followed the action in verse and in 1866 published his
first collection of poems under the title *Battle Pieces
and Aspects of the War*. A position as inspector in the
New York Customs House freed him from the financial compulsion to write, and his only publication during that period was a long philosophical poem, *Clarel,
A Poem and Pilgrimage to the Holy Land,* published
in two volumes in 1876. It was his most ambitious
single work, for within its narrative framework he attempted a descriptive survey of Palestine, a summary
of most of the religious attitudes current in the nineteenth century, and an account of a young man's effort
to restore his religious faith under the influence of holy
places, in an atmosphere of religious debate, and in
spite of severe emotional strain. The octosyllabic verse
he adopted (perhaps in imitation of the narrative
poems of Scott), however, was not equal to the serious demands he made upon it; and the poem as a
whole, though picturesque in many of its details, vivid
in its characterizations, and moving in some of its
scenes, is difficult to follow. Perhaps the major reason
for this is that Melville's interest was by now more
centered upon people than upon philosophy, and the
old conflict between Transcendentalism and empiricism—here expressed in the post-Darwinian symbols
of religious belief versus scientific doubt—was of less
concern to him than the individuals who were by
temperament or conditioning inclined to one side of
the controversy or the other. At any rate, many of the
characters in the poem were finely and sympathetically drawn, while the philosophical problem was left
unresolved by Clarel's bitter disappointment and by
the author's advice, in an Epilogue, that he should

nevertheless keep his faith. Once again Melville had found himself incapable of committing himself without reservations to a rational empiricism, but this time the tensions, once inherent in this attitude of mind, were reduced by his awareness of the enormous diversity of human beings and their individual attitudes of mind.

Near the end of his life Melville was to publish two more volumes of poems, *John Marr and Other Sailors* (1888) and *Timoleon and Other Poems* (1891), both mostly concerned with individual people in peculiarly individual circumstances and both printed in limited editions of twenty-five copies for his close friends. He was also to leave a considerable amount of verse for posthumous publication, but the most impressive work of his later years was to be the short novel *Billy Budd*, written between 1888 and 1891 and left unprepared for printing. The story is in part one of conflict between good and evil, innocence and sophistication, exemplified by the handsome sailor Billy Budd and a malignant master-at-arms Claggert who falsely accuses Billy of plotting mutiny and is struck and killed in Billy's outburst of speechless indignation. But the focus of attention is upon Captain Vere, who directs the court-martial which orders Billy to be hanged from the yardarm despite every one's realization that he is morally innocent of any crime. Its basic theme is that of conflict between individual and social morality or between principles of justice based upon the judge's responsibility to the individual or to the society of which he is a small part. Melville represents Captain Vere as a perceptive, sympathetic, and conscientious man who is acutely aware of Billy's personal innocence but chooses to sacrifice the sailor's life and his own ease of conscience to the necessity of preserving dis-

cipline in a navy upon which his country depends for
its existence at that crucial moment. It is not a happy
story but it is a vital one in its indication of Melville's
awareness, in his old age, that he must face the facts
of life in a society grown too complex to tolerate the
tragic heroism of a Captain Ahab or the reckless
naïveté of a Pierre Glendinning.

The transition of Melville's concern from principles
to people and their problems in society is characteristic
of American literature as a whole during the latter
part of the nineteenth century, and it is perhaps most
evident in those writers who were more obviously and
superficially involved in the tensions of the prewar
period and found an easier means of release afterward.
Such a one was John Greenleaf Whittier, the most important of the abolitionist poets, who showed an extraordinary capacity for devoting almost thirty years of
his life to aggressive reform and then, the reform accomplished, settling down to an equally long period
of peaceful productivity. Whittier was a New England
Quaker farm boy and apprentice shoemaker who had
little formal education but was inspired to write
poetry by the example of Robert Burns. One of his
poems attracted the attention of William Lloyd Garrison, who encouraged him to pursue a career of
poetry and journalism while also recruiting him to what
Whittier eventually called the "Moral Warfare" against
"the folly of an evil time"—that is, Negro slavery. His
first important prose work, a pamphlet entitled "Justice and Expediency" (1833), clearly sets forth the
principle on which he based his reforming activities
and, incidentally, provides an interesting contrast to
the attitude Melville was to display many years later
in *Billy Budd*. Whittier, like the somewhat Transcendental Garrison, believed in absolute moral justice

intuitively perceived by the Quaker "inner light." He was sternly opposed to what he considered the immoral expediency of utilitarian social morality based upon an empirical estimate of "the greatest good for the greatest number." For him slavery was a violation of the absolute principle of freedom, and the enforcement of the fugitive slave law, however expedient in terms of national union, provoked the powerful indignation of "Massachusetts to Virginia" (1843); and when Senator Daniel Webster, in the interest of national unity, supported the Compromise of 1850, Whittier poured forth upon him the scorn of "Ichabod." These were the strongest poems written in support of the abolitionist cause and they bear witness to the ringing power of Whittier's feeling.

When President Abraham Lincoln issued his Emancipation Proclamation in the midst of the Civil War, Whittier felt that his cause was won and celebrated the victory in the equally strong phrases of "Laus Deo" and turned to quieter things. He had always been interested in New England history, people, and customs (as illustrated in the beautifully restrained and sensitive "Telling the Bees" of 1860); and "Snowbound" (1866), the best of his long poems, is a fine idyll of country life, filled with sensitive and sympathetic human understanding and touched by a humorous appreciation of the eccentricities of thought and behavior. It also suggests that Whittier, as he approached the age of sixty, was experiencing the feeling so common among the English Romantic poets in their youth—that of the passing of some emotional glory from life and the necessity of taking refuge in the strength of a philosophic mind. He revealed the attitude from which he drew his own strength in "Abraham Davenport" (1867), a poem based upon an incident in colo-

nial history when the legislature of Connecticut fell
into a panic because it believed that an eclipse of the
sun marked the beginning of doomsday. But Davenport, the presiding officer, remained calm. "Let God
do his work, we will see to ours," he ordered as the
darkness thickened: "Bring in the candles." Whittier's
own inner light burned with less heat as it became less
concerned with God's justice than with human foibles,
but it never went out.

An abolitionist of a different sort but with a similar
career was Harriet Beecher Stowe. Her attack upon
slavery was based more upon sentiment than upon any
informing principle, yet, perhaps for that reason, her
Uncle Tom's Cabin (1852) was the most widely read
American novel of the nineteenth century and the
most influential work of literature inspired by the antislavery cause. Mrs. Stowe was careful to direct her
attack against the institution of slavery rather than
against the South or its slaveholders, and she was exag-
geratedly kind toward her southern characters while
making her most notorious villain, Simon Legree, a
New Englander by birth. Yet she crowded her book
with all the abuses she could discover by hearsay and
research and made the old Negro Tom the most saintly
character ever canonized by sentiment. To the extremes of characterization she added almost all the
other ingredients of popular fiction—pathos and humor, the misfortunes of chance, the excitement of the
chase, and the melodrama of violence—and it was successfully dramatized both as a serious propaganda play
and as a new variation on the Negro minstrel show.
When its popularity provoked challenges from the
South she published a *Key* documenting the abuses it
portrayed and attempted to duplicate its success in
Dred: A Tale of the Great Dismal Swamp (1856). But

she had exhausted her effectiveness and on the eve of the Civil War turned, perhaps with some relief, in *The Minister's Wooing* (1859) to the quieter subject of New England village life, which she was to pursue most successfully after the war in *Oldtown Folks* (1869), a book which made an influential contribution to the local-color movement.

Mrs. Stowe was a writer of considerable perceptiveness but no considerable depth, and her work is a popular symptom of the literary drift of the times—a drift, at least temporarily, toward the surface of everyday life and away from intellectual commitments, social passions, and artistic involvement with one's materials. The intemperate passions which preceded the Civil War, the long and bitter conflict itself, and the natural reaction which followed all tended to disturb the tenor of the individual life by which the American writer had learned to test his wisdom. The tradition of an American way of thinking, of assaying literary symbols, and of writing had grown up during the second quarter of the nineteenth century. The question, in the third quarter, was whether it could be defined and preserved before it was lost in the tumult of social and political change.

III

Literary history is a complicated affair because—as we have already observed—it is concerned with the large symbols of communication which have value at a particular time, with the intangible patterns of tacit belief and ways of thinking which are in the process of creating new symbols, and with language, which acquires its own symbolic or suggestive value when it becomes informed with both thought and the power of communication. Herman Melville is a crucial figure in American literary history because he absorbed the full strength of the prevailing pattern of thought, expressed it in terms of old symbols which still retained their power of communication, and found in the combination a vitality of language which gave *Moby Dick* a suggestive quality beyond the power of any author's calculated achievement, Walt Whitman is equally crucial but in an entirely different way. He translated the existing pattern of thought into a new large symbolism which defined it, adapted it to a new idiom of expression, and made it available to a new generation which was being subjected to changes in both conscious and tacit belief.

There was less in Whitman's early background than in Melville's to suggest the role he was going to play. Two months older than Melville and a native of the same region, he also left school at the age of thirteen and got his education from reading and experience. His early reading, however, was less Romantic and less literary; for the Whitman household were followers of the rationalistic Quaker, Elias Hicks, and young Walt seems to have been strongly impressed by the sermons of Hicks, by the political and religious writings of Tom Paine, and by the visions which the French Count Constantin de Volney had of mankind progressing toward some ideal state of nature and allegiance to its laws. He was apprenticed as a printer and moved from printing to journalism, free-lance writing in New York City, and eventually to the editorship of the Brooklyn *Eagle*—a position which he gave up when he became something of an abolitionist in 1847 and the paper remained conservatively Democratic. His serious concern for moral and social issues was rather late in developing, for his early contributions to magazines and newspapers, although they included a temperance novel and a short story attacking corporal punishment in the schoolroom, were superficial and perhaps even cynical in their use of popular reform sentiment for literary journalism. After leaving the *Eagle* he made a trip through the South, lived for a while in New Orleans, and returned to take charge of an antislavery newspaper, the *Freeman,* and continue the independent experiments in verse which were to culminate in the first edition of *Leaves of Grass* in 1855.

Leaves of Grass was an astonishing volume of verse, shockingly new in form, tone, and idiom. The form was free verse, influenced by the lyrical sections of the King James Bible, the irregular ode, and the popular Martin Farquhar Tupper, but not unaffected by the oratory of the Shakespearean stage and the rhythms of the sea, which Whitman heard as he recited his experimental verses on its shores. The clue to its unique tone was given in a sentence in its Preface in which the author described his book as being mainly an attempt "to put *a Person,* a human being (myself, in the latter half of the Nineteenth Century, in America) freely, fully, and truly on record"; and the new idiom is that of a person, as he saw himself or wanted himself to be seen by the public—rude and unconstrained, rebellious against the affectations of society, inclusive in his acceptance of the whole of life, and aggressive in identifying himself with all mankind while maintaining his own peculiar individuality. Emerson greeted him as a living essay in self-reliance, at "the beginning of a great career," and Thoreau saw him as a wild American buffalo breaking through the conventions from which he himself had withdrawn.

The person revealed in *Leaves of Grass* was a representative American man.

The revelation was, in fact, not only extraordinarily comprehensive but remarkably subtle, perhaps more so than Whitman knew. The catalogues of human types, the displays of different attitudes, and the descriptive allusions by which he attempted to "tally" America were all self-conscious exhibitions of his desire for "inclusiveness"—for absorbing his country, as he put it in the Preface, completely and affectionately —and they give his longest and most ambitious poem, later entitled the "Song of Myself," a panoramic quality rarely found in literature outside the novel. And his method of presenting his all-inclusive panorama was an equally self-conscious representation of the method Emerson and Hawthorne had found necessary for the American writer: Whitman was finding within himself a solution in hieroglyphics for the questions he would put and loudly professing a wisdom tested by the tenor of his own life. Beneath this was also a fairly well-balanced reflection of the prevailing American philosophy. The poem later called "There Was a Child Went Forth" is probably the best expression of Locke's empirical theory of knowledge that can be found in verse, yet in the "Song of Myself" Whitman professed to be not only the poet of the body but the poet of the soul and hinted of an intuitive and almost mystical experience by which he had achieved vision. Despite this note of Transcendentalism, however, the poems in this edition and in that of the enlarged edition of 1856 were predominantly poems of sensory perception and experience; and it is indicative of Whitman's attitude of mind at this time that his most striking poem in the third person was that on the philosophically conceived child who went forth every day and always would go forth to form his mind by sensation and reflection. While trying to capture the tangible fact of America for his book, Whitman had also managed to capture its intangible pattern of thought, and *Leaves of Grass* would be far more representative than *Moby Dick* as a reflection of the time were it not for one basic difference: Melville's individualism was in the creative depths from which his book was drawn; Whitman's was entirely on the surface. The author of *Leaves of Grass* discovered the wellspring of creative energy in American literature, but instead of tapping its force he made it gush.

The result was a writer who reveals none of the tensions which made Melville so suggestive and gave suggestive power to Hawthorne, Poe, Emerson, and Thoreau. Instead, in Whitman, the tension was released in reaction against the struggle to control literary material. "Walt, you contain enough, why don't you let it out then?" is the line from the "Song of Myself" which best reveals his own attitude toward his writing. The nineteenth-century American "person" in *Leaves of Grass* is not a coherent individual who adapts literary symbols to his individuality but rather an incoherent one whose individuality itself consists of a multiplicity of symbols. Consequently Whitman is most comprehensible when seen as a symbolic poet whose major literary symbol is the first personal pronoun and whose own changing attitudes may be followed through the shifting meanings he attached to the words "I," "me," and "myself."

These meanings at first were not carefully calculated; for Whitman was never a precise thinker, and the first Preface to *Leaves of Grass* stressed the virtues of a style which would suggest instead of define the poet's vision. Yet by the time he wrote "The Mystic

Trumpeter" in 1872 he was sufficiently aware of this quality in his work to describe his poetic development in clearly symbolic terms, and in later editions of *Leaves of Grass* he revised the opening section of the "Song of Myself" until it defined, with reasonable clarity, the four most distinct ways in which he thought of himself as a person. The first of these and the one of which he was most completely conscious at the beginning of his career was that of the representative man—an "I" which included the entire population of America in all of its social conditions and with all its heritage of experience and history. The second was the "natural," as opposed to the civilized, man who loafed and invited his soul, who felt inclined to lie down with the animals because they lived by instinct rather than thought, and who sounded his barbaric yawp over the roof of the world like the wild hawk. The third was the unique individual poet who appeared here and there in all of Whitman's verses but without achieving a dominant role until after the Civil War. And the fourth was an "I" symbolizing the biological race of man, not very clearly defined in the opening section of the "Song of Myself" and never extensively used although it dominated the magnificent Section 44 of the poem which represented humanity as "the acme of things accomplished" in a long evolutionary process.

There can be little doubt that Whitman's greatest appeal to his readers was in his second symbolic role—that of the natural man, the free-spirited rebel against conventions, who appeared frequently in the "Song of Myself" and dominated the new poems of the 1856 edition of *Leaves of Grass*, where he appeared at his best in the "Song of the Open Road" and caused the most trouble in the poems grouped in the section later called "Children of Adam." It was time perhaps for the rebellion against Victorian conventions, which Swinburne was conducting in his own way in England, and from which Whitman's way differed in that it invoked a wider range of sensuous feeling, was more firmly based upon a philosophical tradition, and was expressed in a more modern and realistic idiom. For Whitman's most distinctive poetic achievement was that of taking the old philosophical concept of an ideal "state of nature" as he had found it in the eighteenth-century rationalists, particularly Volney, and translating it from the old language of abstract intellectuality into a new language of realistic adventure which appealed strongly to a lingering Romantic individualism. "Afoot and light-hearted," he took the open road to physical and spiritual freedom, finding his good fortune within himself, testing all philosophies by the feel of the morning dew, and inviting all men to accompany him on equal terms. He was the Declaration of Independence in the flesh—enjoying life, liberty, and the pursuit of happiness while accepting the doctrine of equality. He was a foot-loose Thoreau whose Walden was everywhere. He made the physical universe his oversoul. He transformed himself into a believable symbol of the union for which Melville yearned—a union between the free spirit of Transcendentalism and the undeniable reality of empirical experience.

Stimulating and inspiring though the role of the natural man was, Whitman could not maintain it for long and formally renounced it in the second half of "Give Me the Splendid Silent Sun" (1865). For the demands of institutionalized society were pressing in upon the individual, and Whitman believed that individual freedom was possible only under the institution of political democracy, which he saw exemplified in the American Union. And the Union, in the late fifties, was being threatened by sectional differences, talk of southern secession, and the imminent likelihood of civil war. Misled perhaps by a peculiar psychological bias of his own, Whitman tried in the third edition of *Leaves of Grass* (1860) to meet this threat in individualistic terms rather than by the exercise of social force. The new poems in the "Calamus" section of this volume preached the gospel of "adhesiveness"—a phrenological term for comradeship or the affection of a person for others of his own sex—as a means of holding the Union together but did so with a naïve candor which was more shocking than persuasive to a public which had been unable to face the implications of Melville's *Pierre*. In any case, the Civil War was by then inevitable, and Whitman followed its developments from Washington, where he was a government employee in the Department of the Interior and a volunteer nurse in the military hospitals. There he collected material for the prose paragraphs of his *Specimen Days* and the poems incorporated in the *Leaves* under the title "Drum-Taps." There too he first attracted widespread public attention when he was discharged by a puritanical Secretary of the Interior (who found a copy of the 1860 *Leaves of Grass* on Whitman's desk), reemployed by the Attorney General, and defended by a group of young journalists including John Burroughs and William Douglas O'Connor, whose pamphlet, *The Good Gray Poet*, gave the prematurely grizzled Whitman a permanent label.

The triumphant conclusion of the war was to Whitman proof of the lasting strength of American democracy, and some of his patriotic exaltation seems to have entered his verse, for some of the poems in "Drum-Taps" and "Memories of President Lincoln"—especially

"Pioneers! O Pioneers!" "O Captain! My Captain!" and "When Lilacs Last in the Dooryard Bloom'd"—share with the earlier "Out of the Cradle Endlessly Rocking" the distinction of being his most lyrical verses. But this note of sadness and triumph was not to last. Postwar America, at least as represented by political Washington, went morally to pieces in the materialistic corruption of what was to be called "the gilded age." In a series of prose essays, *Democratic Vistas* (1871), originally begun in answer to Carlyle's criticisms of America, Whitman was forced to admit that the spectacle was "appalling." Cynicism and corruption abounded on every side, and there was immediate need for a program of reform designed to restore human dignity and decency. Matthew Arnold's gospel of "culture" would not suffice, for it tended to produce a race of "supercilious infidels" instead of men of the robust natural dignity which lingered as an ideal in Whitman's mind from the time he had written the "Song of the Open Road." For the first time, in *Democratic Vistas*, he approached society rather than the individual from a philosophical point of view.

His approach was symptomatic of the new era in that it was based upon a theory of social evolution. American society, as Whitman surveyed it, had to pass through three evolutionary stages. The first had already been completed in the achievement of political democracy on a permanent basis. The second—material growth and economic prosperity—was in the process of being achieved in contemporary activities which he morally deplored. The third stage would be that of greater individualism based upon a new awareness of spiritual values; and his new role, as the prophet and seer he had always thought of himself as being, would be that of hastening his country toward the climax of this evolutionary process by helping create "a new Literature, perhaps a new Metaphysics, certainly a new Poetry" which would be the support for a new American "Religious Democracy." His highest, final theme, he announced in "The Mystic Trumpeter," would be that of "a reborn race" and "a perfect world."

Unfortunately, the first of several paralytic attacks, occurring at about the time of this announcement, limited his energy and prevented the full development of this theme; and the most distinctive characteristic of his later poems is that they were almost all written from the point of view of the individual poet who had abandoned his symbolic role. Consequently it is difficult to interpret such poems as "Passage to India" (1870) and the "Prayer of Columbus" (1874). The first, written to celebrate the completion of the Suez Canal and the Union Pacific Railroad the year before, actually rejoices in the passage of the "soul" to an India conceived as a source of religious thought; and both strongly suggest that the poet had experienced some sort of ecstatic mystical vision. But it seems impossible to determine whether a genuine religious experience led Whitman to his personal interpretation of social evolution or whether his notions of social evolution led him to assume the role of mystic as a means of creating the new poetry of a religious democracy. His growing desire to emphasize the religious element in his verse, however, is clearly indicated by such later prefaces to Leaves of Grass as "Two Rivulets" (1876) and "A Backward Glance O'er Travel'd Roads" (1888) in which his critical retrospection found a stronger strain of spirituality in his early poems than would have been apparent to contemporary readers.

As a whole, Whitman's writings in verse and prose

represent a verbalization or symbolization of an older
tacit belief in the individual as a center of reference
in estimating the value of intellectual systems and
literary material. He was more self-conscious, artificial,
and affected than the writers of the first half of the
century and, for that reason, reflects a decadence of
the creative spirit which brought American literature
to its period of triumph over its inevitable borrowings
from abroad. Yet the transmission of an attitude of
mind from one generation to another must be substan-
tially on a conscious level, and if the spring of individualism had not gushed in mid-century—not only in
Whitman but in political, economic, and other non-
literary manifestations—it might not have attained the
place it did in the American tradition.

PART THREE

The Tradition
1868–1929

CHAPTER SEVEN

The Search for Reality

I

THE externalization of American individuality in Whitman's early work marked the climax of an attitude of mind which for a generation had been working its way toward self-consciousness. It was also symptomatic of a new age in which writers were to search for literary inspiration from without rather than from within, were to reject European literary fashions in favor of material they found around them, and were to attempt to control their work by external observation rather than by some inner wisdom. The word for the new approach was "realism," but it was a realism of appearances rather than of depths and its guides were the eye and ear rather than the mind. What Hawthorne had called "the truth of the human heart" was passed over lightly in terms of the clichés of sentiment and sentiments. When it was still associated with the intellectuality of the older generation, as in the later writings of Melville, it displayed a genuine concern for the characters of people who could hold certain opinions. When it was highly intelligent, as in the novels of John William De Forest, it explored the social scene and the backgrounds of prejudice with considerable skill. When it was simply popular, as in the publications of a host of magazine writers, it was primarily photographic, with an emphasis upon unusual settings or new angles of viewing the commonplace. The authors of the new literature, in general, tried to maintain something of a photographer's detachment from their material except for the display of such expected emotions as sympathy, humor, or, in a few cases, irony.

The only writers who remained unaffected by this prevailing literary climate were those who were out of touch with the main currents of public interest, and the finest of these was Emily Dickinson, who came to poetic maturity during the early years of the Civil War and remained relatively unaffected by external events as she continued to write, without publishing, in the seclusion of the little New England college town of Amherst. Like Whitman, she rebelled against the conventional demands for smoothness in meter and perfection in rhyme; but her rebellion took the form of going her own succinct way within the basic patterns of conventional verse rather than that of a verbose attempt to overwhelm them. For she was as quiet as Whitman was boisterous, and the first personal pronoun in her poems is the "I" of a self-sufficient private individual rather than that of an exhibitionist. Her verse often contains, in fact, the same suggestion of private communication that is to be found in the English metaphysical poets of the seventeenth century and certain English and American poets of the twentieth, but it is more feminine, intimate, and delicate in its emotional transitions, suggesting a thoughtful passion which is deep and sometimes tragic but made endurable by a strict refusal to be solemn.

The result is a rare quality of irony in her verse,

whether she is writing lightly or with deep feeling, gently or sardonically. She could be a sophisticated child describing how "A bird came down the walk," show a tough New England response to tragedy in describing "The bustle in a house" after a death, display a tender grief for a child "Taken from men this morning," or reveal casual scorn in damning a minister when she realized that "He preached upon 'breadth' till it argued him narrow." The subtlety of her poetic inspiration was sometimes extraordinary, as when she wrote that "A thought went up my mind" and tried to capture its fleeting but unidentifiable familiarity; but, on the other hand, she was capable of putting her deepest personal tragedies into the little poem "I never lost as much but twice," suggesting the depth of her feeling in the equally short "Pain has an element of blank," and mocking her own greatest disappointment in the whimsey of "I asked no other thing." Nothing could altogether escape her nimble-witted perceptiveness. She could agree wholeheartedly with the Transcendentalist Emerson in denouncing conformity with the assertion that "Much madness is divinest sense" and then tease her master for the solemnity of his essay on "The Poet" by making fun of his Wordsworthian advocacy of plain living and high thinking in "I taste a liquor never brewed." Always succinct and often cryptic, she addressed herself to the world on her own terms, even though it meant the disappointment of her tentative impulse toward publication and a gradual complete retirement to her garden and her manuscripts.

At the other extreme from Emily Dickinson were the southern poets, who were estranged from the main currents of American literature by the Civil War, the defeat of the South, and the consequent eleven-year

period of military occupation and social upheaval
known as "Reconstruction." Henry Timrod, whose intense love for his native region as shown in such poems
as "The Cotton Boll" and "Ethnogenesis" (1861)
earned him the title of "Poet Laureate of the Confed-
eracy," died before the Reconstruction period was
under way; but his friend and associate, Paul Hamilton
Hayne, revealed in "The Pines" and in various sonnets
the tendency toward escape which in the younger poet
Sidney Lanier produced a genuine outburst of American Romanticism in the purest English vein. At the
beginning of the Reconstruction period Lanier had
seemed a poet of his times, concentrating his attention
upon the people and problems of his own locality and
presenting them with a realism of observation and
dialect which was characteristic of the new "local
color" school in fiction. But as time went on, Lanier,
though still concerned with the economic problems of
the South, escaped emotionally into the conventional
channels of an earlier period—into a preoccupation
with the past (in such poems as "The Revenge of
Hamish" and in his popular books for boys) and into
a devotion to external nature which was as passionate
as Wordsworth's and as sensuous as Keats's. His contemplation of "The Marshes of Glynn" (1878) made
his soul "suddenly free" from a wearier weight than any
earlier American nature poet knew; and although
he realized that beneath the escape symbol of the
Marshes there was something darker than he could
face, he almost deified nature, and in "A Ballad of
Trees and the Master" (1880) gave it the healing
power of the Divine Spirit.

Lanier's other medium of escape—and his most significant one, from the point of view of purely southern
literary history—was through the deliberate glorifica-

tion of emotion at the expense of reason. In part, as
his novel *Tiger Lilies* (1867) had revealed, this was a
product of an intellectual background like Lowell's,
which derived moral principles from innate senti-
finest poem, "The Symphony" (1875)—"Music is Love
ments; and the sometimes puzzling conclusion to his
in search of a word"—reflects a theory of knowledge
comparable to Lowell's in which the moral sentiments
grope upward through various media of communication until they find their perfect expression in the
words of the poet. But "The Symphony" is a more complex poem than anything Lowell wrote, for Lanier was
not simply being philosophical in verses ingeniously
contrived to suggest the instruments in an orchestra.
He was in deep rebellion against a contemporary
world devoted to the calculating materialism of commerce, and he identified "trade" with the intellectual
activities of the "head," while setting in opposition to
it the higher sentiments of the "heart" as exemplified
in the love of nature, the chivalric love of woman, and
the charitable love of one's fellow man as ordered by
Christian doctrine. These were the resources available
to his own downtrodden, poverty-stricken South; and
these were the ideals on which he and southern literature for the generation to follow took a last ditch stand
against the onslaughts of realism.

But the larger literary world belonged to the realists
—of one sort or another—and the sort who flourished in
the popular magazines were the local colorists. The
Atlantic Monthly, Harper's, and *Lippincott's* vied
eagerly for new writers who could present pictures of
new localities with the proper sound effects of dialect
and idiom. They already had Harriet Beecher Stowe
and Rose Terry Cook for New England and were to
find Rebecca Harding Davis for the iron mills of the

Pennsylvania and West Virginia border, George Washington Cable and Grace King for New Orleans and the bayou country, Charles Egbert Craddock (actually Mary Murfree) for the Tennessee mountains, Edward Eggleston for the midwestern Hoosiers, and Emily Dickinson's friend Helen Hunt Jackson for southern California. The *Atlantic's* greatest find was Bret Harte, of San Francisco, who had tried his hand at romantic stories of the West but had turned to a Dickensian treatment of gold digging in such tales as "The Luck of Roaring Camp," "Tennessee's Partner," and "The Outcasts of Poker Flat," (1868–69), which brought him fame through the *Overland Monthly* and an extravagant and highly publicized contract with the *Atlantic,* which stimulated the whole movement enormously but got little of value from the quickly exhausted Harte. In its later stages the movement was to produce such fine regional books as Sarah Orne Jewett's *The Country of the Pointed Firs* (1896) and Kate Chopin's *The Awakening* (1899), but, in retrospect, its early importance seems to lie in the fact that it opened up the field of ordinary life to literary exploitation and seduced readers through the charms of novelty to appreciate the realism of the commonplace.

The broader effects of the new tendency, at its beginning, may be seen in the work of John William De Forest, who turned away from his prewar romances and travel books to write *Miss Ravenel's Conversion from Secession to Loyalty* (1867)—a novel which ranges in scene from New Haven to New Orleans, deals boldly with such a variety of matters as military action, political chicanery, and domestic and somewhat undomestic manners while presenting realistically the variety of characters involved in the southern heroine's change of attitude toward her native region.

De Forest was for some years associated with the Freedmen's Bureau in South Carolina and drew upon his experiences for a number of short stories which were equally free from sentimentality and comparably broad in their comprehension of both individual character and social conditions. But he did not consistently remain in the realistic vein, and although *Kate Beaumont* (1872) and *Honest John Vane* (1875) are solidly based upon the realities of prewar life in South Carolina and contemporary American politics, the serious search for reality within the commonplace was conducted by the younger novelist William Dean Howells.

Howells was a magazine editor—of the *Atlantic* in Boston from 1871 to 1881, and of *Harper's* in New York from 1885 to his death in 1920—who came East from Ohio after four years of service as American consul in Venice. His experiences abroad had provided him with material for two travel books and his first novel, *Their Wedding Journey* (1872), but he was quickly converted to the new realism which the *Atlantic* was encouraging and began searching for his own proper medium of expression. A mawkishly sentimental or humorous realism was not acceptable to his genuine intelligence, and farcical humor, which he attempted from time to time, was not suited to his talents. The fictional technique of Ivan Turgenev appealed to him more than did that of any other novelist, and in the Russian master he found a detachment which did not have to be disguised by any artificial pose and which enabled him to transform his own sense of the ridiculous into stylistic irony. He was able to direct this irony effectively upon spiritualism in the Shaker community of Vardley in *The Undiscovered Country* (1880) and upon the rocking-chair society of a seaside hotel in *Dr. Breen's Practice* (1881), but it was at its best in *A Modern Instance* (1882), which portrayed a possessive young woman, her enterprising but weak journalist husband, and the shrewd Yankee lawyer who was her father. Although the book touched upon the problem of divorce, which was not common at the time, it was a fine example of commonplace realism sustained and lightened by style.

Howells was not entirely content, however, with this sort of empirical fiction, based upon skillful observation and informed only by a surface intelligence. He was looking for a deeper reality and, perhaps naturally enough, looked for it first in the traditional American belief in an innate moral sense or intuition which was capable of rising to an occasion without any evident preparation or training; and in a characteristic gesture he uncovered it in the type of American who was so widely damned for lacking it—the successful, self-made businessman. The hero of *The Rise of Silas Lapham* (1885) was realistically portrayed as a Vermont farmer who had become a manufacturer of paint and achieved financial success by the shrewd management of his business, the ruthless elimination of his partner, and a willingness to splash the countryside with advertisements of his product. At the opening of the book he is ready to retire, build a big house on Beacon Hill, and introduce his daughters to the Boston society in which his wife expects them to find cultivated husbands. The situation was commonplace enough, and so were most of the incidents of the novel—the financial misfortunes of a man who is wise in business but an innocent on the stock exchange, the return of the ruined partner, the family conferences, and the tragicomedies acted out by the *nouveaux riches* amid an established aristocracy. But the real story is of

Lapham's moral rise, and it reaches its climax when he displays an ethical sensibility which causes him to sacrifice an opportunity to recoup his own fortunes and to relieve his ordinary conscience by restoring those of his former partner. It is a sensibility which rises above anything in Silas' training, above the highest concepts of business morality, and above the perceptions of his wife, who normally served as his ethical guide; and it demanded not only self-sacrifice but the sacrifice of the greatest good for the greatest number to some Transcendental abstraction within the man's individual consciousness. The basic reality presented in this book was the essential goodness of man.

But Howells could not hold on to the Transcendental tradition. The America of his day was a country of increasing social conflicts, and when Howells moved to the larger world of New York in 1885, fresh from four years abroad, he became aware of them. His sympathies, as he himself observed, could not embrace two million people; and, influenced by the new doctrines of socialism as he had already been influenced by the literary theories of Hippolyte Taine, he began to see individuals as representatives of social and economic classes. When the Haymarket riots occurred in Chicago in 1886 Howells jeopardized his own position on *Harper's* to defend the arrested anarchists, and their eventual conviction and execution (for their opinions rather than their guilt) helped powerfully to convince him that social forces were more real than an innate moral sense. Accordingly, in *A Hazard of New Fortunes* (1890), the most comprehensive and impressive of all his novels, he turned to presentation of the conflicting points of view he found in the society around him. The framework of the book was autobiographical in that it dealt with the removal of the

March family from Boston to New York, and the action centered around the New York streetcar strike which had occurred soon after Howells' arrival. The characters were mostly associated with the publishing world that the author knew so well, and through them —the capitalist Dryfoos and his liberal son Conrad, the self-centered Beaton, the radically reactionary Colonel Woodburn, and the socialist Lindau—Howells presented a variety of beliefs that all had a stronger operative power than any possessed by the sensitive and open-minded March. In this book the man of sensibility was relegated to the position of an observer of realities outside himself, too powerful for him to control.

And there he remained through all the later novels which provide significant indications of Howells' intellectual position. In his two discursive Utopian romances, *A Traveler from Altruria* (1894) and *Through the Eye of the Needle* (1907), the weak and intellectually ineffective characters are the novelist and the clergyman, who are professionally devoted to sensibility and the moral sense, whereas the banker and the lawyer are best equipped to understand the realities of an altruistic civilization. For the Altrurians did not arrive at their ideal state through abstract reason, intuition, or even the Christian principles to which they so closely conformed, but by a long process of empirical trial and error which taught them that socialism was the best form of government because if men knew enough they would rarely have to be forced to do unto others what they would have others do unto them. Howells' final view of reality was that the forces which controlled men were to be found in the social order rather than within the individual himself, and his belief in the innate goodness of man was translated into

an optimistic prophecy of social evolution toward a
state of human relationships in which altruism would
be indistinguishable from enlightened self-interest.
His principles of morality never changed. In fact, they
became more clearly defined as he decided that they
were less absolute than expedient.

II

While William Dean Howells was finding his way to
the respectable realism of the magazines, his contemporary and eventually his close friend Mark Twain was
becoming involved in a different kind of realism in the
newspapers. For it was in the weekly newspaper that
the western tradition of storytelling flourished. It had
attracted widespread attention for the first time in
1834 with the publication of David Crockett's *Autobiography,* the story of a ring-tailed roarer who had
come to Congress from the Tennessee canebrakes and
who could jump into the air, crack his heels together
three times, crow like a rooster, and come down to
lick his weight in wildcats or run like a streak of
greased lightning. The book may have been ghost-
written in the first place, and it certainly was in later
editions when Whig propagandists used Crockett to
attack Andrew Jackson; but it brought before the
public an authentic frontier hero who was wilder and
more extravagant than Cooper's Natty Bumppo and,
to some tastes, considerably more amusing. The alma-
nacs created Mike Fink, king of the keelboats and hero
of the Mississippi; and, in oral tradition, the sort of
folklore was developing which was eventually to produce the tallest of tall-story heroes in the person of
Paul Bunyan.

But the type of literary taleteller who put such stories into print was best represented by Augustus Baldwin Longstreet, classically educated at Yale, whose *Georgia Scenes* (1835) exemplifies a type of local color which was not to be found in the respectable magazines but flourished in such books as Joseph G. Baldwin's *Flush Times in Alabama and Mississippi* (1853) and hundreds of newspaper stories by known and unknown contributors—so many, in fact, that in 1831 William Trotter Porter had founded a New York newspaper, *The Spirit of the Times*, to disseminate them throughout the country. The stories were both cruel and comic, and the most distinctive thing about them was the manner of their telling: no matter how brutal the incidents or how extravagant the comic fantasy, they were told with the straight unrevealing face that later vaudevillians were to call "the dead-pan technique." The best storyteller, orally or on paper, was the one who could maintain the most complete detachment and allow his audience to build up its own emotions without any clue to the expected response. Unlike the magazine writers, who put their readers at ease by affecting sentiment or humor, the frontier storytellers attempted to make their audiences uncomfortable by playing a cat-and-mouse game with their feelings until detachment itself became the art of arts.

Samuel Langhorne Clemens had been brought up within touch of the frontier in the small town of Hannibal, Missouri, where immigrants crossed the Mississippi on their way west to the Oregon settlements and eventually the gold mines of California. As a journeyman printer in his youth he had become professionally familiar with newspaper humor, and as the pilot of a Mississippi River steamer before the Civil War he was in a position to exchange stories with the masters of the

art. But it was not until he became a newspaper reporter in the western silver-mining town of Virginia
City, Nevada, that he became notorious as the teller
of such tall tales as that of the "Petrified Man" and took
as his nom de plume the cry of the Mississippi River
leadsman, "Mark Twain"—a name which became na-
tionally known to connoisseurs of American humor
after a New York newspaper published in 1865 "The
Celebrated Jumping Frog of Calaveras County." He
had by this time moved to California, and a trip to the
Sandwich Islands provided him with material for his
first successful appearance as a humorous lecturer in
the autumn of 1866 and for a series of newspaper
articles which he later was to revise for *Roughing It*
(1872). His first great success, however, came in 1869
with *The Innocents Abroad,* a book in which he used
the technique of frontier storytelling in an account of
a grand cruise through the Mediterranean and to the
Holy Land. Here he could solemnly assure his readers
that there was no conflict in the claims of two rival
monasteries for the skull of Adam because a difference
in size indicated that one was the skull of Adam as a
boy and the other that of Adam as a man; and by such
an application of a new art to old material he could
not only delight the western readers of the *Alta California* (which sent him on the expedition) but also
the eastern clients of a religious publishing house
that distributed the book with misgivings which were
quickly overcome by its sales.

The success of *The Innocents Abroad* enabled Twain
to take an eastern wife and settle down as a western
writer and lecturer in an eastern home. The western
pose was the secret of his success as a comic writer or
funnyman, for it enabled him to affect a crude detachment from the sentiments expected of the well bred

and thereby keep his readers in a constant state of shock. He cultivated the manner in various anecdotal sketches he published from time to time and in the autobiographical narrative of *Roughing It,* and he transferred it to the novel in *The Gilded Age* (1873), which he undertook in collaboration with Charles Dudley Warner. Although primarily an attack upon the materialism, speculation, and corruption of the postwar period, especially well personalized by the grandiose Colonel Sellers and the cynical Senator Dilworthy, *The Gilded Age* also contained autobiographical elements in the experiences of the Hawkins family; and it may be that Twain's partial identification of himself with young Washington Hawkins turned his thoughts back to his Missouri boyhood and caused him to write *The Adventures of Tom Sawyer* (1876). At any rate, Tom Sawyer was strongly reminiscent of his own boyhood and effective in its influence upon his imagination because it opened his eyes to the possibility of a boy's view of the world as a means of relief from that of the western humorist. He remained western, however, in his next autobiographical books, *A Tramp Abroad* (1880) and *Life on the Mississippi* (1883), although he used the boy's approach in *The Prince and the Pauper* (1882)—a historical novel which grew out of a long-time plan to satirize English customs and institutions but was transformed into a children's book as he tried out his approach on his own family. But all the while he was trying a completely new role, that of a boy who was totally unlike the young Sam Clemens or the mature and somewhat hackneyed humorist and who therefore offered him a freedom of outlook he had never before possessed. The boy had strolled into *Tom Sawyer* swinging a dead cat, and his name was Huckleberry Finn.

The *Adventures of Huckleberry Finn* appeared in 1885 and brought to a peak the creative achievement of Mark Twain and the western tradition in which he developed. For in writing this book Twain found what every outward-looking novelist seeks—that "lucid moment of balance" in which he becomes freshly involved in the world while remaining artistically detached from it. The fresh involvement came through the point of view of a boy character for whom the author felt no social or personal responsibility, a "poor white" in a class-conscious village, but through whom he could recapture the past and release a store of memories and associations that sophistication had suppressed. The detachment was achieved by maintaining the fiction that Huck Finn was a fictitious character, the representative of an insensitive class whose dead-pan attitude toward the world gave the false impression that he had "no more morals than a mud turtle" and made him an ideal storyteller in the western tradition. And so Mark Twain could let him drift from adventure to adventure down the river, the great central highway of prewar America, and take a fresh look at the richly varied society which the author himself knew so well. The book is as plotless and as anecdotal as any of Mark Twain's autobiographical writings but infinitely more natural, human, and, in a sense, intimate. The reader knows Huck Finn as he never gets to know Mark Twain, and in fact the best thing we know about Mark Twain is that he was able to create this boy who is one of the most completely and deeply imagined characters in literature.

The faults of the book (and they are many) came from the loss of balance, as a result of either the author's excessive involvement in Huck or his occasional efforts at self-conscious detachment. For Huck knew everything that his creator knew, and he sometimes displayed more learning than he could have acquired in character. When he struggled with the moral problem of freeing the Negro Jim, for instance, he knew from an inward humanity very close to a "moral sense" that the conventions of a slaveholding society were harsher than his own abstract notions of hell; but he knew this as a boy would know it, impulsively and irrationally, and we accept it more readily than we accept Mark Twain's arguments against the southern feudal system in *Life on the Mississippi*. But when he explained the abuses of royalty within the European feudal system, he revealed what Mark Twain had learned from his recent researches for *The Prince and the Pauper* and became implausible by reason of the same identification with his creator which generally makes him so convincingly human. The greatest flaw in the novel, however, is the conclusion, where the detachment implicit in Huck's point of view is lost and he becomes a substitute narrator for the author of *Tom Sawyer*. Here the artificial detachment of the self-conscious storyteller reveals the hackneyed quality of a role Mark Twain had played too long and from which he had had the great good fortune, in the better part of his book, to escape.

Twain was subtly aware that the spontaneity had disappeared from his storytelling, and on the lecture platform he tried to introduce variety into his performances by placing them in contrast to those of an author whose manner and temperament were completely different from his own. It was George Washington Cable, serving this purpose for a season, who gave him Sir Thomas Malory's *Morte d'Arthur* to read and so provided the inspiration necessary to turn a fantasy in his notebook into *A Connecticut Yankee in King Arthur's Court* (1889). For this new book was the tallest of all Mark Twain's tall tales, based upon the notion of translating into the fifth century a man with the nineteenth-century genius for trading and manufacturing and then having him remake its civilization in the modern American image. It was also the best sustained of his tall tales, for both the romantic chivalry and the artificial language of Malory provided fresh material for burlesque. The notion on which it was based could be exploited in innumerable ways, and it enabled Twain to carry out his long-time plan to satirize English institutions—especially those relics of "feudalism" which offended his rationalistic mind, the aristocracy of class distinctions and privileges and the established church. Into it he could pour the thoughtful results of his reading which had been suppressed in *The Prince and the Pauper* and had been struggling for expression in *Huckleberry Finn*. The *Connecticut Yankee* is a book as rich in artificial invention as *Huckleberry Finn* is in the re-creation of memories.

Yet *A Connecticut Yankee* is not an emotionally coherent book. The impulses back of it were more varied than those in any of Mark Twain's other writings. The prevailing impulse seems to have been that of fantasy and burlesque, but the intellectually sustaining one was undoubtedly that of satire. For Twain was growing indignant about the world toward which he had been, as a humorist, so professionally cynical. His satire of institutions was from an eighteenth-century rationalistic point of view, but he added, from the point of view of disillusioned humanity, bitter attacks upon insensitivity and cruelty; and, with a new pessimism, he attacked eighteenth-century rationalism itself by denying the possibility of educating superstition out of a people. The only touch of mellowness in the story comes from the sort of personal nostalgia found in *Tom Sawyer, Huckleberry Finn,* and the first half of *Life on the Mississippi,* for in their tour of the country, King Arthur and the Yankee Sir Boss slip into the characters of Huck and Tom in a subtle indication of the author's feeling that humanity was tolerable only when it was childlike.

Mark Twain referred to *A Connecticut Yankee* as his "swan song" and, although the feeling back of the reference may have been only a lack of energy, the book actually does mark the climax of his career as a humorous storyteller and the beginning of emotional and intellectual insecurity. He had felt a reality beneath the surface of the life he observed so accurately and had sought it in an individual point of view—that of a humorist and impressionistic satirist, that of a nostalgic man and the various boys who were products of his nostalgia, and that of a rational satirist who was also filled with humane indignation. But none of these points of view was stable. The humorist and casual satirist had grown tired, nostalgia was only an occasional means of escape, and reason itself seemed untrustworthy. Like the Emerson of "Experience" he was becoming aware that life was a string of moods, and temperament was the wire upon which they were strung, but like Poe his own temperament was that of an actor who had appeared in different moods without achieving a private intellectual stability. Unlike Melville, who experienced similar but more profound stresses, he could not settle into a limited scale of living. Money—the enormous sums of money he earned from his writing and threw away in speculative investments—meant too much to him. In his mid-fifties, as he

approached the later stage of his career, he could do
nothing but write according to his moods while at the
same time searching for something he could accept as
intellectual reality.

The mood he tried to sustain in the many potboilers
of his later years was that of the comedian, but the one
which moved him most deeply was that of indignation.
He became violent on such subjects as copyright laws,
the political organization of Tammany Hall, and certain capitalists and corporation executives; and he became the defender of the underdogs of history in his
essay "In Defense of Harriet Shelley" and his *Personal
Recollections of Joan of Arc* (1896), and of the Negro
race in *Pudd'nhead Wilson* (1894). But amidst these
outbursts of indignation he was seeking for some form
of belief. He implicitly denied the existence of an internal, uncorruptible moral sense in his story "The Man
That Corrupted Hadleyburg" (1899) and sought refuge in a form of mechanistic determinism in his essay
"What is Man?" which he withheld from publication
until 1906. The best and most revealing book of his
later years, however, was his posthumous novel *The
Mysterious Stranger* (1916). Written in the nostalgic
mood which caused him to revive his boy characters in
Tom Sawyer Abroad (1894) and other stories of the
nineties, it tells of three boys in medieval Austria who
were visited by an angel named Satan and taught by
him, first, that living beings were the playthings of
their creator, that the moral sense was a quality in man
which made him lower than the brutes, that life was
in the chain of necessity, and, finally, that all this and
existence itself was nothing more than an illusion of
the mind. Cynical in theme, it was astonishingly tender
in tone, and it presented Mark Twain's search for re-

ality ending in a sort of discouraged philosophical idealism.

This was not the real conclusion. The author stopped here because he could go no further, and his friend Howells persuaded him that he had reached a perfect artistic if not a satisfactory philosophical conclusion. Mark Twain was never able to accept the empirical realities to which Howells learned to conform, nor could he find within his own mind a philosophy which he could accept as something more real than the world that was too much with him. His search led to disillusionment and bitterness but to no belief—perhaps because he began it too late, after his role as a detached, uncouth western humorist had separated him for almost a generation from other seekers after a personal philosophical refuge from the overwhelming forces of society.

III

The intellectual guiding spirit behind these other seekers, whether they accepted the fact or not, was Herbert Spencer and his theory of social evolution. Two ideas from Spencer were particularly influential upon American literature after the publication of the *First Principles* in 1862. One was his general formula for the evolutionary process, which moved from the simple to the complex in terms of an increasing tendency toward the specialization of parts and a greater integration of these parts into a coherent whole. The other was contained in the famous phrase he contributed to the Darwinian theory of evolution, "the survival of the fittest" in this process of change. With reference to society, the first of these ideas implied movement away from a simple culture in which people were more or less alike and were independently engaged in similar activities to the development of a complex civilization in which individual activities were highly specialized and closely integrated with each other. The second implied competition, ruthlessness, and allowed some of Spencer's American followers to see Darwin's law of the jungle within the highest form of civilization. Spencer's notion that "the integration of matter" was accompanied by a "concomitant dissipation of motion" was also influential in its suggestion, to some people at least, of wasted energy in modern life. The peak of social evolution would be reached in a highly organized society of completely heterogeneous individuals, and the implication was that these individuals would be fiercely competitive for their places in the organization and enormously wasteful of energy.

The great contribution that Darwin made to the intellectual climate of the late nineteenth century was that of increasing men's confidence in empirical knowledge by showing that it could answer questions which writers like Hawthorne had found beyond the empirical range—questions involving creation itself, which had hitherto been questions of faith or speculative reason. Spencer, as the philosopher of the evolutionary movement, was therefore offering a new and more solid version of natural law, partially verifiable by every man's observation in accord with a method now proved practicable for such a large inquiry. It was eminently suited to the defense of such economic tendencies in America as the exploitation of natural resources, the rapid growth of industrialization, and the establishment of large corporations and trusts; but it was also eminently suited to create discomfort among those old-fashioned individualists whose concepts of natural law were ethical and intuitive, who valued morality above success, or who longed for the security of the absolute. It was a new philosophical reality, in short, which some people were eager and others felt obliged to accept; and the literary response to it reflected the difficulty of fitting it into the American cultural tradition.

The first response, by Walt Whitman, suggested no difficulty at all. For Whitman, though intellectual enough to seize upon the idea of social evolution as a means of explaining the faults of democracy, was either too optimistic or not alert enough to grasp the implications of the Darwinian theory; and in *Democratic Vistas*, as we have seen, he simply welcomed the forthcoming age of individualism and redirected his aims as a poet toward hurrying it up and improving its moral tone. But the impulse of the younger writers whose lives spanned the Civil War period was to escape. They could neither deny the new reality nor reconcile themselves to existence within it, and the simplest and most direct of the escapists was Lafcadio Hearn.

Hearn had been born of an Irish father and a Greek mother on the Aegean island for which he was named, reared in Britain and France, and impelled to come to America as a youthful Bohemian devoted "to the worship of the Odd, the Queer, the Strange, the Exotic, and the Monstrous" in such varied places as Cincinnati, New Orleans, and the French West Indies. He had expressed his devotion in such newspaper sketches as those later collected as *Fantastics and Other Fancies* (1914) and *Creole Sketches* (1924), in a colorful novel *Chita* (1889), and in an autobiographical *Two Years in the French West Indies* (1890); but he was a noncompetitive individualist, financially unsuccessful and out of place in the world of Spencerian evolution which he had intellectually accepted in his early newspaper pieces. In 1889 he read Percival Lowell's *The Soul of the Far East* (1888), which interpreted Japan in Spencerian terms, and there discovered a land in which he could worship his own peculiar gods and at the same time escape the turbulent evolutionary stream by settling into the quiet eddies of an older culture of stable values where "impersonality" rather than "personality" was the ideal. There for a while he found what he was seeking and made effective literary use of the strange and exotic aspects of old Japan in several volumes of ghost and fairy stories. But his two most serious books on his adopted country, *Glimpses of Unfamiliar Japan* (1894) and *Japan: An Attempt at Interpretation* (1904), show a distressed recognition of the fact that Japan would have to become industrial and commercial if it survived in the modern world, and the old system of stability and unselfish ethics was being lost in the evolutionary current. By the time of his death he was disillusioned about the possibility of escape and anxious to return to America.

Even less successful in his effort to escape the overwhelming forces of social evolution was Henry Adams. The great-grandson and the grandson of American presidents and the son of America's most influential minister to Great Britain, Adams seems to have identified himself early as one of the ablest members of his family and one of the least likely to succeed. The trouble was with the world, not with the Adams breed. For the Adamses were men of character and merit in a world whose standards of values had grown so poor that real merit was no longer recognized and a man of character could no longer be called from his plow to

manage the ship of state. The political arena after the
Civil War had become a place for wild beasts and
wilder men, unfit for a Roman, and so Henry Adams
became a man of letters—a journalist and editor of the
North American Review, a historian of early nineteenth-century America, and an anonymous and pseu-
donymous novelist with *Democracy* (1879) and *Es-
ther* (1884) when the continued attractions of politics
induced him to move to Washington and attempt to be
influential behind scenes. Protected by a thin wall of
sardonic irony, he stood aside from the social forces of
his own day and tried to understand them. But the
protection broke under the severe emotional blow of
his wife's suicide in 1885, and he made the same attempt to escape that Hearn was to make a few years
later—first to Japan, where he was uncomfortable and
ill at ease, and later to Tahiti, where he sought through
the memories of old men to find the pre-evolutionary
civilization which existed before the French came to
the islands.

Although he traveled much, Adams' refuge was in
the past. He published his monumental *History of the
United States during the Administrations of Jefferson
and Madison* (1884–89) in nine volumes and devoted
the next fifteen years of his literary life to the meticulous reconstruction of a world he might have loved and
the analysis of one he hated. His love was focused upon
twelfth-century France, and he described it in *Mont-
Saint-Michel and Chartres*, which was eventually published privately in 1904. There he partially found and
partially created a homogeneous culture whose energy
was not dissipated but was directed toward an end
which could be readily symbolized by the worship of
the Virgin and which was expressed in the magnificent
cathedral at Chartres. It was a civilization more deper-

sonalized than Hearn's Japan, and the anonymity of
the architect of Chartres was, to Adams, one of the
most significant facts in it. He loved it with the meditative passion of a weary man's dream of nirvana, and
sacrificed his historical conscience to it as he re-created
it as a sanctuary which would be tragically violated by
the evolutionary processes which produced modern
America. In contrast to it he placed the world of his
own lifetime in *The Education of Henry Adams*
(1907), where the man of character, an Adams, was
lost in the rush toward heterogeneity and the undirected dissipation of power for which he found a symbol in the dynamo. The *Education* purported to be an
autobiography, but, in actual fact, it skipped the most
important period in Adams' life and, instead, revealed
the state of mind of a man whose consciousness was
haunted by evolutionary symbols—the Terebratula
which had failed to survive or evolve, the Limulus or
horseshoe crab which had survived unchanged from
the Silurian period, the sharklike Pteraspis which was
the first of the vertebrates and hence the ancestor of
man, and the Cunard liner which was the symbol of
social man's most spectacular dissipation of power.
Evolution was a reality he was forced to accept, but he
hated it with an intensity which made him long for the
period of dissolution which would inevitably follow;
and the last activity of his sardonic mind was the composition of two essays (posthumously published by his
brother Brooks as *The Degradation of the Democratic
Dogma*) in which he attempted to find a mechanistic
formula for dissolution in the second law of thermo-
dynamics and apply his brother's "rule of phase" to the
evolutionary process in a way that might hurry it to an
end within his own lifetime.

Another reluctant Spencerian of Adams' generation

was Ambrose Bierce, who served in the Civil War, began his career as a journalist in San Francisco, and went to London in 1872, where he cultivated the rather grim and ghastly humor which led him during the nineties into a cynicism as bitter as that of Mark Twain. Less a seeker than an escapist, however, he expressed his cynicism in his column of "Prattle" for the San Francisco *Examiner* and in the form of artificially constructed short stories of the sort perfected by Edgar Allan Poe, cultivated by Rudyard Kipling, and brought to a state of decadence in America by the popular O. Henry. But Bierce's cynicism was not the stuff for popular publishers, and his best collection of stories, *Tales of Soldiers and Civilians* (1891), owed its existence to the generosity of a San Francisco merchant and did not appear commercially until seven years later and then under the title *In the Midst of Life.* This, with another collection of stories, *Can Such Things Be?* (1893), and a collection of epigrams, first called *The Cynic's Word Book* (1906) and later *The Devil's Dictionary,* formed the basis for his reputation as one of the leading eccentrics of the era, who dramatized his reputation by disappearing into Mexico at the age of seventy-one to join the army of the insurgent Pancho Villa and removing himself permanently from the civilization he so despised.

The younger American writers who were born into the age of Spencer and Darwin were less rebellious than Hearn, Adams, and Bierce and more willing to accept the principle of evolution as a natural law under which they must live and to assume a certain amount of individual freedom within the framework of social necessity. Some of the more humane and optimistic souls, in fact, were able to turn their backs on Darwin, ignore Spencer's theory of the dissipation of motion as society became more coherent, and hope that social evolution would eventually result in a civilization of finer individuals who were freed from their animal impulses by the perfection of their communal organizations. Howells was to fall into this group in *A Traveller from Altruria,* but by far the most popular and influential of these Utopians was Edward Bellamy, whose *Looking Backward, 2000–1887* (1888) pictured a society in which abundance had been achieved by the intelligent direction of the power of the machine, selfishness and material competition had disappeared, and something like Whitman's "re-born race" of superior persons had been developed. The book's achievement of a tremendous popularity bore witness to a widespread belief that social evolution was not something to escape but to control, and the first problem of the realists who shared this belief was that of indicating what needed to be controlled.

In an age of large fortunes and abject poverty, exploitation and the abuse of privilege, the greatest need for control seemed to be within the economic system; and of the later realists young Hamlin Garland was the most acutely conscious of the economic forces which made life, as he had known it, on the western plains, so drab. An ardent Spencerian, he had moved to Boston and attempted a history of American literature on evolutionary principles; but as he turned to more creative work in the short stories of *Main-Travelled Roads* (1891) and *Prairie Folks* (1893), he devoted himself to the impressionistic use of his own early experiences in a way which suggested the need for reform before any development could occur in the direction that another of his literary heroes, Whitman, had foretold. He had already found the means of reform in the single-tax system advocated by Henry George in *Progress and*

Poverty (1879), and the economic bias of his stories
was against landlords and mortgage holders who prof-
ited by the increased value of land at the expense of
its users. There was a vividness of realistic detail in
these stories, like that of such earlier books from the
Middle West as Edgar Watson Howe's *The Story of a
Country Town* (1883) and Joseph Kirkland's *Zury*
(1887), but there was no great power in Garland's
thought, and he was easily diverted to the artificial romances which became popular at the end of the
century.

The strongest and most effective writers of this
group, in fact, were those who exhibited the intellectual detachment claimed by Émile Zola for naturalism
and the experimental novel. Although probably not influenced by the French naturalists, Stephen Crane was
of their temper in his desire to present the brutal facts
of life that needed public attention and to do so with
a power which invited reform without attempting to
direct it. Crane was a minister's son and a rebel against
his upbringing whose two volumes of free verse, *The
Black Riders* (1895) and *War Is Kind* (1899), reveal a
young man who was almost the calculated opposite of
the hero Christian in John Bunyan's *Pilgrim's Progress;*
and he sent a copy of his first novel, *Maggie, A Girl of
the Streets* (1892), to a clergyman with a note to the
effect that it tried to show how tremendous a thing environment was in the shaping of lives. His most successful book, *The Red Badge of Courage* (1895), owes
its effectiveness to Crane's imaginative feat in capturing the private soldier's environment during a military
action and making him subject to it. The same quality
is to be found in the best of his short stories published
in *The Open Boat* (1898), and one story, "The Blue
Hotel," concludes with a brief comment upon crime

and causation which is purely naturalistic in its implication.

Crane's contemporary, Frank Norris, was an avowed
naturalist who had studied art in Paris and perhaps
learned there about the new school of writers whose
principles he adopted while in a writing course at Harvard where he wrote the posthumously published
novel *Vandover and the Brute* (1914) and partially
wrote his most famous novel *McTeague* (1899). Before
completing the latter, however, he tried his hand at
two kinds of popular romance in *Moran of the Lady
Letty* (1898) and *Blix* (1899); and he experimented
again with an adventure story of the Far North in *A
Man's Woman* (1900) before deciding that the naturalistic method was the most desirable one to use for
the epic trilogy of wheat which was left uncompleted
at the time of his early death. *McTeague* is a memora-
bly detailed story of simple people driven to destruction by chance, circumstance, and the primitive passion of greed; and, despite its moments of western
melodrama, it is the best example of French naturalism
in nineteenth-century American literature. It lacks the
feeling for the power of social and natural forces, however, which is evident in *The Octopus* (1901), the first
of the wheat trilogy, in which Norris throws the California ranchers of the San Joaquin Valley into conflict
with the corporate railroad octopus and allows them to
be destroyed. More powerful than the economic organization with all its political ramifications, though, is the
power of nature as symbolized by the wheat which
flows through this book and into the next, *The Pit*
(1903), as a stream which can neither be dammed nor
controlled by all the efforts of human ingenuity exercised on the Chicago grain exchange. It is not clear
whether Norris really felt the power of nature or was

merely using it for dramatic purposes, but it is clear from these books that he thought of the strongest, most intelligent, and most heroically determined individuals as being subject to forces over which they had no control. Reality for him, as for most of his contemporaries, was something outside himself; and, in common with many of them, he was inclined to see it as some onward-moving, irresistible natural force.

CHAPTER EIGHT

Society and the Individual

I

WITH so strong a feeling for external reality dominating late nineteenth-century America, it is perhaps not surprising that the writer who best preserved the traditional confidence in the individual human spirit was the expatriate Henry James. For James had been educated mostly abroad by a father who gave an international exhibition of the sort of individualistic, eccentric Transcendentalism that Thoreau had displayed at Walden Pond; and the effect of this education was to give the future novelist external familiarity with international society and the internal detachment of an observer who studied social conventions without allowing himself to be dominated by them. To James these conventions represented social reality, and he observed them acutely and with what must have become a fascinated interest in their subtlety. He knew little or nothing of the commonplace middle-class life which was so real to Howells, he could not realize (even by a calculated act of the imagination, as in his novel *The Princess Casamassima*) the economic and class conflicts which obsessed so many of his contemporaries, and he was completely indifferent to the theory of social evolution. The grandson of an Irish immigrant who had made a fortune in the new world, he did not feel with Henry Adams that he had inherited a judicious position at the center of the universe, nor did he have Mark Twain's compulsion to strike an outsider's pose. He felt free to choose his own world and adapt himself to it, and in 1876 he chose London because he preferred it as a center of operation for a man of letters who, at the age of thirty-three, had published two novels, some twenty-five short stories, and twice as many reviews but was just beginning his serious career as an artist.

The primary aim of the elder Henry James in educating his four sons had been to give them freedom—freedom to pick and choose not only among countries but among occupations, ideas, and religions—and he was successful enough to affect the minds of all of them as they reached maturity. In young Henry it seems also to have affected his literary style in the earliest of his short stories by causing him to hesitate over an observation as he was later to hesitate over his choice of residence, displaying an anxiety to pick and a reluctance to choose which gave him a tendency to see everything through the eyes of fictitious observers rather than commit himself directly to paper. Like the insecure Poe and the escapist author of *Huckleberry Finn,* he found his best release from constrictive self-consciousness by pretending to be somebody else; but, with James, the pretense never became a role that the author obviously played. Instead, it was incorporated so early into his technique of storytelling that it became the very basis of his art and the source of his greatest strength and greatest weakness. For as he matured and his choosing became more firm, his picking

developed into a mannerism which made some of the
most imaginative novels in American literature intolerable to many readers.

There were certain choices, however, that James as
a writer had to make fairly early, and one was of the
general area of his interest or the major symbols with
which he would deal. He began to make it in several
of his early stories, most notably "The Passionate Pilgrim" (1871), and confirmed it in the second of his
two early novels, *Roderick Hudson* (1876); it would
be the impact of European society, which so evidently
fascinated him, upon the stranger within its gates who
had been "prepared for culture" (as he thought that
he himself had been) by an American background. In
Roderick Hudson he could only find the impact overwhelming, and he concluded his story with Roderick's
suicide. But such a conclusion was essentially unreal-
istic in view of his own decision to live as an American
abroad and also impractical in the restrictions it placed
upon him as a novelist interested in this theme. Accordingly he was forced, perhaps without fully being
aware of it, to the second major choice in his literary
life—that of a belief in some reality which would enable a man to survive, as an independent human being,
the social pressures to which he was exposed. For a
basically shy person of James's upbringing, the choice
was probably inevitable; and he made it in *The American* (1877), which told the story of an American appropriately named Christopher Newman who went to
Paris, fell in love with the daughter of an aristocratic
French family, was rejected by family pressure which
sent the girl into a convent, and finally found evidence
of a crime which put the family under his complete
control. As a matter of course he destroyed it, sacri-
ficing his own feelings and perhaps those of the girl

who loved him to some internal moral sense which was superior to all ordinary standards of tolerable self-interest and conventional justice. Like Howells in *The Rise of Silas Lapham* a few years later, James found his highest reality in the American tradition of Emerson, Thoreau, and his own father.

The difference between the two friends and literary rivals was that James held onto the tradition, refining the concept of morality and removing it from its more sanctimonious implications by identifying it with innocence, goodness, perceptiveness, and artistic sensibility. The much-misunderstood and consequently greatly denounced *Daisy Miller* (1879) showed the vicious potentiality of conventions in their effect upon unprotected innocence, but the finest of his early novels, *The Portrait of a Lady* (1881), presented Isabel Archer as another American girl abroad whose innate goodness triumphed over disillusionment and gave her, it would seem, moral control over a situation which within a system of values other than James's would be tragic. James had published a biography of Hawthorne only two years before, and there may have been a bit of Hester Prynne as well as a good deal of his cousin Mary Temple in the character of Isabel; but when she returned to her husband she returned with a strength of character which had been revealed rather than developed by suffering, for James believed in the spirit rather than in the will, the emotions, or the intellect.

For a long while after *The Portrait of a Lady* James made little use of what may be called, in retrospect, his greatest theme—that of an individual, usually American, with a moral sense in a European society without it. He had already attempted a wholly American novel in *Washington Square* (1881) and was to do another in *The Bostonians* (1886); and he was to write, with unusual suspense, of a slum-bred revolutionary's growing awareness of the amenities of upper-class life in *The Princess Casamassima* (1886) and of the rebellion of the artist against these amenities in *The Tragic Muse* (1890). But such popularity as he had enjoyed through his early books was on the wane, and he was turning to the essay, the short story, and the drama. The most notable of his essays during this period was "The Art of Fiction" (1884), in which he defended the novel as a serious esthetic form, based its appeal upon the author's individual "sense of reality" and identified its quality in terms of the intelligence of the writer with particular reference to the "point at which the moral sense and the artistic sense lie very near together." The essay provides a significant indication of James's place in the American tradition, for its theme was that of Emerson's definition of art as "a nature"—that is, some chosen aspect of the external world —"passed through the alembic of man" and it contained the germ of the later novel in which James most clearly revealed his Emersonian concept of man.

The novel, *What Maisie Knew* (1897), was evidently James's attempt to do what the essay said Edmond de Goncourt had "failed deplorably" to do in *Chérie*—to trace "the development of the moral consciousness of a child"—and in it James struck a subtle blow against both the empirical naturalists and the affected morality of Victorian conventions. For he gave the child Maisie a thoroughly corrupt environment in the form of her parents and their associates, relieved it only by the person of the governess Mrs. Wix and her prattling "moral sense" of the proprieties, and allowed Maisie to develop within these surroundings the sort of sensitive perception of good and evil which was characteristic of the innate goodness he had portrayed in Isabel Archer. Maisie's "moral sense" was so delicate that some critics have refused to take it seriously, but if James had not clarified his belief in its innate quality in this book he might never have been able to assert its power in one of the finest of his mature novels, *The Wings of the Dove* (1902)—a book which resolved the ambiguity of the final sentences in *The Portrait of a Lady* by declaring, in dramatic terms, that individual goodness could not only face and perhaps endure the viciousness of a materialistic society but actually overcome it. Milly Theale in the later novel is another Isabel Archer, and Kate Croy and Merton Densher are closely related to Madame Merle and Gilbert Osmond; but the story is extended beyond that of *The Portrait of a Lady* when the "wings" of Milly's influence are transformed from the symbol of wealth to the symbol of unselfish generosity and their moral influence is spread as effectively over Kate and Densher at the end as their mercenary influence was at the beginning.

James's mature novels, however, were not merely the products of a growing assurance of belief—an increasing firmness of choice between the values of a society which fascinated him and those of the various individuals who could remain free from its worst influences. The maturity was also the result of a rare art which had been brought to perfection in the experimental short stories composed during his period of lost popularity and of disappointment with the drama. Some of these were experiments with themes that he was later to handle in longer works, as "The Pupil" (1891) anticipated the problem of the moral consciousness of a child in *What Maisie Knew* and was related to the influence of innate goodness asserted in *The Wings of the Dove* and to the portrayal of sophistication embarrassed by

innocence in *The Awkward Age* (1899). Others such
as "The Lesson of the Master" (1888), "The Real
Thing" (1893), "The Death of the Lion" (1894), and
"The Figure in the Carpet" (1896) affirmed with increasing sureness and subtlety the quality of creative
intelligence which must belong to the true artist; and
the last went so far as to suggest that it is beyond discovery, or at least definition, by the analytic or discursive intellect. In these stories James was, in effect,
identifying the artistic intelligence with that refusal to
commit himself which he had revealed in his own
earliest style and of which his own mature imagination
was certainly compact—an anxiety to pick the right detail or word which had become so pronounced that it
disguised the fact that his choice was no longer hesitant
but was firmly made for the artistic purpose of achieving suggestiveness on a higher level of consciousness
than can be found in the ambiguities of Hawthorne,
Melville, or any of his predecessors in American or
English fiction. Consequently the most technically interesting of the short stories are those tours de force
he used to test his range.

Several of them, like "The Jolly Corner" (1908) and
the related fragment of a novel *The Sense of the Past*
(1917), dealt with the supernatural; and of these the
one which has proved most fascinating is "The Turn of
the Screw" (1898), which used the governess of two
small children as a means of narration and also as a
means of avoiding commitment as to what happened
in fact and what might have occurred only in the
young woman's morbid imagination. The details were
selected with a masterly teasing designed to bring the
reader's own imagination into the story, and the several
critics who have been seduced into rational expositions
of it bear strong witness to James's claims for the su-

periority of "silken threads suspended in the chamber
of consciousness" over discursive reason, even when the
artistic mind is not, as he would have it be, "sincere."
The critical inclination to look into James's personality
rather than into his art for an explanation of his stories
might perhaps be better applied to "The Beast in the
Jungle" (1903), another tour de force in its creation of
intolerable suspense without action. For John Marcher
is what Henry James might have been had he not been
a writer, and his fears are of the same stuff as that
with which James created his fiction—anxiety and an
"enormous sensibility," which, in Marcher's case, is not
informed by the energy of creation.

But James's energy was as enormous as his sensibility, and in the decade from 1897 to 1907 it found expression in not only *What Maisie Knew* and *The Awkward Age* and a considerable number of shorter stories
but in the perfect and ironic short novel, *The Spoils
of Poynton* (1897), the less successful *The Sacred
Fount* (1901), and in the great major novels of three
successive years: *The Wings of the Dove* (1902), *The
Ambassadors* (1903), and *The Golden Bowl* (1904).
In addition he was able to produce a two-volume biography of *William Wetmore Story and his Friends*
(1903) and (after a return to the United States at the
age of sixty) a travel book full of the fresh immediacy
of *The American Scene* (1907). It is in the three great
novels that James's literary achievement reached its
climax in a combination of artistic skill and firmness of
belief. The refined Jamesian version of the moral sense,
whose power he asserted in *The Wings of the Dove*, became identified with the artistic sense in *The Ambassadors* when Lambert Strether, an elderly businessman
from Woollett, Massachusetts, achieved his emancipation from the conventional and vulgar American no-

tions of Paris and learned to see things as they really were and appreciate a certain rightness in the atmosphere and relationships of a city from which he withdrew in evidence of his freedom even from its charm. *The Ambassadors* has been the most popular of James's last novels, perhaps because it revived the American-in-Europe theme most pointedly and effectively and perhaps because it is the most carefully controlled through the use of Strether's single point of view. But for the latter reason it is also less appealing than *The Golden Bowl* to the confirmed Jamesians, who prefer to capture their author's vision of life through the intellectual or perceptive montage which was the peculiar outgrowth of his style and the final flowering of his art. For in this queer quadrangular romance of Maggie Verver, her father, her friend and stepmother, and her husband and stepmother's lover, James weaves a web of relationships which captures "in the chamber of consciousness" a perception of *how* the combination of intelligence, sensitivity, and goodness which was his moral ideal could possess the strength he had so often attributed to it. The most tortured example of the mannered picking of his way through a narrative, it is also the surest evidence of his choice of spiritual freedom—freedom not only from materialism but from the demands of resentment and the protests of passion—as the main figure in his own slowly woven but at last complete literary carpet.

II

Against the background of the American tradition the pattern of Henry James's mind should be both familiar and clear. He was devoted to careful observation of the world around him, skillful in drawing inferences, indifferent to the prevailing rationalistic notions of necessity, and convinced that reason was choice and that individuals could freely choose to follow some supreme intellectual light within them. The significance of the reappearance of this pattern at the end of the nineteenth century, however, may be better realized if it is placed in contrast to that of his leading disciple, Edith Wharton, who thoroughly learned the lesson of the master without ever being able to follow the figure in his carpet. For Mrs. Wharton possessed to a greater or less degree many of the qualities James drew upon for his fiction—a more intimate knowledge of international and especially of American society, a comparable sensitivity to the nuances of human relationship, and an equal sympathy for the individual in society—without having his capacity for belief in the reality of freedom. As with James, her books tended to have as their central characters heroines rather than heroes, but hers were morally defeated rather than triumphant. In the best of her novels of contemporary society, *The House of Mirth* (1905) and *The Custom of the Country* (1913), Lily Bart and Undine Spragg jeopardized or sacrificed their integrity in vain efforts to hold and to gain places in a social order which rejected them for their lack of wealth or of cultivation; and in her finest full-length novel, a nostalgic recapturing of *The Age of Innocence* (1920), she told the story of two lovers whose deep, genuine, and lasting emotion could make no headway against the barriers of convention which kept them apart. Even in such stories of New England country life as the extraordinarily succinct and deeply moving *Ethan Frome* (1911) and *Summer* (1917) chance and circumstance exercised their control over rebels and kept them in their places.

There was, in short, a certain individual negativism or pessimism in Mrs. Wharton's sophisticated view of the world; and the struggle against this negativism is the most evident common characteristic of the less sophisticated writers of her generation who continued the search for reality within the framework of evolutionary theory and who did not have Mrs. Wharton's personal excuse for doubting an individual's power to resist the pressures of his social environment. Of these, the one who achieved the greatest stature was Theodore Dreiser, the hulking, awkward, self-conscious son of a severe moralist and a gentle mystic who learned a great deal about the struggle for existence as he worked his own way upward from the position of a common laborer to that of a newspaper reporter and magazine editor before he became a successful novelist. An early convert to the theory of social evolution, he was more impressed than most Spencerians by the concept of a mysterious life force, which the English philosopher had called "the Unknowable," and seems to have felt that the business of the literary artist was to find this life force in the raw materials of human life, as George Bellows and other members of the "Ash Can School" of painters had found it in the derelicts and alleys of the slums. Exposed at second hand to French naturalism through the writings of a fellow reporter, Robert H. Hazard, Dreiser was actually a more avid reader of Balzac than of Zola; but his background was more journalistic than literary, and his novels were generally based upon real incidents and people and involved detailed reporting informed by his own view of life.

He expressed the essence of this view in his first novel when he referred to contemporary civilization as being in "a middle stage" of evolution in which man was "far removed from the lairs of the jungles, his innate instincts dulled by too near an approach to free-will, his free-will not sufficiently developed to replace his instincts and afford him perfect guidance . . . even as a wisp in the wind, moved by every breath of passion, acting now by his will and now by his instincts, erring with one, only to retrieve by the other, falling by one, only to rise by the other—a creature of incalculable variability." And the novel itself, called *Sister Carrie* (1900) despite the temptation to change its title to *The Flesh and the Spirit*, was a story of the rise of Carrie and the fall of her lover, Hurstwood, without an attribution of a determining free will to either of them: they profit or lose by chance and circumstance as they are pushed onward by social forces over which they have no control. Yet it is obvious to the reader that although Carrie was the partial portrait of the author's own sister he realized the character of Hurstwood more effectively and believed more firmly in his reality and in the reality of his fate. Carrie the good and Carrie the fortunate had to be written out of his system in his second novel, *Jennie Gerhardt* (1911), whose heroine's goodness caused her to sacrifice her good fortune, before he could write the novels in which the real strength of his belief was expressed.

The first of these were the two parts of a trilogy, *The Financier* (1912) and *The Titan* (1914), completed by the publication of *The Stoic* (1947) after his death, in which Dreiser undertook to tell the story of a transportation magnate named Frank Cowperwood, who began his operations in Philadelphia in the first book and landed in jail but began anew in Chicago in the second and eventually gained control of the street railroad system. It was a story of the law of the jungle in modern civilization—of a magnetic personality whose sexual and financial ruthlessness made him "fit" to survive and whose magnetism is explained in chemical terms which would have allowed him to take no account of the goodness suggested in Carrie and portrayed in Jennie. Dreiser's world was a moral chaos to be mastered by animal energy and a willingness to meet society on its own terms, and his basic conviction that these terms were materialistic and economic is indicated by the comparative failure of his next novel, *The Genius* (1915), in which Eugene Witla displayed many of the qualities of Cowperwood but proved a weakling in his pursuit of art rather than financial power. These novels, however, revealed only one side of Dreiser's attitude toward the world. The other side was revealed in the tenderness and sentimentality of several autobiographical works, and in the sympathy amounting to an enormous pity for the misfits and the unfortunate most notably displayed in the unactable drama, *The Hand of the Potter* (1918), and the essays of *Hey, Rub-a-Dub-Dub* (1920), which was aptly subtitled *A Book of the Mystery and Terror of Life*. For life, even as he had found it interpreted by Herbert Spencer and the various scientists he had been reading since, remained a mystery to Dreiser; and his early belief that "it was not so much the business of the writer to indict as to interpret" was always modified by the notion that such a code was cruel unless the failure to indict society was compensated for by a display of pity for its victims.

Something of a balance between detachment and sympathy may be found in the collections of short stories, *Free* (1918), *Twelve Men* (1919), *Chains* (1927), and *A Gallery of Women* (1929), but it was best achieved in his most carefully controlled and impressively detailed novel *An American Tragedy* (1925). The story of the weak but attractive son of two street evangelists, it presented in the person of Clyde Griffiths a young man who was the plaything of his environment. Forced by an automobile accident to abandon his employment as a hotel bellhop and leave town, he moved to a smaller city where he had wealthy relatives who provided him with employment in a factory. The breath of passion involved him with an attractive fellow worker, but he decided to abandon her for a wealthy marriage made possible by the social contacts provided by his relatives. Learning that she was pregnant, he made elaborate preparations to fake an accident which would get her out of the way, only to lose his nerve at the last moment and allow her to drown by the genuine accident of an overturned boat and his own panic. Suspicion was aroused, however, by his preparations; and he was arrested, convicted on circumstantial evidence by a politically inspired prosecuter, sentenced to death, and executed. *An American Tragedy* is one of the most powerful of twentieth-century American novels, and much of its power comes from the combination of Dreiser's sympathetic interpretation of Clyde as a "wisp in the wind of social forces" and his steadfast refusal to issue an explicit indictment against the society which tossed him to destruction. For the book is one to provoke an infinite amount of discussion of guilt and innocence, moral and social responsibility—a book of many ambiguities which are made to seem as real as life by the meticulous detail of Dreiser's reportorial technique and the lumbering, uncalculated, awkward honesty of its style.

By the time Dreiser wrote *An American Tragedy* he seems to have lost his belief in social evolution, for he gave his book a general implication by the use of the indefinite article in its title and by making its last scene a repetition of the first, with a younger boy taking the place of Clyde. And in the remaining two decades of his life he was to waver curiously in his search for a philosophy, leaning toward communism in a sympathetic book on Russia and toward Transcendentalism in a collection of social and political essays on Thoreau before he created, in the posthumous novel *The Bulwark* (1946), his last hero in the person of Solon Barnes, who was as sternly religious as the author's own father but more sympathetically comprehended as a member of the Society of Friends than as a Roman Catholic. The most consistently close to the naturalists of all major American novelists, Dreiser always revealed an undercurrent of rebellion, part intellectual and part emotional, against the biological and social determinism which he asserted as his major article of faith.

The other aspect of the struggle against negativism in the early twentieth century was more logical than that represented by Theodore Dreiser, more "rational" in what had come to be the Continental meaning of the word. Its exponents did not question the power of the social order to overwhelm the ordinary individual or the prevalence of the law of tooth and claw in the existing order. They simply reasoned that since human misery was a widespread product of the social organization, then society should be reorganized to promote happiness. This was the implication which lay back of the "muckraking" journalists of *McClure's Magazine*—Ida M. Tarbell, Ray Stannard Baker, and Lincoln Steffens (whose *Autobiography*, published in 1931, is the best account of the movement and its social philosophy)—and of such early novels as David Graham Phillips' *The Great God Success* (1901) and Robert Herrick's *The Common Lot* (1904). It was most succinctly expressed, however, in the poetry of

William Vaughn Moody, whose "Ode in Time of Hesitation" (1900) and other poems of the Spanish-American War bear witness to the moral impulse back of his social consciousness and whose "The Menagerie" is the most amusing expression of evolutionary belief in American literature. For in "Gloucester Moors" Moody represented the earth as a "ship of souls" gallantly moving forward without knowing its port. As he saw it with some men in the cabin and some before the mast, with a noisome hold full of men kept down because "the ship sails faster thus," he thought it "better captainless" than brought to harbor by leaders who would break the souls of men rather than turn them into brotherly shipmates. The new suggestive implication of this imagery, like that of the muckraker's attacks on large fortunes, was social revolution.

Yet there were few American writers prepared to advocate revolutionary socialism as opposed to the optimistic Fabian dreams of William Dean Howells. Jack London, in fact, was the only one to be widely read at home and abroad; and the violence of his socialism was less impressive at home than the romantic love of violence which made him one of the most popular writers of his day. Sailor, laborer, hobo, and adventurer in the Far North and the South Seas, London began as a teller of tales and gained his greatest popular success with a dog story, *The Call of the Wild,* in 1903. In the same year he published his first attack upon contemporary society in *The People of the Abyss,* which grew out of his observations of the London slums; and the following years saw a strange alternation of popular adventure stories and books of social protest—*The Sea Wolf* (1904) and *War of the Classes* (1905), *White Fang* (1906) and *The Iron Heel* (1907), *Burning Daylight* (1910) and *Revolu-*

tion (1909)—with a tendency toward the end of his life to such troubled autobiographical novels as *Martin Eden* (1909) and *John Barleycorn* (1913). Where his heart lay may perhaps be seen in a comparison between the vitality he gave to the brutal Wolf Larsen in *The Sea Wolf* and the woodenness of the self-sacrificing hero of *The Iron Heel* and the remnants of life still to be found in the style of the first and the dull heaviness which pervades the second. An avowed Spencerian, London was eager for the help of Karl Marx in the direction of social evolution; but he was basically an escapist, a he-man Lafcadio Hearn or a Cro-Magnon Henry Adams, whose primary impulse was to go over the horizon or revert to primitivism because his hatred of the existing order was more real than his hope for changing it.

In the less violent area of political revolution, however, the socialist cause found a brilliant and single-minded recruit in the prolific and well-bred young romancer Upton Sinclair whose novel *The Jungle* (1906) displayed such extraordinary naturalistic power that one critic was moved to complain of its propagandist conclusion, with more bitterness than wit, that its author had "sold his birthright for a pot of message." Growing out of Sinclair's own investigation of the Chicago stockyards, *The Jungle* told the story of the merciless exploitation of a Lithuanian immigrant family from the moment of their first hopeful settlement in a home of their own in the new world until the only survivor escaped the toils of capitalism and its law and found refuge in the socialist party and new hope in its belief that "the country will be ours." Its description of the economic jungle and the helpless human creatures who suffer in it is the most vivid and convincing in American fiction, and the power of its vividness, in fact, defeated its purpose. For, as Sinclair was to complain, it was an appeal to its readers' heads and hearts which, instead, hit them in their stomachs. Its casual but sickening accounts of the unsanitary conditions in the meat-packing industry set up a public hue and cry which hurried the passage of the federal Food and Drug Act and left its rationalistic appeal for socialism almost unnoticed. Sinclair had proved himself magnificently capable of achieving the naturalists' aim of diagnosing the evils of society so effectively that the legislators would be forced to find a cure for them, and had he been content with this aim he might have become America's greatest realistic novelist.

But Sinclair proved to be the rarest type of American writer—the man of great individual talent who could not use it without the support of an orthodoxy. His own logic had provided him with socialism as the legislation needed, and his later investigations of social evils were not designed to demand some cure but to argue for his own cure. For two decades he vigorously attacked a great variety of capitalistic interests in such novels as *The Money-Changers* (1908), *King Coal* (1917), *Jimmie Higgins* (1919), *Oil!* (1927), and *Boston* (1928) and in such journalistic muckraking as *The Profits of Religion* (1918), *The Brass Check: A Study of American Journalism* (1919), *The Goose-Step: A Study of American Education* (1922), *The Goslings: A Study of American Schools* (1924), *Mammonart* (1925), and *Money Writes!* (1927). He was almost alone among American socialist writers to stick tenaciously to his principles after the party was almost destroyed by its pacifistic stand during the First World War, and it was not until he himself seriously entered practical politics in his unsuccessful California guber-

natorial race in 1934 that he relaxed his rigid orthodoxy
in a way which permitted him to turn in fiction to a
representation of individual good works in the Lanny
Budd series of novels which began with *World's End*
in 1940. There is a certain fascination about the Lanny
Budd novels, for their detailed effort to cover the whole
of the contemporary world through the activity of a
single man of good will suggests that Sinclair is doing
more than trying to perpetuate his own view of modern history. He may be recapturing the true literary
personality of a man who was always a behind-scenes
romantic at heart and who had held too rigidly to his
dogmatic principles because he did not know quite
what to do without them.

III

Although the main stream of American fiction in the
early twentieth century appears in retrospect to have
been realistic and dominated by social consciousness,
the popular fiction was a literature of escape into
Romanticism and sentimentalism. The historical novel
flourished under the temporary dominance of Winston
Churchill, whose *Richard Carvel* (1899), *The Crisis*
(1901), and *The Crossing* (1904) surveyed American
history from the colonial period through the Civil War;
and various writers who were to achieve greater literary stature contributed to the genre—Upton Sinclair
with *Manassas* (1904) and Ellen Glasgow with *The
Battle-Ground* (1902)—while others in a semihistori-
cal vein tried to capture the color of the past as Joseph
Hergesheimer did in *The Three Black Pennys* (1917)
and *Java Head* (1919). Sentimentalism dominated the
popular magazines and the widely read later writers

of the local-color schools and was both used and
mocked by the most complex of the Romanticists,
James Branch Cabell, whose short stories collected in
The Line of Love (1905) and whose medieval novel
The Soul of Melicent (1913) were, in their original
versions, highly sentimental but whose novels of contemporary life, leading up to *The Rivet in Grandfather's Neck* (1915) and *The Cream of the Jest*
(1917) were increasingly inclined toward mockery.
Cabell, however, was an unusually alert and sophisticated writer for this period, who tried to define certain
historical attitudes of mind in the contrasting short
stories of *Gallantry* (1907) and *Chivalry* (1909) and
who dealt interpretively with historical figures in the
stories of *The Certain Hour* (1916); and his maturity
belongs to the period after the First World War when
he himself realized the full implication of the tendencies displayed in his early work.

These implications were of the creative importance
of a return to individual values rather than a turn to
conventional Romanticism as a means of escape from
the oppressive weight of social consciousness whether
felt in terms of evolutionary theory or the need for
reform; and this return was led not only by Henry
James but by a new group of poets who found in
poetry itself an escape from that shadow of social consciousness which had so darkened the realistic novel.
And the earliest of these poets was Edwin Arlington
Robinson, on whom the shadow of the world lay heavy
but who was second only to the expatriate James in
the persistence with which he followed his own intellectual "light" and attributed such a private illumination to a host of fictitious characters.

Educated for two years at Harvard and there exposed to the residual influences of Emersonian Tran-

scendentalism, Robinson published his first public volume of verse in 1897 with the significant title *The Children of the Night*. Most of the individuals in this volume and in *Captain Craig* (1902), *The Town Down the River* (1910), and *The Man Against the Sky* (1916), too, were people who received no guidance from the shrouded world around them but were somehow greater than they would have been had they simply made a "blind atomic pilgrimage" because their brains and bones and cartilage would have it so. The sex-ridden "John Evereldown," the gentlemanly suicide "Richard Corey," the broken "Annandale" who "went out" by instrumentality of a kindly physician, the drunken and romantic consumptive "Miniver Cheevy," the gracious beggar "Flammonde," and the mysteriously secluded victim of "Eros Turannos"—these are only a few of the many characters in Robinson's poems who are in no way conventionally admirable but who attract a sympathetic respect because they have a quality of individual independence never given to the characters in the novels of Edith Wharton, Theodore Dreiser, or Upton Sinclair. If they are social misfits it is because they have been created out of the poet's own private preoccupation with the infinite variety of the human impulse toward self-destruction which he found even in the greatest of men and which enabled him, in "Ben Jonson Entertains a Man from Stratford," to draw one of the most sympathetic portraits of Shakespeare in literature by allowing the plain-thinking Jonson to meditate upon the significance of his friend's new house in his native town.

In many of these early poems Robinson showed a mastery of disciplined verse forms and an epigrammatic wit which makes him one of the most quotable of modern American poets, but his novelist's interest in people was also accompanied by a tendency toward verbosity which led him into a kind of colloquial verse narrative that was effective in the carefully controlled "Isaac and Archibald" (1902), in the earlier Arthurian poems, *Merlin* (1917) and *Lancelot* (1920), and in the somewhat melodramatic *Avon's Harvest* (1921), and that became subtly magnificent in the restrained passion of *Tristram* (1927). But this was a dangerous tendency in the sort of person who could look outward only when the larger world affected his own private convenience (as the Prohibition amendment did when he composed *Dionysus in Doubt* in 1925 and the economic depression did when he wrote the allegorical *King Jasper* at the end of his life), and the bulk of his later work from *Roman Bartholow* (1923) to *Amaranth* (1934) was of an introspective flatness which aroused enthusiasm only among his most confirmed admirers.

Less prolific and less ambitious in range than Robinson, Robert Frost was also much less given to errors in judgment and the mistakes of introspection; for there is probably no twentieth-century American poet who has been more firmly and soundly devoted to the principle that wisdom should be tested by the tenor of one's own life or that literary symbols should make sense in terms of one's own experience. Although he was born in San Francisco and made his poetic reputation in England (with *A Boy's Will* in 1913 and *North of Boston* in 1914), his work is more strongly marked than Robinson's by the New England physical environment and by the New England tradition of Emerson, Hawthorne, Thoreau, and Dickinson. The poems in *A Boy's Will* are mostly lyric and those in *North of Boston* dramatic, with both forms appearing in *Mountain Interval* (1916), and they are all packed with thought and feeling realized in terms of simple personal experience. "Mending Wall," for example, is a meditation upon an annual spring chore undertaken with a neighbor which suggests more than the novelists of the time were able to say about the difficulty of impressing the conventional consciousness with an individual sense of values; but Frost records the difficulty with a serene humor which also suggests that he looks upon convention as a tolerable eccentricity rather than as a depressing weight. Similarly, "Birches" suggests a philosophy of aspiration and contentment with earth which explains why Frost was able to capture so much of the tragedy of the New England back country in these volumes without losing its humor or his own capacity for enjoying his "Good Hours" of intense awareness.

In *New Hampshire* (1923) and *West-Running Brook* (1928) he became somewhat more discursively philosophical (as in the title poem for each volume and the amusing verses on "The Bear" in the latter) but without losing the suggestiveness which makes "Stopping by Woods on a Snowy Evening" so haunting, the lyricism which makes "Spring Pools" so perfect, or the intensity of personal feeling which makes the sonnet to "A Soldier" so moving. In later volumes, composed in more pressing times, this reflective discursiveness was directed toward contemporary problems—labor in *A Further Range* (1936) and politics in *A Witness Tree* (1942) and *Steeple Bush* (1947)—and broadened into the larger issues of his verse dramas, *A Masque of Reason* (1945) and *A Masque of Mercy* (1947). Yet even when he showed signs of impatience and irritability with the contemporary world Frost maintained an attitude of wry humor which preserved the individuality of his own values and kept him in the position he has assigned to himself—that of one who "had a lover's quarrel with the world."

Compared with Frost and the best of Robinson, the prewar poets of the Middle West seem artificial and excessively self-conscious—as in fact they were, for they bore the same relationship to the revival of individual-ism that Whitman bore to its earlier triumph in that they paraded it and made it a symbol rather than a tacit attitude of mind. The oldest and the most flam-boyant of them was Vachel Lindsay, the dreamy would-be artist son of a Campbellite minister who fed his dreams on Edgar Allan Poe, William Blake, and Emanuel Swedenborg in his native Springfield, Illinois, and eventually took to the open road in an effort to beat the economic "system" by trading rhymes for bread. His success, however, came with his acceptance of the system and his rebellion against the poetic con-ventions of his own early verse; and the title poem of *General William Booth Enters into Heaven* (1913) was written to the strong rhythm of a Salvation Army song with an indicated drum and brass accompani-ment. Such a poem was written for reading before a mass audience, and Lindsay found a means of captur-ing audiences in the tom-tom beat of *The Congo* (1914), which enabled him to spend the next decade and a half in what he called "the higher vaudeville," reading these and such other poems as "The Ghosts of Buffaloes" and "The Santa Fé Trail" with a variety of sound effects ranging from the thin cadences of *The Chinese Nightingale* (1917) to the roaring and cater-wauling of "The Calliope." Lindsay was a new kind of folk poet—with public-school teachers as his folk—who could be nostalgic in "The Building of Springfield" and tender in "Abraham Lincoln Walks at Midnight" but was probably at his best when capturing the gaudier aspects of the American scene and translating them into verses for ears primarily attuned to popular songs.

Carl Sandburg also looked upon himself as a people's poet, but he was, like Whitman, more the poet of the people than for the people. Like Whitman, too, he was devoted to the long lines of free verse, but he was less able to find a consistent compromise between prose and the imagistic delicacy he sometimes achieved. The opening line of his description of Chicago, "Hog Butcher for the World," shocked the readers of his first volume of verse, *Chicago Poems* (1916), into an awareness that a new kind of poet had appeared on the scene; and, although he achieved a certain balance in the title poem of *Smoke and Steel* (1920) and broadened his range in *Cornhuskers* (1918) and *Slabs of the Sunburnt West* (1922), he struck no new note until he turned folklorist, folk singer, and imaginative biographer of Abraham Lincoln and incorporated his new interests into a volume of definition and affirmation called *The People, Yes* (1936), which defies literary classification but which contains some of Sandburg's most effective work.

Both Lindsay and Sandburg were protégés of Harriet Monroe and the Chicago *Poetry: A Magazine of Verse,* which was established in 1912 and had the distinction of printing the early poems of Hilda Doolittle, Amy Lowell, William Carlos Williams, John Gould Fletcher, Wallace Stevens, Edgar Lee Masters, T. S. Eliot, and Marianne Moore as well as those of Robert Frost, Vachel Lindsay, and Carl Sandburg. It also printed in its first issue two poems by Ezra Pound, the Idaho expatriate who became its "foreign correspondent" and proved to be the best informed, most influential, and most sophisticated example of the individual on parade which the "new poetry" movement

brought into the limelight. He had the curiosity but
not the patience required for graduate work in Romance philology at the University of Pennsylvania, and
in 1908, at the age of twenty-three, deserted the
academic world for London. By the end of 1912 he had
published eight small volumes of original and translated verse which revealed his interest in Latin, Greek,
and Provençal poetry, in the work of such modern
French poets as Laurent Tailhade, and in the new
English "Imagist" movement inspired by T. E. Hulme
and F. S. Flint. Pound's interest in medieval France
was probably affected by the same sort of academic
Romanticism which his fellow admirer of Eleanor of
Aquitaine, Cabell, was displaying in the popular American magazines but with the difference that he had
seen for himself a harsh reality in Provence which re-
minded him of the "half-savage country" of his native
West and made him feel that with its people, and with
the Imperial Romans and the Greek sailors who preceded them, he would have been at home.

So with his heroes from the past he rebelled against
what a softer age demanded (and what it was getting
in a man like Cabell), and he found in his young English contemporaries men who could appreciate his
learning and not only share his rebelliousness but direct it into the productive channel of creating a new
poetic style. The style which Hulme demanded would
be "cheerful, dry, and sophisticated" in a free-verse
pattern which would permit concentration upon the
image rather than the metrical line; and although
Pound was no model of cheerfulness, despite the implied claims of his "Commission" to his poems, he
strove passionately for dryness and sophistication.
"Dryness" was the particular aspiration of the Imagist
movement whose manifesto in *Some Imagist Poets*

(1915) called for concise, clear, hard, exact poetry; but by this time the energetic, self-made but well-heeled poetess, Amy Lowell, had captured the movement for Boston, and Pound was contemptuously referring to it as "Amygism" and fulfilling its aims in his own way. He increased the sophistication of the new poetry by turning, through Ernest Fenellosa, to Chinese and Japanese poetry for new models of imagistic succinctness, by recruiting new talent and ruthlessly editing it (as he edited the manuscript of Eliot's *The Waste Land*), and by beginning his own most ambitious life work in a long series of "Cantos" of which the first three were published in *Poetry* magazine in 1917 and, with revisions, in *Quia Pauper Amavi* in 1919. A year later he abandoned London with severe strictures upon its Victorian traditions and commercialization of literature, in *Hugh Selwyn Mauberley* (1920), and made his way to Paris and eventually to a permanent home in Italy.

Pound's influence upon modern poetry has been so great that it can be treated here only in terms of a manner which is displayed in the early "Cantos" as well as anywhere else. The first, which reads like a free rendering of an Anglo-Saxon adaptation of Homer, bears witness to the eclecticism of Pound's manner—a manner which enabled him to range in allusiveness from the Greeks and Romans, through Dante and the medieval troubadours, to ancient Chinese and modern French poetry while pursuing his general theme of the decay of civilization under the particular influence of usury and in terms of a great variety of personalities ranging from the Italian *condottiere* Sigismondo Malatesta to John Quincy Adams and Henry James. The style is dry in the sense that it is imagistic and colloquial rather than rhetorical, although it reveals a fondness for primi-

tive epithets and often does create the rhetorical effect of deliberate harshness and rudeness. The most
striking quality found in the *Cantos* and in Pound's
poetry in general, however, is a calculated sophistication achieved by the trick of substituting literature for
common human experience as a source for those allusions by which a poet suggests more than he says.
Pound's method, then, is the very reverse of that used
by such a poet as Frost in that it asks the reader to admire the breadth of his knowledge and take his sensitivity on faith; and it is for that reason that his ultimate
influence, by basing poetry on essentially private
rather than intensely personal experience, has been to
make a substantial body of modern verse academic and
erudite rather than popular and simple.

While Pound was avoiding the hackneyed by leading poetry back into the academic environment from
which he thought he was revolting, another American
expatriate, in Paris, was quietly anticipating and actually achieving the "cheerful, dry, and sophisticated"
style which Hulme had set up as the ideal of the
Imagists. Gertrude Stein's education had been in
psychology at Radcliffe and medicine at the Johns
Hopkins University before she went to London in 1902
and then settled permanently in France, where she was
to find kindred experimental spirits among the Expres-
sionist painters Pablo Picasso and Henri Matisse, who
became her friends, and the many talented young
American writers who sat at her feet. Her influence has
been greater upon modern prose than upon poetry, but
the most interesting of her experimental work has been
in what might be called the verses of *Tender Buttons*
(1914) and *Portraits and Prayers* (1934). Unlike
Pound, who attempted fresh communication through
the implications of a vast erudition, Miss Stein at-

tempted to communicate her profound knowledge of people as well as things by means of a calculated simplicity, which is almost always fresh and challenging even when incomprehensible. Her incomprehensibility, however, is the result of her most persistent aim—that of abstracting from her considerable knowledge of a subject the peculiar or "essential" quality of it and attempting to communicate that quality with a minimum of irrelevant associations. When she was experimenting with the communication of peculiar qualities by unconventional means (as in *Tender Buttons* when she undertakes to give the visual image of a moving dog in a rhythmical arrangement of words which literally refer to a monkey and a donkey, or when she gives her opinion of the opera in the rhythmical suggestion of a line drawing of a top hat, cape, and cane), comprehension immediately follows a realization of what she is doing; but when she is dealing with essential qualities, as in her "portraits" of real or typical individuals, comprehension often depends upon the reader's having a sufficiently adequate knowledge of the subject to appreciate the wit and wisdom of what she abstracts as "essential."

Consequently the understanding of Miss Stein's work is likely to be only partially increased by the sort of elaborate annotation which Pound's poetry demands; and readers of her most ambitious novel, *The Making of Americans* (1925), are likely to find some parts of it extraordinarily entertaining and other parts intolerably dull, according to their own background of experience, and turn with greater delight to her first work of fiction, *Three Lives* (1909), and her last, *Brewsie and Willie* (1946), or to the autobiographical works, in which the peculiar directness of her genius can be seen at its comprehensible best. But whether one appreciates the cheerful dryness of her sophistication or not, there was a freshness about her approach to writing which left a good mark on the literature of the twenties and made her one of the most historically important writers of her time. Combining the direct and wholesome wisdom of Frost with the erudite eccentricity of Pound, she joined with them and with the unhappy Robinson and their more flamboyant contemporaries—against the solid background of Henry James—in leading American literature back to the traditional fountain of individual judgment from which it had emerged for its first period of greatness.

This new individualism, however, was different from that of the mid-nineteenth century. For with James and his successors a new consciousness became evident in American literature—a pervading awareness of the conflict between the individual and society. Man was no longer free, as he had been in the mind of Emerson, to vault into his throne and lord it over the creepers and crawlers of the conventional world. He had to assert his individuality, by self-sacrifice, by isolation, by flamboyant rebellion, or by a parade of eccentricity, in order to be sure that he maintained it. The weight of a complex social organization was depressing the confidence of even those who were most determined to declare their independence, and it remained to be seen whether the American tradition would survive as a deep quality of belief or whether it would remain as no more than a symbolic refuge for the maladjustments of second-rate talent.

CHAPTER NINE

Tradition in the Twenties

I

THE consciousness of society was strong in the intoxicating twenties. No period in American history, perhaps, gave greater encouragement to freedom in literary expression, but it was the freedom of iconoclasm rather than that of inspiration. The decade between 1919 and 1929 was an era of rebellion in which writers revolted against the narrowness of their prewar world, against the conventions so dramatically symbolized by the Volstead Act, which made the distribution of alcoholic liquors a crime, and against America itself, as people turned against the idealism of Woodrow Wilson or flocked abroad to take advantage of the favorable rate of exchange which was one of the evidences of their country's new and more powerful position in the world. It was a decade of new writing growing out of the experimental attitudes of the prewar period, of the new psychology of Sigmund Freud, and of a new freedom to do what one wished. It was, in short, a time when the individual walked at large in the literary scene and wrote as he pleased with the assurance that some ambitious young publisher would willingly offer his work to a tolerant and eager public.

The core of the rebellion was against the narrowness of background—particularly against the small town in which so many American writers grew up—and, like most literary manifestations of the twenties, it was foreshadowed by the prewar poetry. In retrospect it can be seen symbolically anticipated in the first poem of Edna St. Vincent Millay, *Renascence* (1912), which told of death and burial, realization that narrowness is of the spirit, and rebirth to greater awareness of the values of the world. But the appropriateness of the poem, welcomed more for its youthful freshness than for its significance, was not appreciated at the time; and the poetic leader of the revolt from the village was Edgar Lee Masters, whose *Spoon River Anthology* (1915) was one of the most popular volumes of verse ever published in America. Cynical and bitter, Masters used the form of the free-verse epitaph as a method of revealing the meanness that lay beneath the sanctimonious surface of village life, and his poetry appealed strongly to young rebels who wanted to get away from it all and into the freer life of the city. Both poets, however, proved to be rather sterile. Miss Millay got to the city and with the gay impertinence of *A Few Figs from Thistles* (1920) became the poet of Bohemian Greenwich Village and the idol of a postwar generation of undergraduates; and although she achieved a fine lyric quality in *Second April* (1921) and in *The Harp Weaver and Other Poems* (1923) and grasped at the fringes of greatness in the sonnets collected in *Fatal Interview* (1931), she suffered from the reaction to overpraise and the disillusionment provoked by the socially conscious poems in *Conversation at Midnight* (1937) and *There Are No Islands Any-*

more (1940) and has been almost forgotten in the critical devotion to the "new" poetry. Masters, already a Chicago lawyer when he wrote *Spoon River*, continued to imitate himself, in *Domesday Book* (1920) and *The New Spoon River* (1924), in a vain effort to repeat his early success.

The more influential and fruitful leader of the rebellion against the village was Sherwood Anderson, who had written two novels, both expressing a vague dissatisfaction with life, and a volume of poems before he clarified his own point of view in the related stories of *Winesburg, Ohio* (1919)—a book which was to have an extraordinary influence upon the American short story by freeing it from the well-knit formalism of Poe, Bierce, and O. Henry and making it the medium for that perceptive record of a significant moment of experience which was to be perfected by Ernest Hemingway. Anderson's point of view in these stories was like Masters' in that he was interested in the grotesque reality beneath the smug surface of village life but unlike Masters' in that he was sympathetic rather than bitter or cynical toward the "grotesque" or unconventional and nonconforming element in human character. Like Miss Millay, although more inclined to express himself in psychological than in spiritual terms, he was something of a Romantic rebel himself, who found freedom in an irresponsible reaction to conventions; and that attitude provided him with the theme for the best of his novels, *Dark Laughter* (1925). But his finest work was in the short stories of *Winesburg* and of *The Triumph of the Egg* (1921) and *Horses and Men* (1923) which followed, and his literary achievement was that of bringing the reader closer to those queer, frustrated, and sometimes tragic individuals who in Robinson's poems had been appealing characters but who in Anderson's stories became neighbors and friends.

The technique of capturing the reader's entire sensibility and making it—rather than some specialized reaction like sympathy, humor, or respect for the author's quality of mind—a part of his literary response, in fact, became a characteristic of the rebellious realism of the twenties and is nowhere better illustrated than in the novels of Sinclair Lewis. He used it effectively for the first time (after five earlier novels of the American scene) in *Main Street* (1920) and developed it most skillfully in *Babbitt* (1922). The Gopher Prairie in *Main Street*, although located in the Middle West, was everybody's small town, and the characters in it could be identified by practically every small-town resident as his friends and neighbors. The first novel of genuine realism ever to be widely read in America, *Main Street* owed much of its popularity to the accuracy with which Lewis caught the spirit, speech, and mores of small-town life, and also, among intellectuals, to the strong strain of satire which ran through it. But, more than that, it allowed every reader—the satisfied villager, the intellectual who had escaped to the city, or the complacent foreigner—the free play of his own individual consciousness in interpreting what he was enabled to see and hear. Similarly in *Babbitt*, which is a better novel because the central character was more fully conceived and because the small city was more representative of America in transition, every reader was made to feel and rejoice in a secret superiority to the ordinary humanity with which he might, to all appearances, be identified. Even businessmen read the book and began calling themselves Babbitts with a complacency which grew out of a private sense of identity which even so complete an observer as Lewis had not been able to capture and so take from them. Instead of dominating his readers as Howells had done through his style and James through the complexity of his perceptions, Lewis somehow managed at once to open their eyes and give them a feeling of superior vision.

How much Lewis knew about what he was doing is doubtful, for the denial of a spiritual center to his characters is a weakness in a novelist; and it would not have led to popular success in any age other than the twenties, when individualism was rampant and standards of value were more unstable than even Henry Adams might have anticipated. At any rate, it was a sign of increasing maturity when Lewis tried in *Arrowsmith* (1925) to create a character who could rise through a chaos of multiple values and achieve universal respect. He chose a scientist who would move through the academic and medical worlds to a position of eminence and opportunity, only to fail in his great experiment because of a humanizing flaw in his scientific temperament. This plot produced the best of his novels, and it might have been a great one had Lewis chosen to stop at this point and emphasize a tragedy which was genuinely moving because it had been developed in an atmosphere of satire which conquered the chaos of multiple values and made those of Martin Arrowsmith seem real. But a certain intellectual weakness and a strain of sentimentality caused him to lead the reader away from the threat of catharsis and disengage him from the story in its concluding parts; and these qualities affected both of the two other important novels he was to publish during the decade, giving to *Elmer Gantry* (1927) the values of the self-conscious intelligentsia rather than those of the understanding realist and touching *Dodsworth* (1929) with a slight suggestion that he was trying to apologize and make up for the injustice he had done the American businessman in *Babbitt*. With the possible exception of the antifascist hypothetical story *It Can't Happen Here* (1935), Lewis failed in later years to achieve a literary success comparable to his five major novels of the twenties; and these failures perhaps confirm the suspicion that he was peculiarly the representative of the postwar decade—a man whose experience was wide and perceptive but who was so dimly focused within himself that readers in a chaotic age could absorb his experience, bring it to terms with their own inner consciousness, and find satisfaction in the awareness of their own individuality.

Unlike Lewis, the other major novelist stimulated to new artistic achievement by the revolt against smalltown life had done some of her best work during the prewar period. Many critics, in fact, consider Willa Cather's early stories of simple people on the Nebraska plains, *O Pioneers!* (1913) and *My Ántonia* (1918), the finest of her novels, and her story of the opera singer who came out of such an environment, *The Song of the Lark* (1915), comparable to them. Certainly her admiration for these immigrant daughters, inured to toil and with the inner strength to rise above adversity, was warm and moving; but the intellectual basis for it was obscure, for she kept them separate in body or in spirit from the social entanglements which tested and revealed the beliefs of Henry James and Edith Wharton. It was not until she undertook the story of a young man who went to and returned from war, in *One of Ours* (1922), that she faced in a full-length novel the problem of a heroic spirit in a frustrating society and found that a feeling for heroism was not enough to sustain the integrity of a realistic story. Her first solution was pessimistic, and in *A Lost Lady* (1923) she produced a compact tragedy of moral and spiritual decay which confirmed the attitude toward village narrowness she had indicated in such early short stories as "The Sculptor's Funeral" and "Paul's Case" (from *The Troll Garden* in 1905) but had generally avoided in her novels. Her next two books, *The Professor's House* (1925) and *My Mortal Enemy* (1926), revealed a continued preoccupation with environmental frustration; but within the first of them was an avenue of escape in the form of an inserted novella called "Tom Outland's Story"—an escape into the American Southwest, which she loved with a passion never felt for Europe however much her early European experiences may have affected her art.

Actually, the theme of the Southwest had been anticipated in *The Song of the Lark* when Thea Kronborg, worn out by the pressures of the city and unable to find the artistic restoration she sought in her native town, took refuge among the cliff dwellings of "the ancient people," listened to "a voice out of the past, not very loud, that went on saying a few simple things to the solitude eternally," and in this communion with the past found a renewal of strength and character. The story of the archaeologist Tom Outland and his Blue Mesa was designed to have the same effect by letting in a breath of fresh air from the mesa in the form of Outland's fine disregard for the triviality of "petty ambitions," "quivering jealousies," and "American proprieties" with which Miss Cather had deliberately made Professor St. Peter's house "stuffy." In these episodes she was reflecting personal experience and feeling, but it was experience and feeling from which she was to create a new theory of values which were environmental but not social and on which the individual could depend for a strength she was not quite willing to attribute to his Transcendental spirit—a system based upon a few simple things said externally from the past and thereby uniting the past and present in one timeless reality.

Miss Cather could have acquired from Henri Bergson or Marcel Proust the ideas that led her into her *recherche du temps perdu* in *Death Comes for the Archbishop* (1927), but her own comments upon the inspiration of the novel suggest that she was simply following the same sort of sensitivity that caused Hawthorne to become preoccupied with the past prolonging itself into the present as a sort of "gray legendary mist." In any case, her success in recapturing the legendary quality of the early Santa Fé missionaries, Bishop Latour and Father Vaillant, harmonizing it with the existing atmosphere of the region is one of the finest achievements in American fiction in one of the most secure of modern classics. The fineness of her achievement in interpreting the distinctive atmosphere of a peculiar locality in terms of the past and the few simple things it whispers to the present can be tested by any one who reads her other novel of the same type, *Shadows on the Rock* (1931), set in modern Quebec, where the shadows seem to be more delicately but definitely etched than in New Mexico. But *Death Comes for the Archbishop* is the deeper book, emotionally, in the witness it bears to a sense of the past not as history but as life, and nothing in Miss Cather's later work ever rivaled it.

Comparable to Willa Cather in the opinion of some critics and certainly possessed of more wit if less sensitivity and feeling is Ellen Glasgow, another Virginian by birth but one who remained in her native state and found her literary material almost exclusively there.

Miss Glasgow's early ambition was to give in fiction a panorama of Virginia history, but she developed from a historical novelist into a novelist of inbred character and finally, during the twenties, into a witty and sardonic commentator upon contemporary southern life. Born in Richmond rather than in a small town, Miss Glasgow's revolt was against the southern devotion to Romantic illusion, which she so skillfully presented in *The Deliverance* (1904); and she began it early with the realistic story of the Reconstruction period, *The Voice of the People* (1900), which preceded her Civil War novel *The Battle-Ground* (1902). Her method was that of emphasizing the importance of the lower middle class in southern life in a series of novels culminating with *Barren Ground* (1925), whose heroine, Dorinda Oakley, is comparable to Willa Cather's Alexandra Bergson and Ántonia Shimerda, and of holding up for admiration those people who broke with the southern conventions as did the heroine of *Life and Gabriella* (1916). Under the influence of Cabell, her wit came to full flowering in the three novels of "the Queenborough trilogy," *The Romantic Comedians* (1926), *They Stooped to Folly* (1929), and *The Sheltered Life* (1932), in which she mocked the manners of contemporary Richmond and—in the second and perhaps the best of the three—gave an amusingly ironic representation of the change in attitude toward three generations of lovely ladies who slipped or stepped from the path of virtue.

Miss Glasgow had as deep a feeling for the past as did Miss Cather, but she felt it within a pattern of evolutionary ideas rather than as something from which time selected certain absolute values and incorporated them into the present. To her the past was a cultural heritage which might destroy or preserve, a myth one might live but against which it was better to rebel, a period of selective breeding in a strictly biological sense. It was this last concept which finally prevailed in the most profound of her novels, *Vein of Iron* (1935), in which she paid tribute to the hard firmness of her own Scotch-Irish strain and suggested that the stern cultural heritage of the Presbyterian intellectual was weaker than the inbred qualities of character.

II

The rebellion against conventions, for which Edna St. Vincent Millay wrote the lyrics and H. L. Mencken beat the drum, had the advantage of its own periodical in *The American Mercury,* which Mencken founded in 1923 with the assistance of George Jean Nathan, who had been associated with him in the editorship of *The Smart Set.* Mencken himself had been an aggressive Baltimore individualist for more than two decades, an early admirer of George Bernard Shaw but an outspoken opponent of socialism, a defender of the philosophy of Friedrich Nietzsche, an eclectic critic whose essays had been collected in *A Book of Prefaces* (1917), and a bull in the conventional china shop with *Damn—A Book of Calumny* and *In Defense of Women* (both in 1918). He was also an independent and explosive user, student, and creator of the American language, who had already begun his monumental work of scholarship on that subject with the publication of its first volume in 1919; and he had collaborated with Nathan in an ironic study of *The American Credo: A Contribution toward the Interpretation of the National Mind* (1920). His major literary works of the postwar period consisted of the six-volume series of essays called *Prejudices* (1919–27) which began with a literary emphasis but became increasingly sociological, and with the damning *Notes on Democracy* (1926) and a cynical *Treatise on the Gods* (1930).

His greatest influence was exercised through the *Mercury*, in which he published a quarterly collection of "Americana" gleaned from the country's press and revealing the national life at its sanctimonious worst, denounced the "boobosity" of the country as a whole and especially the service club "wowsers" and the smugness of the "Bible Belt," and defended generously every new or old writer who seemed to be striking at or through the moral or social conventions of which he so vigorously disapproved—Theodore Dreiser, Sinclair Lewis, and especially James Branch Cabell. For the Cabell of Mencken's era had become quite different from the earlier representative of popular if somewhat sophisticated Romanticism. In 1919 he had published in the essays of *Beyond Life* an urbane defense of Romanticism on the grounds that man alone of all animals was able to play the ape to his dreams and that Romantic illusions were necessary if he was to raise himself out of the biological mire. But in the same year he had also published the novel *Jurgen*, which told the story of an old and cynical pawnbroker whose youth was renewed by magic; his renewed youth was devoted to biological activity under the influence of his single remaining illusion. With an intellect entirely too active for the sort of writing he had been doing, Cabell had reached the point of having to decide whether he would develop as a sort of Romantic evolutionist or become a satiric and cynical commentator upon the world as it was. As he approached the threshold of the new era, the choice, in fact, was made for him: he became the latter, writing a companion novel for *Jurgen*, called *Figures of Earth* (1921), in which the hero, Dom Manuel, followed his own thinking and his own desires under the motto "The world wishes to be deceived," until he achieved every high position the world could offer without ever changing his original simple self.

During these years *Jurgen* was generally suppressed throughout the country on the grounds of indecency, and Cabell busied himself revising all his earlier books in order to bring them into a common pattern. He went so far as to give a new title to the revised version of *The Soul of Melicent* (*Domnei,* in 1920), but most of the revisions were designed to sharpen their cynicism of tone and place them within the mythological framework of his pseudomedieval world of Poictesme, in which Jurgen (as the exponent of the cleverly intellectual way of life which he called "gallantry") and Manuel (representing the simple-minded way of "chivalry") were the two protagonists from whom all his other characters were descended. His whole ingenious plan was charted in *The Lineage of Litchfield* (1922), filled out with the eighteenth-century gallantry (and sexuality) of *The High Place* (1923) and with the chivalric fellowship of *The Silver Stallion* (1926), and rounded off with *Something about Eve* (1927), which is the most sympathetically human of his novels in its representation of the effects of marriage and of a father's transfer of his own dreams to his hopes for a child. Cabell's own greatest illusion, stoutly maintained in the essays of *Straws and Prayerbooks* (1924) at a time when every tendency was in the opposite direction, was that lushness and sophistication were the proper qualities of a good style; and, although critics of a later generation may find in him the stylistic and intellectual ambivalence which has become so attractive in Hawthorne, his immediate successors have ignored him to such a degree that he has become least known of all the major literary figures of the twenties.

Yet Cabell was only one of a considerable group of rebel sophisticates which included the later Joseph Hergesheimer of *Cytherea* (1922) and *Balisand* (1924), the young Thornton Wilder of *The Cabala* (1926) and *The Bridge of San Luis Rey* (1927), and the aging critic James Gibbons Huneker whose privately printed collection of short stories, *Painted Veils* (1920), appeared the year before his death. Huneker's literary successor—and also the successor of Edgar Saltus, whose death in the same year revived an interest in his precious, erotic writings of the previous century—was Carl Van Vechten, music and art critic and devotee of cats, whose novels *Peter Whiffle* (1922), *The Blind Bow-Boy* (1923), and *The Tattooed Countess* (1924) were supposed to contain practically everything a young man should know during the early twenties. Van Vechten's interest in the offbeat aspects of New York life, however, was both genuine and intelligent; and he went on in *Nigger Heaven* (1926) and *Spider Boy* (1928) to explore Harlem and the sporting world with a knowledge which was not to be exceeded in American fiction until Ralph Ellison wrote *Invisible Man* (1952) and Bernard Wolfe *The Late Risers* (1954). But Cabell's closest rival was the short-lived Elinor Wylie, who handled a Romantic style with much more delicacy and taste and produced two minor classics in *Jennifer Lorn* (1923), the story of a young Englishman in the East India Company whose elegant discrimination kept him a year or two in advance of the great minds of his age, and *The Venetian Glass Nephew* (1925), an imaginary episode in the life of Giacomo Casanova told from the point of view of complete innocence. She achieved popular success in

The Orphan Angel (1926), a Romantic fantasy of
Shelley pioneering the American continent, and maintained it to a certain extent in the year of her death
with *Mr. Hodge and Mr. Hazard* (1928), a novel which
suggestively portrayed in human terms the impact of
Victorianism upon the Romantic spirit; but she has
been remembered more by a later generation for her
poetry (from *Nets to Catch the Wind* in 1921 to *Angels
and Earthly Creatures* in 1929), which shares some of
the qualities of Edna St. Vincent Millay but is much
more clear-cut in style.

While Mencken was encouraging his group of rebels
in fiction, George Jean Nathan found his major literary
protégé in the person of Eugene O'Neill, who brought
to the dreary boards of the American theater a quality
of excitement never felt before in serious native drama.
O'Neill had got his start with the Provincetown Players
on Cape Cod and in the Provincetown Playhouse of
New York, and several of his early realistic dramas had
been published in *The Smart Set* before he attracted
widespread literary attention with the publication of
*The Moon of the Caribbees, and Six Other Plays of the
Sea* in 1920. O'Neill was primarily a dramatist of
frustrations, whose background of realism and whose
technical skill, acquired through the early one-act
plays, enabled him to be convincing while he made his
theme exciting by expressing it in terms of the new
theater and the new psychology. *Beyond the Horizon*
(1920), the story of a dreamer and would-be wanderer
who is held to the farm by a woman's passion while his
solid brother is set awandering, was a realistic representation of the basic conflict in most of his plays—a
conflict between dreams and desires on the one hand
and temperament and practicality on the other. *The
Emperor Jones* (1921) translated it into symbolic and

psychological terms by making a ruthlessly calculating Caribbean dictator the victim of the little formless fears that arose in his own mind, and *The Hairy Ape* (1922) experimented with its symbolic expression by the use of masks and stereotyped figures. This experimentation was carried in 1926 to its utmost length in *The Great God Brown* (which used masks, not altogether successfully, to stage the conflict in terms of the divided personality of a single character) and in the almost unactable *Lazarus Laughed* of 1927 (in which Lazarus found, through the experience of death, a life beyond desire and a laughter which split the masked personalities of the world to which he returned). In the meantime O'Neill had been developing his more naturalistic means of expression in the unresolved pathos of *Anna Christie* (1922), in the stronger pathos of miscegenation in *All God's Chillun Got Wings* (1924), and in the unadulterated passions of sex and greed in *Desire Under the Elms* (1925), until he was able to bring his realistic and experimental tendencies together in the most ambitious of his dramas—*Strange Interlude* (1928), in which the characters spoke their secret thoughts in motionless pauses between the passages of conventional dialogue.

Much of O'Neill's power seems to have come from the fact that in the infinitely varied twenties he could accept frustration as a way of life and find in that acceptance a source of energy comparable to that which Anderson found in irresponsibility, Lewis in superiority, Cather in the past, Glasgow in inbred character, Mencken in irreverence, and Cabell in cynicism. He was less prolific and less exciting in the more serious decade which followed, when he tried in vain to modernize the Greek tragic spirit in *Mourning Becomes Electra* (1931), was more successful with the nostal-

gia of youth in *Ah, Wilderness!* (1933), but became
lost trying to deal with the religious impulse in *Days
Without End* (1934). Positive commitments were not
easy for a man who sank into silence for more than a
decade before he revealed the essence of his problem
in *The Iceman Cometh* (1946): he could neither be
content with a drunken dream nor accept the conventional realities of life as sanity. And the reason for his
dilemma was to become clear in his revealing posthumous drama, *A Long Day's Journey into Night* (1956).
Frustration, violent impulsiveness, and theatric expression were bred in him and formed the tenor of a
life which could never quite find ease in irony or really
reach the depths of tragedy.

For people who enjoyed the revolt against conventions during the twenties, Mencken, Cabell, and Millay preserve its true flavor; but, for later readers who
just missed it, Scott Fitzgerald became the novelist of
the great rebellion. Perhaps this is so because Fitzgerald himself did not quite believe the age but played
its game with an air of wonder, a double sense of involvement and detachment which made him the immediate historian of an age he was half living and half
creating. At any rate, *This Side of Paradise* (1920)
was a reminiscent novel at the time he wrote it, drawing upon his experiences as a romantic, Irish-midwest-
ern egoist in prewar Princeton; but it was put together
with a postwar feeling that made it a model of emula-
tion for a new generation. Similarly the short stories of
Flappers and Philosophers (1920), *Tales of the Jazz
Age* (1922), and *All the Sad Young Men* (1926) were
careful and often fascinated observations of the new
era which were widely distributed in popular magazines as examples of a way of life which, as Mencken
observed, was "imitated by the flappers of the Bible

Belt country clubs" in the weeks that followed. Fitzgerald was more ambitious as a social historian in
The Beautiful and Damned (1922), a somewhat chaotic portrayal of the attractions and the futility of the
New York world to which his success had admitted
him; but it was not until *The Great Gatsby* (1926) that
he managed to triumph over his early faults of style
and achieve a novel which seemed to T. S. Eliot "the
first step that American fiction has taken since Henry
James." There was, in fact, a Jamesian quality in the
book, emphasized by the use of a narrator and the
method of presenting the story in scenes, in its conception of flamboyant bootlegger Gatsby as an individual of greater moral sensitivity than the wealthy
and well-bred Daisy and Tom; and, although it lacks
Jamesian faith inasmuch as Gatsby is killed instead
of being allowed to experience some inner triumph, it
is this quality which makes it Fitzgerald's most human
book rather than another fine example of social history.

Fitzgerald was to preserve this humanity in his next
and much later novel, *Tender Is the Night* (1934), by
making the reader feel pity rather than respect for
the young psychiatrist Dick Diver, whose most successful case was his wife who had no need for him
after she was cured. He also carried it over into many
of the later short stories collected in *Taps at Reveille*
(1935) and into the fragmentary novel, *The Last
Tycoon* (1941), which he attempted after his Hollywood experiences and while he was himself going to
pieces in the way he so candidly described in *The
Crack-up* (1945). But his great achievement was that
of capturing, in the person of Gatsby, the major symbol of the rebellion against conventions during the
Prohibition era and identifying it with that quality of
humanity which Americans traditionally admired.

Among the less high-spirited but more pretentious leaders of the rebellious twenties Thomas Stearns Eliot was to have, by far, the greatest literary influence. A native of St. Louis, he had been educated at Harvard and, like Pound but with much better academic training, he had gone abroad to complete his work for the doctorate. There, like Pound, he decided to remain; and at the outbreak of the First World War he settled in England, married, recognized in Pound a poet of kindred interests, and in 1917 published a pamphlet on Pound's metric and poetry and brought out a thin volume of his own verse entitled *Prufrock and Other Observations*. Some were early satires dating from his Harvard days, a few paid passing allegiance to the Imagist fad, and two of them ("Portrait of a Lady" and "The Love Song of J. Alfred Prufrock") resembled Pound's "Portrait d'une Femme" in suggesting a bystander's fascination with the world of Henry James. At the end of the war he made a collection of his literary essays in *The Sacred Wood* (1920), prepared for publication a new volume of *Poems* (1920), and, suffering from nervous strain, made a trip to Lausanne, where he composed the first version of *The Waste Land*, which was to be extensively cut and edited by Pound before it was published in 1922. With the publication of *The Waste Land* (which appeared in two periodicals and in book form in the same year) against the background of his *Poems* and his critical essays, Eliot became the most controversial poet of the new era.

Consequently his development during these first postwar years is of unusual interest. Some of it can be traced in the *Poems* and attributed to the influence of Pound, who undoubtedly encouraged him in the greater devotion to the French Symbolists which this volume revealed, who taught him the trick of weaving a poem out of allusions to erudite knowledge, and who set him an example for the sophisticated bad-boy pose, which had been foreshadowed by his early satires and the "Portrait of a Lady" but which became pronounced in "Whispers of Immortality" and "The Hippopotamus" and in the suggestion of self-identification in "Mr. Eliot's Sunday Morning Service" with a crude character named Sweeney. Pound's influence is also strongly marked in some of the ideas and in the shift away from the Symbolists toward the Dantesque quality of "Gerontion," which led directly to *The Waste Land* in the new quality of its imagery and in the somber seriousness of its tone and attitude. Yet the *Poems* were also a declaration of independence from Pound. For Eliot did not share his friend and mentor's evangelical determination to sacrifice metrical charm to imagistic hardness, and his words sang their way into their readers' consciousness with all the insidiousness of nonsense verse. Much of Eliot's early fame was probably due to this insidiousness and to the prestige given him by intellectuals who partially mastered his erudition and found that achievement created in them a feeling of complacency comparable to that which Sinclair Lewis was creating in the general public; but Eliot had much more to offer, especially in *The Waste Land,* than the charm of Lewis Carroll and intellectual satisfaction for the initiate. He had a theme in the decay of modern civilization which possessed a strong appeal for a generation which was beginning to read Oswald Spengler and was to consider O'Neill a great dramatist, Cabell a man of wisdom, and Fitzgerald a tragic novelist; and his poem had a quality of inner coherence, a suggestion of focus in depth, which was notably lacking in the poetry of Pound.

The search for a point of focus in *The Waste Land*, however, has been confused by the fact that in the critical essays of *The Sacred Wood* Eliot had set forth two quite different theories concerning the relationship of the poet to his work. One (to be found in "Ben Jonson" and "Hamlet" of his *Selected Essays* of 1932) held that the creation of a work of art consisted of the process of transfusing the personality of the author into it and maintained that literary appreciation depended upon understanding the author rather than the "archaeology" of his materials. The answer to the riddle of *Hamlet*, for example, lay in Shakespeare's biography, perhaps on a subconscious level; and the play was an artistic failure because Shakespeare had transfused into his character an emotion too deep and complex to be evoked in the audience by any of the symbols he used to justify it. For "the only way of expressing emotion in the form of art is by finding an 'objective correlative,'" Eliot explained; "in other words, a set of objects, a situation, a chain of events which shall be the formula of that *particular* emotion; such that when the external facts, which must terminate in sensory experience, are given, the emotion is immediately evoked." This was a theory in the tradition of Emerson and James, who thought of art as a selected portion of the external world passed through "the alembic of man." Yet it was almost completely opposed by another theory (found in "Tradition and the Individual Talent") which held that the mind of the poet was merely a catalytic agent that enabled very special or very old feelings to enter into new combinations with a new effectiveness. These feelings would have no necessary reference to the poet himself. For "the more perfect the artist, the more completely separate in him will be the man who suffers and the mind which creates." Consequently "it is not in his personal emotions, the emotions provoked by particular events in his life, that the poet is in any way remarkable or interesting"; and poetry itself "is not a turning loose of emotion but an escape from emotion; it is not the expression of personality, but an escape from personality." Here Eliot was presenting a more subtle and sophisticated version of Poe's "The Philosophy of Composition."

The line which Eliot himself has followed most consistently since has been the second (most emphatically in the lectures *After Strange Gods* of 1934), and it is from this line that there has developed a whole school of "New Critics" in America, who have violated Eliot's notions of "The Function of Criticism" (1923) by falling into the "autotelic" heresy of creative interpretation and have filled university classrooms with creative and catalytic agents rather than instructors. Because of this—and because the author's own notes for *The Waste Land* suggested an anthropological rather than a personal inspiration for the poem—the interpretations of Eliot's most influential work have been in terms of its superficial theme. But if one assumes that his first theory of poetic creation is the more real one—that he was actually writing in the American tradition of insisting that literary materials make sense in terms of his own experience—and if one makes the further assumption that his literary allusions were selected for their genuine allusiveness rather than as bits of arbitrary structural material for an emotional engineer, then the poem itself and Eliot's peculiar power both become more comprehensible.

Under such assumptions, the key to *The Waste Land*

might be found in its concluding section, "What the Thunder Said," and especially in the final lines, beginning with the voice of the thunder, which are introduced by the interwoven imagery of the biblical journey to Emmaus and the approach to the Castle Perilous in Jessie Weston's *From Ritual to Romance*. The associations of this imagery suggest a moment of time after the Passion and before the Resurrection, a moment when the Fisher King of the Grail romances sits waiting for the word which will cause the waters to flow and restore fertility to the stony places. Then, out of the author's Harvard studies in Indic philology, comes the voice of the thunder—"*Da*," which was variously interpreted, according to fable, as the first syllable of the words meaning "give," "sympathize," and "control." The reflections upon these interpretations seem to be intensely personal in their references to the gift of "the awful daring of a moment's surrender," to the key of sympathy which had turned in the door once and once only, and to the control which would have brought a gay and willing response had it been exercised upon another's heart; and the implication of personal failure in the last reflection is emphasized in the following lines in which the poet identifies himself with the Fisher King, sitting with the arid plain behind him and asking whether he should not at least set his "lands in order." The ordering is in the manner of Pound, by a collection of apparently random quotations which, however, are highly coherent in their allusive context. The first conjures up the inevitable association of "my fair lady" with the catchy words of "London Bridge is falling down," the second calls to mind the Provençal poet who was being purged of lust in Dante's Purgatory, the third is a part of a cry from the violated and mutilated Philomela who

wants to be like the swallow and from dumb distress
set free, and the fourth recalls a gloomy, widowed, and
unconsoled Prince of Aquitaine standing before a
ruined tower. "These fragments" of literary feeling
from the past, said the poet, "I have shored against my
ruins"—in the manner, he implied, of Thomas Kyd's
Hieronimo, who escaped from real distraction by pretending madness and agreeing to write a play by
which he achieved his rational purpose—and the poem
closes with the Sanscrit words of guidance and a
benediction inviting an infinitude of peace.

The rights of privacy which any man can claim in
his lifetime make it impossible to relate these allusions
to a specific experience, but the coherence of its conclusion seems personal enough to invite a reading of
the whole poem in such terms and finding in its earlier parts a sustained emotional balance between old
dreams and current reality. Cleopatra and Lil, the London of Spenser's "Prothalamion" and that of Mr. Eu-
genides and the carbuncular clerk, the Thames of
Elizabeth and Leicester and that of the cockney boats
off Richmond—these represent a balance of opposites
which culminates in the foreboding of "Death by
Water" and in the resolution of its conclusion. From
this point of view it would seem that Eliot's "waste
land" is his own emotional waste land and that contemporary civilization is an "objective correlative"
which the public, under the guidance of his criticism,
has found adequate for its justification. And from this
point of view, too, his later and less influential writings
may be summarized in terms of a search outside of
literature for other means of shoring up his life. He
seems to have dwelt in his waste land at least through
"The Hollow Men" (1925); made a determined effort
to escape in the essays For Lancelot Andrewes (1928)

when he announced himself a classicist in literature, an Anglo-Catholic in religion, and a royalist in politics; and confirmed himself in the institutional refuge of the church with the poem *Ash Wednesday* (1930) and the poetic drama *Murder in the Cathedral* (1935), while trying, in *Sweeney Agonistes* (1932), to exorcise his bad-boy self along the way. But the indications are that he has not found the institution adequate, and in what appears to be the finest and most mature of his poetical works, the *Four Quartets* (1941–43), he has turned to a past which is neither literary nor institutional but one which whispers "a few simple things" eternally. When he came to the belief that "Time present and time past are both perhaps present in time future, and time future contained in time past," he may have been finding his own personal support in the concept of reality which Willa Cather had tried to capture in *Death Comes for the Archbishop*. Or perhaps his final philosophy represents a return to a subjective concept of time derived from Bergson, under whom he had studied in 1910. At any rate he had explored much and arrived back where he might have started had he been able to know the place the first time.

The basic difference between Eliot and Pound can be expressed, though oversimplified, in terms of the old assumption that a man's wisdom should be tested by the tenor of his own life. Eliot, despite his philosophy of composition, seems to have followed this assumption, whereas Pound has formed his life around the fixed ideas of his early rebelliousness. Of the other participants in what has been called "the melody of chaos" it is more difficult to judge. Among Eliot's younger contemporaries the one most closely linked to him, by reaction rather than by imitation, was Hart Crane, whose first collection of verse (*White Buildings*

in 1926) showed a genuine originality in experimenting with the suggestive power of words. But Crane,
unlike the troubled Eliot and the eccentric Pound, was
using poetry to struggle against a genuine derange-
ment of mind, and the ambitious culmination of his
desire to provide a constructive answer to *The Waste
Land* took the form of "an epic of modern consciousness," *The Bridge* (1930), which gathered together
the myths of American history, literature, and folklore
and related them to impressions of contemporary New
York but achieved neither epic quality nor inner
coherence. E. E. Cummings, whose novel *The Enormous Room* (1922) was one of the most psychologically effective products of the First World War, makes
a more lasting impression with his distinctive combination of delicate sensibility and mischievous independence from linguistic conventions; and his volumes
with such queer titles as *Is 5* (1926) and *1 x 1* (1945)
contain some memorable poems in rather startling ar-
rangements of word forms, grammar, syntax, punctu-
ation, and typography. The most deeply independent
minor poet of Eliot's generation, however, was Marianne Moore, who emphasized the objective quality of
her work by calling one volume of poems *Observations*
(1924) and who has since, by constant revision,
stripped her originally stark verses on simple things to
the simplicity of skeleton poetry.

Yet among the host of singers in the chaotic twenties
there arose only one new voice strong enough, for a
while, to rival Eliot's; and that was the voice of the
California poet Robinson Jeffers. As well educated as
Eliot, though interested in the sciences as well as in
the classics, Jeffers had studied abroad and published
one volume of rather conventional verse before mar-
rying and settling upon the California coast near Mon-

terey, where he built the stone tower in which he
was to live the rest of his life in retirement. His
volume of verse, *Californians,* appeared in 1916, but
he attracted little attention until rumors of the privately printed *Tamar* began to circulate in 1924 and
Roan Stallion, Tamar, and Other Poems reached a
startled public in 1925. He had been completely un-
touched by the "new" poetry of Pound and Eliot, but
his own was new enough in its own right. His long
lines invited comparison with Whitman but were more
regular, suggesting at once classical hexameters and
the strong beat of Old English verse, and his images
had the strength of one who had dedicated himself to
absorbing his own wild surroundings. But a greater
wildness was in his subjects: *Tamar* was a story of incest and *Roan Stallion* of a woman's frenzied passion
for a horse, and both ended in violence. That they
owed much to the new psychology was evident, but
they possessed a feeling beyond Freud, as though
their author was releasing subconscious forces for the
purpose of destroying something more than the inhibitions of excessive civilization.

Philosophically, *Roan Stallion* suggested as much,
for in it Jeffers wrote: "Humanity is the mold to break
away from, the crust to break through, the coal to break
into fire, the atom to be split." And this proved to be
his central theme as successive volumes developed
and clarified it, and, though equally violent, modified
the impulsiveness of its first statement. In *The Women
at Point Sur* (1927) the incest motif became more
clearly symbolic of the introversion of society and of
Jeffers' belief in its destructive effect; and the poem
was also more clearly indicative of his condemnation
of man and his civilization, as though the course of
evolution had run itself out and it was time for a col-

lapse, as though the decline of the West had actually been speeded up according to the rule of phase, as though the flash in chaos was the light of revelation. Jeffers had found something of his own feeling among the Greek dramatists and in "The Tower beyond Tragedy" (1925) had given Orestes a vision of humanity turning inward upon itself in hate or love and had allowed him to cut himself loose from human passions by falling in love "outward" with the inanimate world. And he too seems to have achieved something like a catharsis through the violence of these poems, for there is pity in *Cawdor* (1928) for the strong man who is betrayed and broken by the primitive egocentricity of a woman and pity in *Dear Judas* (1929) for the betrayer. His own feeling at the end of the decade is perhaps best expressed in this last volume in the best of the shorter poems which reveal both his violence and his philosophy—a succinct version of *The Bacchantes* called "The Humanist's Tragedy." "It is possible for you to break prison of yourselves and enter the nature of things and use the beauty," says King Pentheus. "Wine and lawlessness, art and music, love, self-torture, religion, are means but are not needful, contemplation will do it. Only break human collectedness." A moment later he is torn to pieces by his mother and her frenzied companions, but the "tragic flaw" in the drama appears in the "wild, somewhat too drunken" representatives of humanity rather than in the hero whose "dignity, as a human being, a king and Greek," is maintained and respected. And whether Jeffers would allow himself to be called a humanist or not, his later work, from *Thurso's Landing and Other Poems* (1932) on, seems to be more concerned with violence as an error than with violence as an ideal.

Most of the writers whose spirit was peculiarly that

of the twenties wrote in the spirit of *après moi le déluge,* and Jeffers, the introspective recluse, was perhaps no more than an ultimate example of the spirit of an age in which every individual could find a source of energy in his own sense of values, even the values of destruction. At the moment it is probably too soon to say which of the writers of the twenties reflected a "wisdom tested by the tenor of a life" and which represented a mere rebellion against conventional life. Certainly the energy of many appeared to fade with the energy of their decade: their individualism was not rugged enough to survive the stock-market crash of the autumn of 1929 and the economic depression which followed. The symbol of the American tradition had flourished, gaudily enough for a while, but the real test of its power was to be made in the sterner years to come when a new generation of writers arose and a few older ones continued to mature.

EPILOGUE

The Test
1930—

CHAPTER TEN

Power and the Past

I

THE most radical effect of the economic depression upon the American consciousness was to make the old attitude of *laissez faire* impossible. From the most conservative stockbroker who turned his face to avoid buying an apple from a former colleague on the streets of New York to the most ardent socialist who welcomed the New Deal in politics as "a step in the right direction," people were forced into an awareness that individuals did not stand alone in the complex society they had created. Many, of course, did not want to stand alone. Even the twenties had been marked by a gradual decrease in enthusiasm for the new freedom, a lessened willingness to live in the present, a noticeable tendency toward second thoughts in literature. But these signs were in older writers who may have been simply losing their energy, and so it required a newcomer on the literary scene, a young man with an apparently inexhaustible gusto, to show that this change in attitude was a sign of the times rather than an evidence of individual exhaustion.

This newcomer was Thomas Wolfe, whose first rich and crowded novel, *Look Homeward, Angel* (1929), was a product of the twenties with all its exuberance but with a pervading suggestion that its author felt lost in the chaotic world his older contemporaries had created and enjoyed. Significantly, it was the one major novel of the decade that was wholly autobiographical in design, re-creating the places and persons of Wolfe's North Carolina background with a quantity of detail that suggested total recall but that was actually memory engaged in interpreting the environment from which Wolfe was glad to escape but for which he had found no satisfactory substitute. His next novel, *Of Time and the River* (1935), was equally autobiographical, dealing with the larger world of Harvard, New York, and Europe, and equally suggestive of the lost "hapless youth" to which the title of the first had referred; but by this time he was trying to find a meaning in his wanderings in terms of the mythological figures to whom he referred in the subdivisions of the book. As he caught up with his own actual experiences in his writing, he planned a vast historical panorama dealing with his ancestral background; but the impulse to re-create his own personal past in terms of its current emotional meaning seems to have been primary with him, and the last years of his short life were devoted to a more mature and disciplined reordering of his early experience, with the introduction for the first time of wholly fictitious characters, in *The Web and the Rock* (1939), *You Can't Go Home Again* (1940), and the fragmentary *The Hills Beyond* (1941) —all posthumous publications which contain sections rejected from his two earlier books but which suggest the struggle of a man of enormous literary energy who could neither accept the values of the decade in which he reached manhood or that into which he survived.

If Wolfe is the best representative of the emotional attitude of the transition period, John Dos Passos was the best representative of its intellectual state of mind. A Harvard esthete of the generation after Eliot's, Dos Passos had gone to war and given his impressions of the experience in two novels, *One Man's Initiation* (1920) and *Three Soldiers* (1921), reported on his postwar European wanderings in several travel books, and attracted wide attention as an experimenter with the technique of fiction by *Manhattan Transfer* (1925) —a novel which succeeded in capturing the peculiar quality of New York life much better than Howells had done (in the house-hunting introduction to *A Hazard of New Fortunes*), by the device of using many apparently unrelated scenes and incidents and gradually pyramiding them into a relationship which produced a story. After other travels and travel books he began his ambitious trilogy of twentieth-century America which was eventually to appear under the title *U.S.A.: The 42nd Parallel* (1930), *1919* (1932), and *The Big Money* (1936). His method was impressionistic, consisting of the episodic pursuit of a variety of representative characters and the use of three extraordinary devices for the purpose of transmitting a timely background of impressions to the reader—"the camera eye" of a sensitive and perceptive observer's stream of consciousness, a "newsreel" of headlines and fragments of news stories and of bits from popular songs, and impressionistic biographies of historical figures who were related to the fictitious action. The whole was aimed at an unfocused portrayal of the American cultural scene during the first quarter of the twentieth century, when its economic center was moving westward along the forty-second parallel and the moral energies of its people were collapsing into the postwar search for "the big money."

Time alone will tell whether the technical ingenuity of Dos Passos gave him a new means of vivifying the novel of social history or whether it merely served as a successful mnemonic device for readers of his own generation. But his critical attitude toward the United States in which he developed is both clear and representative of the early thirties: he considered it a moral chaos in which malefactors of great wealth were more powerful than the leaders of labor and in which little men were the victims of social ideals that were largely mercenary. Such constructive implications as it contained were socialistic, and, although Dos Passos was to attempt to modify and correct these implications in *The Ground We Stand On* (1941) and other later works of history and fiction, the attitude revealed in *U.S.A.* was the attitude which controlled the search for new values by most of the writers who came to maturity in the thirties.

The writer who developed most during the decade was John Steinbeck, whose considerable versatility was displayed in the early books through which he sought those values which would give assurance to his creative powers. His first, *Cup of Gold* (1929), was a romance based upon the buccaneer Henry Morgan; his second, *The Pastures of Heaven* (1932), a collection of fine and sympathetic short stories about the ordinary people of a "happy valley" in California; and his third, *To a God Unknown* (1933), a novel packed with religious and sexual feeling so intense that it could pass for mysticism. The relative quality of these early volumes suggests that he had found what he was seeking in the second; and Steinbeck may have felt so himself, for his next book, *Tortilla Flat* (1935), was another collection of stories about simple people, *paisanos* of Mexican descent, which was unified by Quixotic humor and the suggestion of Arthurian fellowship. Sympathetic and happy-go-lucky in tone, it was the best of his early books and the first to achieve, though slowly, a wide popular success. Before its qualities were recognized, however, it was followed by *In Dubious Battle* (1936), a novel of class warfare in the California farm lands, which in effect announced Steinbeck's conversion to the new proletarian movement in American fiction—a movement represented ideologically by Mary Heaton Vorse's *Strike: A Novel of Gastonia* (1930), Robert Cantwell's *Laugh and Lie Down* (1931) and *The Land of Plenty* (1934), Grace Lumpkin's *To Make My Bread* (1932), and Jack Conroy's *The Disinherited* (1934) and *World to Win* (1935). Without more research than has yet been done, however, it is difficult to estimate any writer's affiliation with the proletarians, for even so anti-Marxian an author as Pearl Buck showed a strong sympathy for the poorer classes in *The Good Earth* (1931) and her other novels of Chinese peasants. In any event, the power of Steinbeck's new book suggested that he had found in the proletarian movement the strength lacking in his short stories and necessary for his development as a major novelist.

But Steinbeck hesitated. Although *Of Mice and Men* (1937) identified his human sympathies with the itinerant worker on at least two levels of interpretation, *The Red Pony* of the same year marked a return to his more spontaneous sympathies, and it was not until 1939 that he was able to produce a really fine novel of social consciousness in *The Grapes of Wrath,* which has properly been called "the epic of the great de-

pression." The story of the Joad family, who had been
driven off their farm in the Oklahoma dust bowl by a
combination of natural and economic circumstances,
it follows them in their transcontinental migration to
the promised land of California, capturing the atmosphere of the time with a discreet use of impressionistic devices borrowed from Dos Passos but telling a
genuinely human story of frailty, endurance, and disillusionment. It was not, however, an orthodox proletarian novel; and although the book was praised by
the Marxian critics, it marked the end of Steinbeck's
association with the movement. The good and evil in
the book were not completely separated by class lines;
and, although Tom Joad certainly was allowed to acquire strength from his radical social philosophy, the
strongest personality in the book was Ma Joad, whose
strength came from character and her determination
to hold the family together. Steinbeck's sympathy for
individual human beings had enabled him to avoid the
rigid demands of Marxism, but his difficulty seems to
have been that he did not have much to escape to. An
insistence that "people are people" was not enough, as
he discovered when he tried to apply that principle
to the Nazi invaders of Norway in *The Moon Is Down*
(1942). What was left was emotion—physical, as he
tried to give depth to his interest in the *paisanos* in
Cannery Row (1945), and almost mystically sexual in
The Wayward Bus (1947)—and with it he has maintained his public but not his literary power.

What would have happened had Steinbeck been
able to hold firmly to the sense of values he undoubtedly gained for a while from the proletarian movement? The question is of course entirely speculative,
but it suggests an approach to Erskine Caldwell, who
is one of the most widely read American authors

abroad and who shared many of Steinbeck's characteristics. Caldwell began with a theme of sensational violence and degeneracy in *The Bastard* (1930) and attracted widespread attention when his novel *Tobacco Road* (1932) was made into a play which ran for seven years in New York. Although it was also concerned with violence and degeneracy, *Tobacco Road* revealed a grotesque humor which was developed in *God's Little Acre* (1933) to the point of making the latter book a spontaneously amusing story of the realities and eccentricities of southern poor whites. Both books displayed, too, a deeper quality in their indication of a sympathetic understanding of a peasant-like attachment to the soil which was the last sign of stability among mean people who were being uprooted by industrialism and fascinated by its products. Furthermore there was a Steinbeck-like quality of emotionalism in both books which developed into the intensely erotic religiosity of *Journeyman* (1935). These were the qualities recruited to the proletarian cause and devoted to it, with a minimum of humor, in the grim tragedies of *Kneel to the Rising Sun* (1935), the title story of which is especially powerful in its treatment of racial injustice and of the inability of human attachments to survive racial consciousness and class pressures.

Although never brought into balance in a single book, there was a Gogol-like quality in Caldwell's writing which held remarkable promise at the time he became primarily interested in reporting (with the photographs of Margaret Bourke-White) the human effects of the American depression, the atmosphere of central Europe, and the Russian battle front. For this reason his announcement of a major novel dealing with the Russian popular resistance to the German invasion of the Ukraine was of unusual interest at a time when Nikolai Gogol's Russians were doing the resisting but Leo Tolstoi's *War and Peace* was a best seller in the United States. Yet when the book, *All Night Long* (1942), actually appeared, it was not only a disappointment to literary expectation but a swan song for the proletarian impulse in American fiction. The Germans and their collaborators were beasts. The communists and the peasants of the resistance were martyrs. The passion and the violence, the eccentricity and high spirits, the humor and the sympathy, and the basic love of the land—qualities which had appeared in Gogol's portrayal of the Russians in *Taras Bulba* and Caldwell's portrayal of the meanest of Georgia crackers—these were nowhere. Caldwell held the line as Steinbeck did not when each got his great chance, and the Marxian line disciplined him out of all contact with his material and with his readers.

James T. Farrell, the third major new novelist to mature in the proletarian atmosphere of the thirties, was saved from Caldwell's fate by the rugged Dreiserian honesty which pervaded all his work and by his Wolfeian tendency to engage in a constant reevaluation and reinterpretation of material derived from his own early background. In his Studs Lonigan trilogy—*Young Lonigan* (1932), *The Young Manhood of Studs Lonigan* (1934), and *Judgment Day* (1935) —he was an effective recruit to the proletarian cause, writing of the vicious social environment of Chicago's South Side and its destructive effect upon a member of the *petite bourgeoisie* in a naturalistic way which refrained from preaching but used the symbol of a communist parade to suggest a better way than that followed by Studs. But in the year the trilogy was completed Farrell quarreled with the communist bureaucrats who dominated the American Writers' Congress, prepared *A Note on Literary Criticism* (1936) which came out strongly against the application of political directives to the creative process, and began the Danny O'Neill tetralogy—*A World I Never Made* (1936), *No Star Is Lost* (1938), *Father and Son* (1940), and *My Days of Anger* (1943)—which was more personal in its representation of the O'Neill and O'Flaherty families and more autobiographical in its account of a sensitive hero who set out to get an education and fight in his own way for the betterment of society. Farrell's own way was one of stubborn independence amidst the many shifts of opinion, and when the reaction against radicalism set in he reasserted his freedom in *The League of Frightened Philistines* (1945) and began a new series of novels—*Bernard Clare* (1946), *The Road Between* (1949), and *Yet Other Waters* (1952)—in which the progress of his hero (who was renamed Bernard Carr after a lawsuit over the first volume) marked his own break with the Communist party but maintained the socialistic ideals he asserted in *Literature and Morality* (1947) at a time when so many of his former intellectual associates were recanting their radicalism or taking refuge in silence.

There was more vitality in the Studs Lonigan and the first of the Danny O'Neill books than in the later novels, for Farrell, like Wolfe, was at his best when his material was fresh; and there is no doubt that he and his contemporaries found genuine strength in the values of the new social consciousness of the early thirties. But it was the strength of shock, anger, and impulsive rationalization rather than the strength of an ideology, for creative power survived only in its resistance to the strangling effects of Marxian orthodoxy. Calverton, at the beginning of his reaction, was to blame the ineffectiveness of orthodox proletarian writing upon a compulsion to view America through Russian eyes. But he was only partially right. The writers of the thirties had to learn the larger lesson that so many of their American predecessors had learned before them—that their material had to make sense in terms of their own experience if their writings were to earn the lasting respect of their readers. Farrell alone knew this almost instinctively, and he would have been the great novelist of the era had he been less prolific and more patient in making sense of his experience before transmuting it into fiction.

II

However much the novelists of the thirties may have failed to find trustworthy and durable values in the social consciousness of the period, they nevertheless exhibited greater vitality than the writers in any other form. The lack of vitality was particularly ironic in the drama, for the Federal Theatre Project during the depression offered American dramatists for the first time a nationwide opportunity for expression and also offered the theater as a whole the chance to recapture the audiences it had been losing to the rapidly developing sound films. Furthermore, the American drama itself, which had for so long lacked any considerable literary character, had taken on a new quality during the twenties with the success of O'Neill and with the exploration of new forms and materials in such plays as George Kaufman's *Beggar on Horseback* (1924), Elmer Rice's *The Adding Machine* (1923), the psychological dramas of Sidney Howard and George Kelly, and the folk plays of Hatcher Hughes and Paul Green. There were also actors' groups prepared to take advantage of the noncommercial theater and at least one able dramatist and dramatic theorist, John Howard Lawson, capable of guiding younger playwrights into the proletarian camp.

The best of Lawson's early plays, *Processional* (1926), had drawn sharp class distinctions, and *The International* (1927) had celebrated the labor movement throughout the world; and after his Marxism became more clearly defined in *Gentlewoman* (1934) he was to write a practical handbook for the proletarian dramatist in *The Theory and Technique of Playwriting* (1936), illustrating it with the spectacular tribute to strikers, *Marching Song* (1937), which was voted the best play of the year by the second American Writers' Congress. Lawson's formula for a successful drama was that of achieving "revolutionary clarity" in an action which embodied "both conscious will and social necessity." He believed that the essential quality of drama was social conflict, but not a conflict of mechanistic or fatalistic forces so much as a conflict of wills directed toward specific aims which brought the action to a state of crisis and, regardless of the outcome, contributed to social progress by creating a new awareness of environment. Lawson's own comparative failure and that of most of his followers seem to have been the result of a greater concern for "revolutionary clarity" than for the presentation of a convincing conflict of wills and social necessities, and the most capable of his younger associates, Clifford Odets, was at his best when he was closer to Lawson's precepts than to his practices.

Although Odets achieved a certain spectacular success with his audience-participation play, *Waiting for Lefty* (1935), he proved himself a dramatist with

Awake and Sing (1935), in which interest was centered upon the characters, and explicit revolutionary
implications were left for the final scene and actually
presented as only one means of escape from environmental pressures. The compulsion toward revolutionary clarity, however, pushed him away from realism
in *Golden Boy* (1937) and revealed how difficult it
was for a genuinely talented American dramatist to
compose a tragedy along party lines. For Joe Bonaparte is the victim of his own weakness rather than of
"the system," and his death is symbolic and theatrical
rather than a social necessity.

But the best illustration of the devitalizing effects of
the thirties can be seen in the work of Maxwell Anderson, who has come nearest to being O'Neill's successor
in the field of literary drama. An extraordinarily versatile craftsman, he achieved his first success with a
realistic war play, *What Price Glory* (1924), in collaboration with Laurence Stallings; mastered the light
comedy with *Saturday's Children* (1927); gave expression to his social consciousness (with the collaboration of Harold Hickerson) by indignant comments
on the Sacco-Vanzetti Case in *Gods of the Lightning*
(1928); and boldly turned to historical verse tragedy
in *Elizabeth the Queen* (1930), *Mary of Scotland*
(1933), and *Valley Forge* (1934). He was also one of
the most serious dramatists of the time who had
reached the opinion in "the godless twenties," as he
was to say later, that "the theatre is a religious institution devoted entirely to the exaltation of the spirit of
man." The message of tragedy was "simply that men
are better than they think they are," and it was delivered through an action which included the discovery
of some element in the soul or environment of the hero
which enabled him to face death or life with "a new

vision." Like Lawson's formula for the proletarian
drama, it was a good theory if it could be put into
practice; and Anderson's major shortcoming as a tragic
dramatist was that he could not find anything in the
human soul or environment, during the thirties, which
made death noble or life worth while.

The result was a tendency to identify the tragic
spirit with a compulsion toward martyrdom which had
neither a sound psychological or social justification—an
arbitrary expression of "faith" in human nobility so far
removed from real belief that it might almost be
founded on the notion, expressed in *Elizabeth the
Queen,* that the noble, the valiant, and the admirable
are always destroyed in their prime while "the rats inherit the earth." This was particularly evident in *Winterset* (1935), his first effort to adapt verse tragedy to
the treatment of contemporary problems. Based upon
the same material used for *Gods of the Lightning,* it
was primarily concerned with the effects of injustice
rather than with injustice itself, especially upon a son
who is anxious to clear his father's name and upon the
judge who (like the Captain Vere of Melville's *Billy
Budd*) had sent an innocent man to his death on the
theory that "the common good" was worth more than
"one small injustice." But Anderson did not set up the
clear conflict between individual and social morality
that Melville did, for Judge Gaunt's notion of the common good is as false as the judgment of guilt he had
once directed. Nor does Anderson set up a conflict between truth and falsehood, for Mio Romagna makes
only the most implausible of efforts to avoid the death
he chooses in order to avoid revealing the truth he had
sought so long. The whole implication is not that he
dies because he is noble but is noble because he dies
and allows the rats of the Estrella gang to inherit the

earth. The "tragedy" of *Winterset,* like that of *Key Largo* (1939) afterward, is one which finds virtue in neither struggle nor sacrifice but simply in giving up.

In such a negative atmosphere as this—to which Robert E. Sherwood's *The Petrified Forest* (1935) also bears witness—there was no more breath for the comic than for the tragic spirit; and the instability of Philip Barry and the thinness of S. N. Behrman reveal the difficulty that even the wittiest of playwrights had in finding a solid basis from which to view the world around them. Only in the fresh, uninhibited whimsicality of William Saroyan's *My Heart's in the Highlands* (1939) and *The Time of Your Life* (1939) at the end of the decade did there appear a really positive affirmation of values, even though they seem to be the values of the pure animal spirits reflected in Saroyan's earlier short stories and so well suggested by the title of his first volume, *The Daring Young Man on the Flying Trapeze* (1934). There may have been little more than this, set forth with much more sophistication and greater pretensions to profundity, in Thornton Wilder's celebration of the eternal "something" within man which made the stark simplicity of *Our Town* (1938) so impressive, but in this play and in his affirmation of the constructive impulse in his comic allegory of survival, *The Skin of Our Teeth* (1942), the drama escaped from the false values of proletarian ideology and romantic pessimism and acquired a new vitality.

The vitality of American verse during this period is more difficult to estimate, for the age was one of considerable poetic activity and talent and of even more active criticism, which brought about many changes in poetic reputations and perhaps sustained some of them beyond their deserts. Certainly one of the most influential men of the time was John Crowe Ransom, whose three early volumes of verses—*Poems about God* (1919), *Chills and Fever* (1924), and *Two Gentlemen in Bonds* (1927)—revealed the irony and delicacy of a fine though minor poet but whose greatest influence was exercised through his leadership of the self-designated "fugitives" of Nashville, Tennessee, and through the criticism to which he turned in *God without Thunder* (1930) and reviewed in *The New Criticism* (1941). His attitude and that of his followers, as revealed in the collection of essays *I'll Take My Stand* (1930), was conservative if not reactionary in its retreat from the modern world of science and industry into an agrarian regionalism. During the thirties the members of the group became rather widely dispersed in academic circles, where they found kindred spirits who shared their self-conscious intellectuality and the tendency toward dogmatism which was so characteristic of the decade, and their influence remained strong in American universities long after the dogmatic proletarians became unfashionable.

The result has been a peculiarly academic type of poetry which has as its distinguishing characteristics a more intimate relevance to learning than to life and a ready susceptibility to critical exposition. The most important literary influence upon it has been that of Eliot, especially through his theories concerning the poet's detachment from his work and his use of the "objective correlative" to express emotion; but Eliot's poetic mannerisms have also been extensively imitated, and even the best of the younger members of the original "fugitive" group, Allen Tate, has not been able to avoid frequent echoes of the master's cadences and a haunted recollection of the animal symbols in "Gerontion" and *The Waste Land*. The more productive Robert Penn Warren has tried to escape the excessively intellectual metaphysical quality of his early poems by a greater use of folk material; but the essentially academic nature of his imagination is revealed in the most widely read of his novels, *All the King's Men* (1946), where the reader of William Faulkner's *The Sound and the Fury, Absalom, Absalom!,* and *The Wild Palms,* and of Dashiell Hammett's *The Glass Key* will find a hero who is as recognizable as he is perhaps unconsciously composite. The dangers of an excessive literary consciousness and too great an ideological awareness, however, can be nowhere better illustrated than in the career of Archibald MacLeish, who had been writing poetry for nearly a decade before becoming a follower of Eliot in the early twenties and to a certain extent of Pound in *Conquistador* (1932)—a historical poem even more ambitious than Stephen Vincent Benét's spirited narrative of the Civil War, *John Brown's Body* (1928), of a few years before. For MacLeish, though genuinely talented and perhaps the most adaptable poet of the century, has been so sensitive to the climate of opinion that he seems to have no sensitivity from within; and the incoherence of his work as a whole shows how difficult it is for an American writer to achieve a firm position in literature by taking his stand on intellectual grounds as shifting as those of the twentieth century.

The writer's dilemma after the exuberant twenties, in short, has been that of finding a relationship to the world which would permit his creative energy to develop and mature; and this relationship was not found in proletarian dogmatism, romantic pessimism, or academic self-consciousness. Consequently it is perhaps not insignificant that the two poets who seem to have grown most in importance as they approached the mid-century were both men who had persistently sought to solve this problem in their own individual ways but in ways which were also within an older American tradition. The younger of them, William Carlos Williams, was old enough to have been in the University of Pennsylvania with Ezra Pound, to have brought out his first volume of poems in 1909, to have been one of the original contributors to *Poetry* magazine, and to have been an active participant in the literary excitement of the twenties with novels and essays as well as with poems—all composed while the author was engaged in the busy life of a successful physician. During these years he passed from a conventional lyricism through the influences of Imagism into a distinctive style of his own, based upon colloquial language and unpredictable in such transitions from seriousness to mockery and humor as may be found in his poem on "The Sea-Elephant." Yet there was a stubborn objectivity in his manner (for, as he observed in one complete poem, "so much depends upon a red wheel barrow glazed with rain water beside the white chickens") which kept him concerned with the external world and convinced that there was nothing in it which could not be brought to life and meaning by the force of imagination. His own imagination, especially when affected by the social consciousness of the thirties, was sometimes grotesquely sentimental (as may be seen by comparing his poem "The Yachts" with William Vaughn Moody's "Gloucester Moors") and sometimes aggressively nonsentimental as he moved toward a philosophy of accepting the world, which gives him a firmer place in the Whitman tradition than is occupied by such earlier professed followers of Whitman as Carl Sandburg and James Oppenheim.

Although he has been one of the most genuinely independent poets of the century, Williams has ac-

cepted, by following the Whitman tradition, some of
the limitations of Whitman—especially those involved
in committing himself to independence as a principle
or symbol with the consequent risk of unevenness or
affectation in his determination to accept everything as
material for poetry. And this unevenness is evident in
the first four volumes of *Paterson* (1946–51), the ambitious work undertaken at the age of sixty in an effort
to make a small New Jersey city—its history, its aspirations, and its beauty and sordidness as a physician,
after years of practice, had come to know it—the emblem of his acceptance of the whole of life as something which could be lifted out of the commonplace
and made exciting by the vitality of the poetic imagination.

Wallace Stevens, although four years older than
Williams, was much slower to come before the public
—perhaps because he was inclined by temperament to
place himself in a quite different sort of relationship to
the world, finding in poetry a retreat rather than a
form of acceptance. Although he had been intensely
active in undergraduate literary circles at Harvard at
the beginning of the century and a leading contributor
to the new *Poetry* magazine, he did not publish his
first volume of verse, *Harmonium* (1923), until he had
reached the age of forty-four. By this time he was a
successful lawyer and insurance executive, completely
separated by age and experience and by his matter-of-
fact life in Hartford, Connecticut, from the flamboyant
individualism of the self-consciously "lost" generation
of the twenties. Yet the volume showed that he was at
heart, in his disciplined way, as flamboyant and as individual as any of his younger contemporaries. Two of
its poems are especially interesting as revelations of
their author's point of view and methods of expression.

The earliest, "Sunday Morning" (1915), revealed a
basic but thoughtful and highly sophisticated hedonism—a renunciation of belief in the supernatural and a
conviction that "the blood of paradise" courses through
the heart of any mortal human being who is capable of
seeking enjoyment in the sensations of daily life, of
feeling the power of "enduring love," and of realizing
that "death is the mother of beauty" which would become insipid if it were imperishable. The second was
a short funeral poem which mocked the traditional
majesty of imperial death in sonorous lines which at
once presented a drab picture of the reality and reduced pretentiousness to nonsense with the high-
sounding refrain "The only emperor is the emperor of
ice-cream." In some respects it resembles the poetry
of Williams, but it is much more coherent in its use of
a precise balance of music, visual imagery, and intellectual content in order to communicate a meaning
which could not be achieved in the unbalanced art of
such a poet as Vachel Lindsay who shared Stevens'
belief in "the essential gaudiness of poetry."

But Stevens' gaudiness was accompanied by a rare
elegance; and both became incidental, during his prolific period in the thirties, to a pursuit of more serious
values in poetry. His *Ideas of Order* (1935)—"the
order," as he was to say later, "of a man's right to be as
he is"—had direct reference to the Marxian "panorama
of despair"; and the poems in the volume reaffirmed
the power of the imagination to master darkness by its
own creative force. But it should not be an imagination
based upon tradition or directed by reason, he felt
when he wrote *Owl's Clover* (1936) at a time when the
literary world seemed to be divided between the tra-
ditionalists and the proletarians. It was "enough to live
incessantly in change"—a change caused by an un-

changeable "subman," who exists below the thinking level in every man and corrects the errors of logic by his irrational consciousness. This was not a return to the popular Freudianism of the twenties, however, for Stevens was being impelled by the times to find a more serious substitute for religion than the hedonism of his early "Sunday Morning." In *The Man with the Blue Guitar* (1937) he had clearly found it in poetry, and much of his considerable literary activity during the remaining eighteen years of his life was devoted to an attempt to define poetry in terms of a disciplined perceptiveness. "Poetry is the statement of a relationship between a man and the world," was one of his *Adagia*, and it was a relationship of intuitive creativeness, based upon observation but opposed to formal reasoning. "For a poem is a nature," he said, echoing Emerson, "created by the poet"; and it was in this older tradition of finding reality within himself rather than in the world about him that he stood opposed to Williams and found both a refuge from his times and a strength which made the last two decades of his long life his most creative.

III

Detached though Wallace Stevens was from the professional world of literature, his development begins to appear symptomatic when we turn to the two writers of fiction, William Faulkner and Ernest Hemingway, who emerged after the First World War and proved to be the only two who survived the time spirit of a particular era and continued to grow in stature for more than three decades. Faulkner's first two novels, *Soldiers' Pay* (1926) and *Mosquitoes* (1927), re-

flected the spirit and life of the twenties in a small
Georgia college town and the region around New
Orleans, and it was not until *Sartoris* and *The Sound
and the Fury* (both published in 1929) that he discovered his vital source of literary material in his native
Mississippi where he created the microcosm of Yok-
napatawpha County in which his imagination has
largely dwelt ever since. *Sartoris*, in fact, provides the
geographical and social frame of reference for the
greater part of his later writing. The small town of Jefferson, haunted by traditions, is situated on the edge
of the red-hill country, where tradition has no meaning,
and within driving distance of the lowlands, where
remnants of the Chickasaw Indian hunting culture still
survive. The aristocrats of Jefferson, the Sartorises and
the Compsons, are never quite free from the past, in
which they live or against which they react in accord
with standards of behavior set on the plantations before the Civil War, by the lost cause of the war itself,
and during the speculative period which followed the
Reconstruction era. The poor whites, represented by
the Snopes family, are free from all inhibitions and are
subject to the driving forces of greed and perverse
meanness. Between the two classes, culturally, are the
Negroes—free from all traditions except the tradition of
service, and free also from greed and meanness—and a
few solid white men who trade and hunt with no feeling of class responsibility. Out of these people Faulkner created his literary world.

The Sound and the Fury made it a world in depth
as Faulkner used the extraordinary device of the
stream of consciousness of an idiot named Benjy to
unify a period of thirty years in the history of the
Compson family and show the quality of love which
the unreasoning child could attract while his calculat-

ing brother Jason descended to all the meanness of the poor whites and his sensitive brother Quentin, torn between family pride and sentiment on the one hand and an awareness of family degeneracy on the other, committed suicide. But the story was not complete, as Faulkner was to indicate seven years later in *Absalom, Absalom!* (1936) when he associated its psychological depth with a depth in time by identifying Quentin's emotional stresses with his knowledge of the wild story of Thomas Sutpen, who had tried to establish a plantation and found a family in the early days when cotton was king and the future aristocrats of Mississippi were all pioneers. In the meantime he had ranged widely in his own approach to fiction, writing in the stream-of-consciousness method a grimly powerful novel of a hill family's epic attempt to deliver a corpse to the family burying ground in Jefferson in *As I Lay Dying* (1930), shocking the public and attracting wide attention with the story of a degenerate gangster and a group of moral weaklings in *Sanctuary* (1931), seriously considering some of the social and racial problems of the South in *Light in August* (1932), and returning to his early theme of postwar recklessness in *Pylon* (1935). He was a great storyteller whose tales were sometimes as tall as any that grew out of the frontier tradition, but he was finding it difficult to achieve a firm medium of communication with a public which was puzzled by his rhetoric and experimental techniques and impressed (during a period of proletarian solemnity) more by his preoccupation with violence and degeneracy than by his pervasive humor.

Actually he was finding his medium and stabilizing himself in the short stories he published in various magazines before collecting them in book form. Some of them, like those in *Doctor Martino and Other*

Stories (1934), were simply good tales; others, like the ingeniously heroic adventures of a grandmother and two small boys during the Civil War in *The Unvanquished* (1938) and the chronological account of the Snopes invasion in *The Hamlet* (1940), were coherent enough to form novels; but the most significant group were those in *Go Down, Moses, and Other Stories* (1942), which revealed the strong attraction held for Faulkner by the primitive values of the hunt—values which made "The Bear," within the context of the collection, perhaps the most positive ethical statement its author had made in fiction up to this date. By this time and with the assistance of the two contrasting stories woven together into a single novel, *The Wild Palms* (1939), Faulkner's prevailing attitudes were becoming reasonably clear. He possessed a stronger and more consistent sense of the past than did any other American writer, but he did not find in it the source of strength that Willa Cather and T. S. Eliot attributed to it. Instead, he saw it as a cultural tradition, often romanticized, which sapped the energies and eventually destroyed (through rhetoric, alcohol, or a subconscious death wish) the people who were affected by it. On the other hand, the rapacious, unprincipled, materialistic, and mean impulses of people like the Snopes threatened all values and society itself. What remained to form the basis of any hope for humanity was the blind courage and enduring spirit which could be found in even the meanest of mankind (witness the Bundrens of *As I Lay Dying* and the convict in "The Old Man" story in *The Wild Palms*) and which acquired a simple ethical pattern in the wilderness stories of *Go Down, Moses*.

The qualities of blind courage and persistence were attributed alike to the sophisticated and garrulous lawyer, the old maid, the boy, and the Negro Lucas in

Intruder in the Dust (1948); and this first novel after nearly a decade, though widely misunderstood by critics preoccupied with racial relationships, prepared the way for the Nobel Prize speech of 1950, in which Faulkner surprised the many critics who admired the myth of southern degeneracy more than they admired his books by his positive affirmation of those values he had always recognized and had come to believe in. "I decline to accept the end of man," he said from his "pinnacle." "I believe that man will not merely endure: he will prevail. He is immortal . . . because he has a soul, a spirit capable of compassion and sacrifice and endurance. The poet's and writer's duty is to write about these things. It is his privilege to help man endure by lifting his heart, by reminding him of the courage and honor and hope and pride and pity and sacrifice which have been the glory of his past. The poet's voice need not merely be the record of man, it can be one of the props, the pillars to help him endure and prevail." The speech was Faulkner's declaration of independence from the fears of the atomic age, designed to encourage younger writers to cast off the bondage of fear, and it is not hard to see in it the pattern of thought and the attitude of mind incorporated in the political Declaration of nearly two centuries before: in the course of human events it had become necessary to take a stand and declare a few self-evident truths agreeable to reason only if its observations are guided by an intellectual light within. Since then, in *Requiem for a Nun* (1951) and *A Fable* (1954), he has asserted these truths somewhat more positively in his fiction; and in *The Town* (1956) he has even attributed to the Snopes an inclination toward respectability which may lift them to the level of humanity before their story is finished.

Ernest Hemingway, in most respects, seems to be as far removed from Faulkner as any contemporary could be. A native of the Middle West, he remained in Europe as an expatriate after the First World War, brought out a volume of *Three Stories and Ten Poems* (1923) in Dijon and a collection of short stories and sketches called *In Our Time* (1924), and for reasons of his own published in America a burlesque novel *The Torrents of Spring* (1926) before becoming the leader of the self-conscious members of the "lost generation" with *The Sun Also Rises* (1926) and the short stories in *Men Without Women* (1927). Since then the little part of his life that he has spent in the United States has been lived in such out-of-the-way places as Montana and Key West, and he has made his permanent home in Cuba. He has written of these places and of France, Spain, Italy, and Africa with no implications of a regional microcosm and has written in the style of a laconic observer who stands generally outside his characters and at the opposite pole from Faulkner's rhetorical stream of consciousness. His immediate success was that of becoming Scott Fitzgerald's successor as the spokesman for the period's bored sophisticates and of speaking in an idiom which was at once more striking and more convincing than Fitzgerald's, and his lasting success came from the artistic discipline by which he achieved this idiom and kept his materials within its power of expression.

In its origin the Hemingway style was not new, for the best known of his earliest stories, "My Old Man," and the Nick Adams stories of *In Our Time* are suggestive of *Huckleberry Finn* and the first half of Melville's *Redburn* in that they are told from the point of view of a boy who can see, hear, and feel acutely but has little capacity for analyzing or interpreting his feelings and no desire to explain or do anything more than co-ordinate what he sees and hears. It is only when an adult becomes the narrator in *The Sun Also Rises* and adopts this point of view as his own—acting as noncommittal as an adolescent about the emotions aroused by a bullfight or a fishing trip or the peculiar complications of the relationship between himself and Lady Brett—that he becomes the representative of a generation which prided itself on an ability to accept any experience without judgment. The success of this technique depends primarily upon the accuracy and restraint with which the author presents material which will allow the reader to draw inferences beyond the adolescent power of expression; but it could not be achieved without such stylistic devices as an extensive use of dialogue and of a grammatical tone derived from the spoken language, a simplification of the narrative diction to a level below that of the dialogue, and a syntax which avoids the sort of judgments which are implied by subordination. *The Sun Also Rises* and many of Hemingway's early short stories were pitched on an emotional level so low that his deliberate simplification would have been ridiculous (and it was, in fact, often ridiculed) had it not been new and extraordinarily representative of people who actually were filled with a sense of futility and who would admit few emotions stronger than the desire to escape boredom. Had his work remained on this level it would have been no more than an interesting manifestation of the twenties, and it was not until he began his constant and prolonged effort to increase the emotional content of his writing without violating the fundamental principles of his style that he proved himself the most serious artist in twentieth-century American prose.

As with Faulkner, much of Hemingway's develop-

ment was through his short stories; but the milestones
of his progress may be found, much more readily than
with Faulkner, in his novels. *A Farewell to Arms*
(1929) advanced to the emotional level of romantic
love, but it was love free from all social implications;
and it provides an interesting illustration of the dominance of style over plot in that Hemingway was forced
to kill off his heroine at the end, not because he wanted
to follow the hackneyed plot of the sentimental novel,
he explained, but because numerous efforts at a different conclusion had shown him that he could not handle
his subject outside the restricted environment of a
hospital. During the early thirties he refrained from
any prolonged attempts at fiction, publishing *Death in
the Afternoon* (a serious study of bullfighting, with
some excellent and revealing literary comments) in
1932, a new collection of short stories called *Winner
Take Nothing* in 1933, and the *Green Hills of Africa*
(a book about hunting, with some rather petulant literary comments) in 1935. But the social consciousness of
the new decade was having its effect upon him; and,
after becoming actively interested in the Spanish Civil
War, he published a novel of the depression, *To Have
and Have Not* (1937), in which the cynicism of his
first novel and the romantic love of his second was
supplemented by a proletarian emotion toward the
decadent rich and an evident sympathy for his hero's
despairing belief that "a man alone doesn't have a . . .
chance."

For a while the tone of this novel and of his dis-
patches from Spain suggested that Hemingway was
adopting the ideological line of his major literary associate in the Loyalist cause (the André Malraux of
Man's Hope) which his American contemporaries were
already finding so unproductive; and his antifascist
play, *The Fifth Column* (1938), was so intellectually

undetermined that an extraordinary interest centered around the publication of his Spanish novel, *For Whom the Bell Tolls*, in 1940. The most ambitious and richest of his literary works, it presented a greater variety of characters than any other and went into more individual minds, and it added to the emotional ingredients of the other books a new sense of humanity and of sacrifice. But this new sense had no ideological support. On the contrary, Hemingway was embittered by the "isms" of the war and attributed to his hero, Robert Jordan, only a simple impulsiveness—almost Transcendental in quality—toward the general welfare of mankind. What he might have added to this had he completed his promised novel of the Second World War is uncertain, for the only book to come out of it was *Across the River and into the Trees* (1950), in which his own anticipation of death seems to have thrown him off balance and caused him to forget the heroism he had admired in his journalistic coverage of the Royal Air Force during the Battle of Britain and of the *maquis* of the French resistance. What was left was a celebration of good wine and good food, love, companionship, and good hunting, and a hatred of high brass and of mutilation, bound together with an emotion that only his style kept from appearing maudlin. His more natural development in a world of increasing emotional complexity was displayed, very simply, in *The Old Man and the Sea* (1954)—the basic individual human qualities of compassion, courage, and endurance which Faulkner had affirmed in his Nobel Prize speech and which seems also to be Hemingway's ultimate concept of value.

The difficulty of looking into the future makes it impossible to say what significance there is in the attraction of two such different writers toward a common standard of values which had become traditional in

American literature—an attitude of mind which had developed in the past and from which they derived a power not given to their contemporaries as they gradually realized it in terms of their own experiences. Yet it is possible to find it in the types of popular literature which are most distinctively American. The spirit of courage and endurance and compassion, incorporated in a single individual, has been basic in the western novel from Owen Wister's *The Virginian* (1902) to Jack Schaefer's *Shane* (1949), despite the efforts of some recent writers to get away from it as a convention and make the Western more "realistic" and psychological. The same ideal was carried over into the peculiarly American hard-boiled detective story by Dashiell Hammett, who perfected its technique in a style that rivaled the early Hemingway's until either his capitalistic resources or his Marxian principles (for Hollywood served as a double agent during the thirties) caused him to quit writing. But his successor in the mastery of this genre, Raymond Chandler, has persuasively defended the American type of detective story as the last refuge for these values in popular literature. Yet they are beginning to emerge in the newly fashionable science fiction, and David Karp in *One* (1953) has looked into a future more skillfully regimented than that imagined by George Orwell in *1984* and expressed his faith in the ability of the individual human spirit to survive influences far more diabolical than those which made the hero of the English novel love the dictatorial symbol of "Big Brother."

Of the more serious writers of fiction it is less easy to judge, for the economics of postwar publishing tend to divide the literary scene between the occasional writers of "quality" short stories—such as Katherine Anne Porter, Eudora Welty, and Truman Capote—and the heavyweight novelists like Norman Mailer, James

Jones, and Herman Wouk, whose experiences provide them with a single best seller rather than with the sustenance for growth. The highly competent professional, like James Gould Cozzens, who can do a variety of jobs in the fashion of the moment seems to have a more than ordinary advantage today over the writer who persists in his individual view of the world until his persistence gives it the validity of his own being. Yet it is interesting to note that among those who have persisted through a half score of novels, with more critical acclaim than sales, Wright Morris—in a final passage dealing with the queer psychologist and his even queerer patient in *The Field of Vision* (1956)—has come in his own way of sardonic understatement to express the same belief that was romantically expressed by Wallace Stevens, rhetorically by William Faulkner, and inferentially by Ernest Hemingway. It is a belief in the creative power of the human spirit to endure and prevail and to exist in the meanest and queerest of individuals.

This is the belief which budded beneath Puritan orthodoxy, found its way through eighteenth-century reason to a declaration of independence, transformed the symbols of European literature into something new, and became established as an American tradition which could survive the impact of an almost overwhelming materialism, the disillusionment of false hopes, and the charms of new dogmatisms. Tacit rather than rational in its pervasiveness, its expression has been shaped by so many intellectual contexts that it refuses to become a part of any system or orthodoxy and exists only as a sort of intangible national quality in American literature and an under-the-surface source of that power which contemporary literature—and perhaps America itself—derives from the past.

Index

NOTE: The American authors discussed or referred to in the text may be identified by the birth and death dates given in the Index. References by adjectives derived from authors' names are indexed under the proper names (e.g., Cartesian and Platonic under Descartes and Plato).

OTHER ANCHOR BOOKS OF INTEREST

OTHER ANCHOR BOOKS OF INTEREST